Groups in Harmony and Tension

Under the Editorship of GARDNER MURPHY

Groups in Harmony and Tension

An Integration of Studies on Intergroup Relations

MUZAFER SHERIF

and **CAROLYN W. SHERIF**

OCTAGON BOOKS

A DIVISION OF FARRAR, STRAUS AND GIROUX

New York   1973

Copyright 1953 by Harper & Brothers

Reprinted 1966
by special arrangement with Harper & Row, Publishers, Incorporated

Second Octagon printing 1973

OCTAGON BOOKS
A DIVISION OF FARRAR, STRAUS & GIROUX, INC.
19 Union Square West
New York, N. Y. 10003

LIBRARY OF CONGRESS CATALOG CARD NUMBER: 66-18044
ISBN 0-374-97334-2

Printed in U.S.A. by
NOBLE OFFSET PRINTERS, INC.
NEW YORK, N.Y. 10003

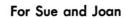

For Sue and Joan

CONTENTS

ЛПЛГЛГЛГЛГЛГЛГЛГЛГЛГЛГЛГЛГЛПЛ

ILLUSTRATIONS

These pictures follow page 272.

P R E F A C E

In the present state of human affairs, the problem of intergroup relations has come irrevocably to the foreground. No other problem today is as important as that of intergroup relations for social psychologists, sociologists, political scientists, as well as for men who find themselves dealing with this problem in a practical way. Both theoretical and practical treatment of human relations necessarily brings in its train considerations of relations among groups. For groups today are no longer closed systems. The unmistakable effects of intergroup relations as they unfold are reflected even in the shaping of policies within separate groups. In fact intergroup relations have an impact in such personal matters as planning family expenditures, whether for a car or a vacation or a college education.

On the theoretical side, the social psychologist can no longer restrict his treatment of group processes simply to *intra*group aspects. The functional relationships among groups have brought increasing interdependence. The understanding of policies and practices prevailing within groups will be inadequate unless relations among them are brought into the picture. If this be the case, it may be that study of relations within groups and between groups are no longer distinct topics to be treated independently of one another. If there is truth in the oft-repeated, but infrequently observed, household dictum of social psychologists that processes can be understood only in their appropriate settings, then the study of group units necessarily involves the setting of intergroup relations.

Recognition of the import of intergroup relations in contemporary study of group processes need not lead to neglecting intragroup processes or the properties of single participating members within them. In our opinion it is feasible to give due attention to the effects of the intergroup setting without losing sight of the properties of intragroup processes and unique properties that individual members bring to the interaction process. This more integrating kind of approach is conceptually feasible if we rid ourselves of the traditional individual-group dichotomy, prepared to study the interaction process giving individual and group factors their due weights. Such a possibility starts with the realization that these due weights of individual and group factors are not fixed and immutable entities for all times and circumstances. The attempt is made in this book toward such an integration of studies on group relations utilizing the implications of literature drawn from various sources. Going a step further, the conclusions thus reached were put to an experimental test which is reported in Chapters 9 and 10.

The preliminary experiment on intergroup relations reported in those chapters was carried out as part of the Attitude Change Project at Yale, under the general direction of Professor Carl I. Hovland, with a grant from the Department of Scientific Research of the American Jewish Committee. Acknowledgment is due to the Committee and Dr. Samuel H. Flowerman, the director of the Department of Scientific Research at the time. Without the effective aid and insightful counsel of Carl Hovland, the study could not have been carried out.

It was fortunate to have the aid of Professor Richard Wittenborn and Dr. Elmer Potter of Yale University in the administration and evaluation of tests given before this experiment. In the arduous tasks required for carrying out the experiment, the senior author was assisted by Marvin B. Sussman and Robert Huntington, as well as by Arthur Jette, Harry K. Ness, and other camp personnel. Grateful acknowledgment is due to Mr. Eugene Van Why, Superintendent of the Gilbert Home, Winsted, Connecticut, for placing the camp site and its facilities completely at our disposal for the duration of the experiment.

Thanks are due to Dr. R. Avigdor who made available her experimental study of stereotype formation which is reported in the last section of Chapter 10.

We feel that the theoretical approach presented in the following chapters is strengthened by Professor Theodore C. Schneirla's contribution on "The Concept of Levels in the Study of Social Phenomena" in Chapter 3. We are grateful to Professor Schneirla for finding time in his busy schedule to write this section for us.

The members of the various group relations seminars at the University of Oklahoma during 1950–1952, especially O. J. Harvey, James Thrasher, Daniel Taub, Edwin Cohen, Charles Shedd, Vera Gatch, Arlene Gibson, Victor Harnack, and Norman Walter, contributed surveys and illustrations, some of which have been utilized. It is a special pleasure to acknowledge the untiring and unselfish collaboration of O. J. Harvey through various phases of preparation of this book.

Dr. Marvin B. Sussman of Union College and Dr. Orville Brim now of the University of Wisconsin collaborated by providing material which was utilized especially in Chapter 8.

We hope that Professor William F. Whyte and Mrs. Whyte will detect in these pages the wholesome influence of our discussions with them on these topics. We are indebted to the kindness of Dr. Temple Burling and Mrs. Burling at a crucial period in the writing.

We want to thank Shirley Ingram and Dorothy Jean Peach for effective help in preparing the manuscript for publication.

Concentration on writing this book was made possible through a grant by the Rockefeller Foundation to the University of Oklahoma, for which grateful acknowledgment is made.

In the background of this book as well as of *The Psychology of Social Norms,* of which it is a logical extension, we feel that a start could not have been made without the unfailing encouragement of Gardner Murphy.

M. S.
C. W. S.

Norman, Oklahoma
February 22, 1953

Groups in Harmony and Tension

ЛЛЛЛЛЛЛЛЛЛЛЛЛЛЛЛЛЛЛЛЛЛЛ

Relations Between Groups: Problem

Relations between social groups, expressed in states of war and peace, conflict and harmony, domination and slavery, business transaction and loot, have always been consequential matters in human affairs. The history books largely consist of records of events concerning intergroup relations, not infrequently selectively chosen and selectively evaluated in the hands of their compilers as influenced by their respective partisan identifications.

But today, it will be hardly an exaggerated statement to say that the balance of the fate of the human race hangs primarily on the course of developments in the area of intergroup relations on both national and international levels. The momentous events in human history of the last decades, and particularly the great changes brought about during and as a consequence of the recent war, have created an unprecedented state of disequilibrium and flux in the relationships of social groups. Modern means of transportation and communication and other modern technological developments have made countries and even the world too small for the isolated existence and functioning of social units—whether they are small or large—no matter how distant or self-sufficient these groups might have been previously. In this general world setting, no human grouping can function as a closed system today; no human grouping, no matter how weak or powerful, has an independent existence today. This state of affairs is ever bringing all social units into closer and closer functional relationship. Increasing interdependence is the tendency both within nations and between nations. In many quarters of the world today (both academic and more practical), there is rapidly increasing concern over the vital and frequently grim problems of intergroup relations. The concern is an inevitable product of this widespread situation.

In order that we may be thinking about at least similar things throughout our discussion, a characterization of our main terms is in order. A group may be characterized as a social unit (1) which consists of a number of individuals who, at a given time, stand in more or less definite interdependent status and role relationships to one another and (2) which explicitly or implicitly possesses a set of values or norms of its own regulating the behavior of individual members at least in matters of consequence to the group. In order that our characterization of a group not be taxed by excessive bulk, we omitted common attitudes, common aspirations and goals. All these shared attitudes, aspirations, and goals are related to and implicit in the common values or norms of the group. (See Chapters 7 and 8.) An adolescent clique or gang, a college fraternity, a club, a church, a union local, a chamber of commerce organization, a political party are examples of social groups. From the point of view of the members within the group these social units may be referred to as *in-groups*. Again from the point of view of the individual, those social units of which he is not psychologically a part or with which he does not identify himself may be referred to as *out-groups*. It follows that the term *intergroup relations* refers to the relations between two or more in-groups and their respective members. Whenever individuals belonging to one in-group, collectively or individually, interact with another group or its members in terms of their group identification, we have an instance of intergroup relations. Group identification and attitudes stemming from it become so much a part of the psychological make-up of the individual in a personally experienced way that the fact of interaction in terms of group membership need not always be consciously recognized as such by the individual himself. Discriminatory practices, for example, are frequently put in terms of personal preferences.

At this early stage of our knowledge we are on safer grounds methodologically if we concentrate on relations between small groups the members of which can be singled out and studied concretely in space and time. But, especially in industrial societies of today, relatively small groups such as a clique, a club, a neighborhood church or union are not closed entities as might have been the case to a large extent in relatively isolated and stable tribes. A club, a church, a union, a manufacturers' organization in the neighborhood is usually a subunit of a larger organization which may have a good number of similar subunits, all tied to each other and to a central authority with definite rules, values or norms, ties, loyalties and responsibilities, and a particular pattern of power relations. This fact, which is the general rule in the complicated societies of today, forces us to take small groups not as distinct and closed entities but as parts or *subordinates* of larger social units, or *superordinates*. The properties of subordinates are determined at times decisively, in other cases to a lesser extent, by the nature of the larger social units of which they are a part. The determination of the properties of smaller units by those of larger units of which they are a part will vary depending on the degree of integration of the various parts within the larger organization and the nature of power relations within it. This fact imposes upon us the precaution of studying small groups and relations between them as affected by their relationship to larger units. These considerations are cogently raised by Arensburg (1), Whyte (5), and others.

Men in various disciplines of human studies (biology, psychology, sociology, anthropology, economics, political science, history, military strategy) are turning in increasing numbers to problems of intergroup relations and carrying out research projects in their own ways. Various committees, organizations, and agencies in both national and international bodies, compelled by more practical considerations, are devoting increasing funds and energy to find short-cut solutions. Such groups are calling on social scientists for effective ways and means to deal with their problems bearing on intergroup relations. In the United States alone, there are hundreds of organizations spending literally millions of dollars year in and year out in attempts to improve relations between various ethnic groups within the country (6).

His subject matter being the study of the experience and behavior of man in relation to stimulus situations, the study of man in his relations to in-groups and out-groups, the psychologist and especially the social brand of psychologist is among those in the foreground in the accounting of intra- and intergroup relations.

The call for psychological accounting is so compelling that a good many writers have not waited for the development of a scientific psychology before advancing "psychological principles" to explain man's relation to man and relations between groups. The scientific study of relations of man to man, group to group has a very recent history—a history that hardly goes back more than a century. During this period psychological theories and principles have been advanced, historical and contemporary "facts" amassed. There have been attempts at experimentation. Yet, it cannot be seriously stated that we now have even the firmly established outlines of a science of group relations. It is one of the first tasks of the psychologist to find out the factors historically responsible for this precarious state of affairs. Equipped with the correctives derived from this unearthing, he can proceed to more positive steps of achieving the perspective necessary to formulate crucial problems, which will lead him to the appropriate approaches and techniques.

A social psychologist has to keep an eye on the actual state of affairs in intergroup relations, if his social psychology is to have any significant contact with the world of reality. Time and again, the psychologist has displayed a tendency to be so absorbed in his own psychological abstractions that he has lost sight of vitally important factors in real-life situations. Consequently, psychological formulations have not been of appreciable use to men in economics, politics, administration, and other more concrete fields. The one healthy outlook that the social psychologist can take in this connection comes from the realization that the problem of intergroup relations is not solely a psychological problem. Hence, the social psychologist alone cannot reach generalizations and write prescriptions for resolving conflicts and tensions of human groupings. Even to deal adequately with psychological problems in this area, he has to keep a keen eye on the concrete vital events in historical, economic, political, military, and related fields. Because of lack of such realistic perspective in human events, psychological accounts of the causes of group frictions and prejudice, human coöperation and competition until very recently have been, on the whole, nothing but one-sided abstractions. Social psychology has not yet established a comprehensive and integrated perspective to problems of group relations. It is still in the stage of formation—erratic and inconsistent at many points.

INTERDISCIPLINARY RESEARCH ACTIVITIES AND LEVELS OF APPROACH

Mainly under the impact of great events in a shrinking world, the call for the development of various disciplines dealing with human relations has been so great that during the last three decades there has been a great deal of elbow-rubbing between psychologists, sociologists, ethnologists, and other social scientists. As a consequence of this widespread elbow-rubbing, and also of the realization of the enormity of their undertaking due to its interrelations with cognate disciplines, the *interdisciplinary approach* to problems became a necessity. It came with the awakening to the fact that universalizing of human institutions and groupings and the attitudes therein by the psychologist in the image of his own microcosm did not square with other facts; and that universalizing on the basis of crude hedonistic generalizations by the general run of economists and philosophers of the last few centuries was *simplistic* psychologizing.

As a consequence of this elbow-rubbing and realization of the need of learning from cognate disciplines, it has become a common practice today to arrange conferences in which biologists, psychiatrists, psychologists, sociologists, anthropologists, as well as representatives of policy makers take their seats around a conference table and express their views on group relations, morale, integration, and so forth. On the whole, the usual practice in such *interdisciplinary* meetings is for every expert to give his piece in line with his special preoccupations. The outcome, on the whole, is simply the juxtaposition of the particular views of specialists in various areas of human relations. A glance at publications that come from such meetings will convince one that there is very little integration and sometimes even little relevance among views expressed. Integration of approaches to the problem at hand is far from being achieved. Mere juxtaposition of utterances made in close physical proximity or between the covers of the same volume certainly does not imply integration. One finds in such meetings contradictory views expressing, for example, ideas based on "instinctive" premises and ideas based on "environmentalist" premises advanced by experts representing contradictory contemporary schools. Even if there is no agreement on fundamental premises in various interdisciplinary meetings, the very facing of opposing views is certainly healthy.

But these interdisciplinary expositions very frequently involve the assumption on the part of contributors and their respective followers that the premises and line of argument offered represent "the" psychological approach, "the" sociological approach, or "the" biological or "the" psychiatric approach, and not "the" views of the contributor himself or, at best, of the "school" of which he is a part.

This important point under consideration can be illustrated by the traditional dichotomy of "psychological" vs. "sociological" approaches. Traditionally the "psychological" approach was taken, on the whole, as the apologist of the individualistic point of view, and the "sociological" approach was taken as the apologist of the cultural environmentalist point of view—of course, both erroneously. In recent years the state of helplessness has forced both parties to borrow from each other. It is becoming clear that mere juxtaposition of little segments from each is not the way out; nor is there the possibility of laying down the two approaches along the same continuum. When in this case the interdisciplinary attempt is made in terms of how far "individual" psychology will take us and at what point we need supplementing by sociological material and ideas, the step taken is a misstep leading to a muddled eclecticism. The corrective for this misstep is the realization that psychological and sociological signify two different *levels* of approach necessitating their appropriate units of treatment and consequently their appropriate conceptual tools (4). If we are working on the psychological level, our unit of study is the individual and hence our treatment must be in terms af his psychological functioning—in such concepts as his motives, perceiving, learning, remembering, imagining, etc. If we are working on the sociological or cultural level, our concepts are in terms of social organization, institutions, kinship systems, value systems, language, art forms, technology, etc. The task of a social psychologist is, therefore, particularly hard. In addition to what he must learn concerning the needs, capacities, homeostatic states, etc., from the biologist, and judging, perceiving, learning, etc., from the experimentalist, he must learn a great deal from the social scientist (sociologist, ethnologist, etc.). For the study of the individual in his sociocultural setting is not a mere label to be tacked on.

Sociocultural stimulus situations mean family structure, kinship system, other social organizations which the individual is facing, and the technological surroundings, the value or norm system of the groups to which he is exposed. The study of the individual in his sociocultural setting implies singling out and knowledge of these sociocultural products. Psychological improvisations concerning these sociocultural products, which constitute the stimulus situations for the individual, have fallen pitifully short of the careful specification they deserve. Sociocultural products as stimulus situations certainly deserve careful and meaningful specification in the same way that the nature and proportions of the maze used in learning experiments need specification. And for this specification the psychologist certainly needs the help of social scientists.

It seems to us that the notion of *levels* is a useful one in making interdisciplinary attempts really effective (3). It will give men working on human relations the realization that they are approaching similar or the same problems at different levels, which necessitate that each formulate its appropriate approaches, units of analysis, concepts in referring to events. This will save us from the patchwork of mere juxtaposition of unrelated ideas from various disciplines and fruitless arguments concerning the units of analysis and concepts to be used.

With the notion of levels in mind we can proceed to check the findings obtained on our level of approach with the findings obtained at other levels of approach to the same or similar topics. If it is valid, a generalization reached at one level on some topic is not contradicted and in fact is supported by valid generalization reached at another level of analysis. For example, if a person is found to be color blind by the psychological approach (exposing him to a series of discriminable color series), there must be something wrong some place in the structure and functioning of his visual apparatus, which may be in the receptor organs, sensory nerves, central areas, or some physiologically related function. If the physiologist declares that there is nothing physiologically wrong with the man in this respect and he should be able to discriminate colors, there is something wrong either with the psychology or the physiology in question—or with both. Valid findings on one level cannot be contradicted by the findings contributed at another level on the same topic. Carrying the illustration closer to our present problem; the sociologist's finding that collective action of a group has properties peculiar to itself should be (and is) verified by the findings of the psychologist in his more detailed and elaborate analysis of the unique experience and behavior of the individual member participating in the group activity. Checking and cross-checking of the findings obtained at one level against the findings obtained at some other level on the same topic will make interdisciplinary collaboration the integrating meeting ground that it should be.

ACTION GROUPS AND THE STUDY OF INTERGROUP RELATIONS

As mentioned before, there are literally hundreds of agencies and organizations specifically attempting to find devices for handling intergroup relations effectively, to develop techniques to eliminate intergroup prejudice and tension, or to bring about coöperation and peace among social groups. The social psychologist has to follow closely the devices and techniques used by such action groups and carefully study their effects in practice. These developments may serve as practical testing grounds for various theoretical approaches. In the last analysis, the test of *validity* lies in the field of action, in the actual relations of groups. A careful analysis of the success and failure of various devices used by action groups can give healthy leads in formulating fruitful hypotheses and in planning research designs. A comprehensively valid theory can develop only if it is firmly rooted in the actuality of daily events of intergroup relations. In actual development of a science, what is called applied and pure act and interact with one another. For example, in the wonderful developments in physical sciences in recent times, the great impetus was provided by the demands of a growing industry, and even current military demands. Likewise, the tremendous expansion of the research activities in the area of group relations is made possible by the demands created by the compelling prominence that group relations have acquired with the increasing state of interdependence among human groupings.

Yet, not infrequently action groups are interested parties having at least primarily the concern of this or that social group which subsidizes them. Their sense of urgency comes from being so closely tied with the actualities of a living world full of immediate frictions and tensions; they are after immediate short-cut solutions here and now.

Attempts to reach scientific formulations thus far have shown that there are no short solutions and generalizations in this most complicated of all topics (viz., intergroup relations), if the aim is the formulation of an adequate theory that is not dated, that is not one-sided, that does not merely advance some sovereign principle to explain all, that is not written from the point of view of a particular group or a combination of groups. Every group represents a point of view, as that group stands in relation to others. Each has a set of premises whether explicitly stated or not. Of course, denial of the desirability of efforts by action groups (such as forward-looking liberal citizens, church groups, minority groups, etc.) in the way of elimination of harmful intergroup tensions of prejudice is not even implied here. Actual life conditions precede any scientific formulations. Action cannot wait for the formulation of an adequate science of human relations.

In the long run an effective action program for the elimination of intergroup prejudice, friction, and tension will be coördinated with an adequate theory of intergroup relations. Such a comprehensive theory of intergroup relations, which does not omit or neglect any factor that counts, cannot be formulated with a few sovereign concepts (e.g., "instinct" or "environment" or "frustration" or "national character") even though every one of them may count in the total picture.

SOME OBSTACLES IN APPROACHING ADEQUATE THEORY

There are certain factors which stand as serious obstacles against attaining an approach which will lead us to the formulation of a comprehensive, adequate theory of intergroup relations. We have to mention a few most relevant of these obstacles to guard against the pitfalls to which they lead us before we can take the positive trail of our discussion.

It is repeated time and again that we have to shed our personal biases, vested interests, subjective views in order to achieve the scientific objectivity, the necessary impersonal perspective in dealing with the problem at hand. Otherwise our treatment of the problem is a partisan one, which leads us to formulations of expediency dated in time and limited in applicability. Achieving the necessary objectivity and perspective was hard enough and took centuries of repeated efforts in dealing with the subject matters of physical sciences. The established grooves within which even the physical world was viewed, the sanctions coming from powerful groups and "public opinion" of the times which were disturbed by what appeared to be heresy, screwball views, deviation, were effective deterrents to achieving and establishing the necessary perspective in the formulation of problems and carrying their indications through along the lines of actual research. The examples of a Galileo or a Pasteur are only too well known. In the area of human relations, such deterrents are still more formidable. And the obstacles are not only external to the research man. Especially for the research man in the human relations area, some of the most powerful negative influences come from within himself.

The research man has his own group identifications. We have noted that every group represents a point of view as it stands in relation to other groups. Every group has its own explicit or implicit premises as to the nature of human relations, as to the directions that the values and goals of group relations should take. From the outset, research and generalizations are doomed to be deflections or mere justifications of the point of view and premises of the group or groups with which one identifies himself, if one does not start his work by clear, deliberate recognition and neutralizing of his personal involvements in these issues. If this painful process of deliberate recognition and neutralizing of one's own personal involvements is not achieved, his autisms will greatly influence his design of the study and his collection and treatment of data. The direction of the study design will be such that it will be more suited to hit upon data in line with his own involvements. The likelihood of collecting data in a selective way (selective in the sense not called for in the explicitly stated propositions) will be considerable. If the social psychologist attempts solution of the intricate problem of intergroup relations without first neutralizing his personal involvements as a consciously or unconsciously identified member of a socioeconomic class, as a member of a majority group, or a minority group, or religious group, or a "school" or "laboratory atmosphere," with their more or less well-established premises, he may (as experiments indicate) be contributing his bit to the already existing muddle and not to the adequate formulation of intergroup relations.

This matter of the negative influence of our personal involvements in structuring and categorizing our views, in rendering us highly selective in the collection of data, highly selective in putting weighted stress on certain parts of our data, is not idle academic talk. Even in areas of study which are not likely to arouse human passion as intense as does the area of intergroup relations, negative influence of personal involvements is definitely shown to operate. During the first decades of the present century some psychology laboratories consistently found sensations as elements of mental life; others consistently failed to find such elements. In both cases the findings were in line with the publicly announced theoretical commitments of these research centers.

Another illustration may be cited from the present-day commitments to particular theories of learning. Some laboratories consistently found "trial-and-error" type of learning; others found results in learning explained primarily in terms of "insight" or "hypotheses." Such more or less consistent, yet differential, results on the same topic may be partly due to the preferred experimental designs used in respective laboratory "atmospheres." But the specific cause of this state of affairs in this area is not our problem here.

The unmistakable effects of personal involvements on the course and results of research can be shown to be operative at times in even more solidly established sciences than psychology.

Recently this point was raised and concretely illustrated by Leighton:

Although their science was sheltered from most of the pressures that beset social scientists, it was exposed to the constant danger of too much attachment to a theory. It takes fortitude to reject an idea that has filled your mind for months or years and which has come to be the star to which your wagon is hitched. One may readily begin reading the signs in its favor and omit thinking of the experiments which might disprove it. Precision instruments are no sure protection, for they are always in the hands of the human being who uses them. One afternoon a biochemist from Caius College sitting on a lab bench told me of how he had spent many months on an experiment which served to confirm the theory of a professor whom he respected. Years later, he said, it became evident that the theory was inapplicable. He repeated his experiments and got a different result, one which fitted the newer ideas.

"I thought I did those first experiments with objective accuracy," he said, "but I know now that I was unconsciously influenced by the professor's scientific stature. As a result, whenever I read the swinging pendulum in weighing a substance, or determined the end point of the color change in an indicator I introduced a slight bias in favor of my expectations. The many slight errors in the same direction mounted up. You can't be too careful." [2, pp. 211–212]

The well-nigh decisive influence of subjective factors, personal involvements, in the area of human relations has become almost a truism today. Some scientific quarters still hang on to modern sophisticated versions of the race superiority doctrines in spite of the overwhelming evidence piled up during the recent decades all pointing to the pitfalls of explaining the pattern of group relations on the basis of biologically inherent traits of the groups in question.

GENERAL APPROACH

At the present time a great deal of work is being carried out studying relations between labor and employer groups, relations between the majority and minority groups, relations between political groups. The international organizations like UNESCO have organized a vast research program for the scientific study of nations, their standards of living, their national character, the relations between them with a view to elimination of friction and tensions, especially in some critical areas of the world.

We can learn a great deal from all these studies in building up an integrated formulation of intergroup relations. So far, attempts to pull together the implications of all these special cases of intergroup relations have been few. We shall gain a common vantage point in studying them if they are all considered as special cases of intergroup relations. The fundamental feature common to all of these cases is that they involve relations between in-groups. To be sure, some are well integrated, others are in a state of flux; the causes of friction do involve different kinds of clashing interests, different kinds of factors underlying cleavages—cultural, economic, political, military, etc. But all being special cases of inter-group relations, there should be a minimum of features common to them all. If we succeed in abstracting these minimum features common in all cases of intergroup relations, a few basic hypotheses underlying all group cleavages, then we shall be moving toward comprehensive principles valid beyond just a few manifestations of intergroup relations. Sound specific hypotheses can be derived from these minimum common features to proceed to carefully designed *experimentation,* which is the final crucible for testing hypotheses whenever we can attain this rigorous stage of verification. Formulated and designed after going through a wealth of material from the concrete world of actualities, the *experiments* thus planned are less likely to be just some more additions to the lists of laboratory artifacts.

In other words, this is a plea for viewing the many cases of intergroup relations (whether manifested between ethnic groups, between labor and employer groups, or between political groups) as part and parcel of persistent major problems in this vital area of study. Of course, spelling out in so many words the essential character of the persistent problems is a many-man-sized job, which may appear, at the outset, too time consuming, too round-about an approach to urgent concerns. Especially action agencies may be impatient with (what they might label) such "academic" hairsplitting. For they function under a feeling of urgency to do something about these problems "here and now." It is not unnatural for them to see their own particular case of intergroup relations as unique, as something no other people faced before. We suppose all psychological tensions are experienced in this unique way by the individuals subjected to them. In the long run, we believe, the long-range approach is the best short cut to solutions. Once the major character of problems is crystallized, these problems will force upon us the necessity of finding the effective methods of study and analysis. After such a basic course is under way, it will be a relatively less difficult matter to do justice to the special unique properties of each case.

A parallel situation to this has been the area of *attitude* studies.

During the last two decades or so literally hundreds of attitudes were studied, on the whole without serious efforts to find common principles operating in all of them. Attitudes toward war and peace, attitudes toward capital, labor, Jews, Negroes, and other groups, attitudes toward romantic art have been tapped, on the whole, as if there were a separate psychology operative for each. Pollsters announced attitudes of people ("public opinion") on almost every conceivable current issue—usually obtained through their short-cut devices. Many of these attitudes were naturally dated. In recent years, however, serious efforts have been made to tie up this welter of attitude studies with major problems of psychology. One line of development along this line, for example, has been the attempt to tie up attitudes with some major findings in *perception*—especially perceptual selectivity as influenced by motivational factors. This is already exerting a precautionary and unifying effect on the work in the extensive area of attitudes. Even the dated attitude or opinion data of pollsters may acquire a lasting significance when considered in this framework.

REFERENCES

1. Arensberg, C. H. Behavior and organization: Industrial studies, Chap. 14, 324–352, in J. H. Rohrer and M. Sherif (eds.), *Social Psychology at the Crossroads*. New York: Harper, 1951.
2. Leighton, A. H. *Human Relations in a Changing World*. New York: Dutton, 1949.
3. Schneirla, T. C. Problems in the biopsychology of social organization, *J. abn. & soc., Psychol.*, 1946, *41*, 385–402.
4. Sherif, M. Introduction, Chap. 1, 1–28, in J. H. Rohrer and M. Sherif (eds.), *Social Psychology at the Crossroads*. New York: Harper, 1951.
5. Whyte, W. F. Small groups and large organization, Chap. 12, 297–312, in J. H. Rohrer and M. Sherif (eds.), *Social Psychology at the Crossroads*. New York: Harper, 1951.
6. Williams, R. M., Jr. *The Reduction of Intergroup Tensions: A Survey of Research on Problems of Ethnic, Racial, and Religious Group Relations*. New York: Social Science Research Council, Bull. 51, 1947.

CHAPTER 2

Some Traditional Approaches

If each generation of men had to learn the facts and relations of social life through direct experience, scientific study would be a hopeless pursuit. Mankind's supreme advantage in attempts to understand and master the physical environment and, more recently, the social environment, lies in the historical accumulation of knowledge and concepts and their transmission to succeeding generations. This almost limitless continuity of historical products in economic, cultural, and social areas is made possible by man's attainment and transmission of a system of standardized symbols, that is, of language. But this good fortune of mankind is not without its penalties. Some concepts marshaled by one generation as "knowledge" may later prove to be inadequate in dealing with realities of physical and social life then known. Perhaps those who developed such concepts and approaches were laboring in too narrow a sphere; perhaps they were strongly moved to advance "knowledge" in such a way that the interests of their group or their society at the time would be well served.

It is the task of scientists of a new period to make corrections, or to eliminate erroneous concepts and approaches, and to formulate new approaches to problems and new concepts on the basis of newly gained facts. But the task of the newer generation is not so simple. The history of approaches, concepts, ideas concerning social problems and social relations tells us all too clearly that, once sanctioned by powerful or influential groups (in science, politics, religion, etc.) as "truth," such approaches and concepts tend to persist even though subsequently shown to be inadequate or erroneous. Especially concepts and ideas concerning social relations become, for the individual member, "his own" concepts and ideas. Concerning as they do the characteristics and relations of individuals to other individuals and groups, such concepts, ideas, and approaches to problem situations in every age become a part of the individual's personal identity. Once learned—at the time of their development, or later through books, or from the lips of parents and teachers—they seem as "natural" to the individual as breathing. They form a system of tacit assumptions in terms of which he views the social world. The scientist is not of a different breed from the rest of humanity. Approaches, concepts, ideas coming from previous generations, whether valid, inadequate, or erroneous, may be so completely a part of himself that he may be unaware of them. They may appear so "naturally correct" that objective realities which "his" approach or concepts cannot adequately handle are ignored or distorted until they fit comfortably into the familiar way of looking at things.

Problems of group relations have naturally been of concern to many groups—small groups and large groups, each with its own goals, aspirations, and special interests. As a consequence, there are many approaches and doctrines which have been promulgated, consciously or unconsciously, in the interests of a particular group. Others may represent sincere attempts to deal with problems of group relations in a scientific fashion which, because of unquestioned background assumptions, have proved inadequate to deal with all the problems and findings of this area. The latter attempts usually are related to certain aspects of these problems, and may not be wholly erroneous. But, dealing with only certain aspects of the picture, they are one-sided approaches. If taken as comprehensive approaches to group relations, such one-sided emphasis results in ignoring certain facts or twisting them into the narrow framework provided.

To attain an approach to group relations with promise of comprehensiveness and validity to all aspects of these problems, the task of understanding the limitations of certain historically important concepts and trends and eliminating their negative influence is a necessary preliminary step.

In this and the next chapter we shall consider briefly a few historically important approaches to group relations which still seem to constitute barriers in the attainment of a comprehensive and valid approach to our topic. Some of these approaches are almost entirely without scientific basis and can best be understood in terms of the interests and directions of those promulgating them. *Racist doctrine* represents such an approach. Others deal with certain important problems in the area. The study of *national character* involves important problems, but this study suffers especially from unsavory antecedents and inadequate methodology. Others, such as explanations of group relations solely in terms of *deep-seated impulses of man* or of a *leadership* principle, demonstrate the distortions which occur when concepts (correct or incorrect) derived from one aspect of the problem are used for sovereign explanations of relations within and among groups. Aside from factual errors and circuitous reasoning, such approaches are bound to be one-sided, hence inadequate.

In the next chapter, Professor Schneirla examines the pitfall of *reductionism* in the study of human groupings.

THE RACIST APPROACH TO GROUP RELATIONS

Race doctrines assume not only that various human groups are essentially different from each other in physical characteristics and in intellectual, emotional, and cultural characteristics by reasons of differing heredities but that such differences result in a hierarchy of superior and inferior groups. It is assumed that groups of relatively "pure" racial stock (with more or less homogeneous hereditary endowment) exist, that any individual belonging to one or another of these groups by definition possesses the superior or inferior characteristics of his group, and that the hierarchy of inferiority and superiority, being determined by heredity, has always been and will continue as long as "intermixing" among "superior" or "inferior" groups does not occur. Intermarriage between individuals of "inferior" and "superior" racial stock, according to race doctrine, can result only in biological and cultural leveling or deterioration of the "superior" stock.

Modern study of genetics, of physical anthropology, and of intellectual, emotional, and social characteristics has unequivocally demonstrated that these major assumptions and conclusions of racist doctrine are not based on sound scientific evidence. Summaries of these findings by Anaṣtasi and Foley (1), Benedict (3), Dunn and Dobzhansky (10), Huxley and Haddon (25), Klineberg (28, 30) and Montagu (39) all point to the weakness of such assertions and need not be duplicated here. In 1950 a body of experts from many countries assembled to formulate a statement on race under the auspices of UNESCO (39).

Racist approaches to group relations, explicit or implied, can do nothing but hinder our scientific understanding. But our understanding of group relations is advanced by knowledge of the development, the elaboration and uses, and the perpetuation of race doctrine. These points will have specific pertinence in later chapters on prejudice or social distance.

Race doctrines prevalent today are based largely on arguments which are relatively modern in content. Although notions of biological superiority are as old as the Old Testament, attempts were not made to classify men into races until the seventeenth century (Bernier). In 1738, the great classifier of plant and animal life, Linnaeus, assigned mankind to one species, Homo sapiens, and subdivided this species into four varieties. There followed a series of attempts to classify human groupings on the basis of one or more physical characteristics which continue to the present day. Historians have noted relatively few arguments prior to the seventeenth century for superiority or inferiority of human groupings based on allegations of hereditary or biological differences (4, 5, 35). However, history gives many examples of arguments for the superiority of one group over another for different reasons. Aristotle, Vitruvius, Ibn-Khaldun, Bodin are but a few of those who recorded for history their belief in the superiority of their own group and the peculiarity and inferiority of other peoples. This superiority of their own group was seen not so much in terms of biological differences as due to the influence of various external forces, such as climate or astrological influences. Group superiority was to be based also on acceptance of religious faith—the

Christian and the heathen, the Moslem and the infidel. In the name of all these superiorities, men suffered and died, were persecuted and killed.

Some writers point to the almost universal phenomenon of ethnocentrism for an understanding of these superiority doctrines. It is true that there is a powerful tendency in every group to view the appearance and behavior of other peoples in terms of the scale of values prevailing within the group. This tendency might be called "natural" in the sense that when the values of the group are learned by each individual member they become a part of his personal identity—of his self. As long as he is exclusively identified with the group and its values, as long as his sights are not raised beyond the value scale of his group, he will judge other peoples in its terms. But ethnocentrism does not lead *ipso facto* to superiority doctrines, or to the group conflict explicit in such dogmas.

A characteristic that appears to be common to the major group-superiority doctrines of all ages is that they are promulgated in groups seeking to rise above, or to maintain ascendance over, other groups—to subjugate, exploit, or eliminate as rivals certain other groups. As Benedict wrote, it is for this reason that: "The fundamental step . . . in understanding race conflict is to understand conflict. . . . The first lesson of history in this respect is that when any group in power wishes to persecute or expropriate another group it uses as justification reasons which are familiar and easily acceptable at the time" (4, p. 41).

When the early European explorers came into contact with the colored peoples inhabiting the African, Asian, and American continents, they felt and expressed their own superiority. But these initial reactions were based to a large extent on the fact that the newly found peoples were not Christians and their societies were less developed technologically.

It is probably not coincidental that beliefs in inherent superiority and inferiority of various races are traceable to that period when exploration of the new geographical areas became expropriation of their wealth and exploitation of their populace with substantial rewards in store for the dominant groups (4, 5, 10, 35). From the point of view of understanding group conflict, it may make relatively little difference whether slavery, persecution, and killing are justified in terms of economic necessity, or religious ideals, or race superiority. But doctrines of race superiority have certain advantages to powerful groups which probably account for their widespread utilization and their perpetuation. Unlike justifications based on environmental forces or on beliefs, race doctrine places groups in relative positions of power and privilege on the basis of characteristics which are presumed to be *unchanging* so long as the groups are kept at some social distance from one another. For these positions are alleged to inhere in differences in the biological make-up of every individual in the respective groups. Ideally, race doctrines envisage a world in which "superior" groups rule forever and "inferior" groups forever maintain their subordinate positions. Even in the more modern and somewhat more tactful versions, this assumption is apparent. As Dunn and Dobzhansky state: "Many people declare it to be the 'white man's burden' to rule men of all other colors. And so anxious have some white men been to lay this burden upon themselves that they used their superior weapons to fight and kill colored people, and incidentally other whites, for this privilege" (10, p. 108).

Race doctrines have had the further advantage in modern times that they have been supported historically by certain "men of science" or by distortions of scientific data. Such explicit or tacit support in an age in which wonders have been wrought by science has been most useful to promulgators of race doctrines. However, it is quite misleading to suppose that race doctrines have ever been squarely based on biology. Certainly Count de Gobineau's *Essay on the Inequality of Human Races* (1853–57) is not an exposition of the biology of his time but a passionate plea for the dominance and "purity" of European aristocrats. As Benedict pointed out, race doctrines were, at first, primarily aimed at lower-class people, whether the laboring members of one's own country or colonial peoples whose resources and labor were desired (3). It is not surprising in a setting of rising modern industrialism and nationalism that findings of physical anthropology and theories of evolution formulated in the nineteenth century should lend themselves to the support of race doctrine. But developments and emphases in these sciences have only aided the formulation of race doctrine, not caused it. The real bases can be detected in statements of modern race doctrine. Thus in the rising tide of German nationalism Houston Chamberlain incorporated into the Chosen Race all those who followed the Leadership Principle. Race was based on ideas, on character, not biology. The Nazi race doctrine exposes these actual bases in their most naked form— Italians, Japanese, Turks, and others shared the enviable status of the Master Race as honorary Aryans whenever it suited the political, military, expansionist designs of the Masters of the Master Race.

In certain regions of the United States the social definition of Negro is certainly not based on biology. An individual with "one drop of Negro blood" is, by definition, a Negro. This is in contrast even to the definition of the American Indian, which is much more flexible. Unless the individual desires to keep his name on tribal rolls for practical considerations, he will probably not be considered Indian because of one remote ancestor.

Race is a biological concept. Racial classifications have been many and varied, and will probably continue to be (39). Geneticists and historians alike agree that there are no "pure" races (10, 25). Indeed, no classifications of human groupings have been found which satisfactorily include all human groups, or upon which all scientists agree. Racial classifications are in terms of characteristics which are *superficial* in the biological make-up and the adaptability of the organism. Along any dimension chosen, variability is always found within a population. No criteria for racial classification have been found which do not result in overlapping of the distributions of different groups. The characteristics used, such as skin color, cephalic index, facial characteristics, and the like, are all continuous, that is, present in some degree in all human groupings. They are inherited independently of one another. This fact results in inconsistencies in classification when more than one characteristic is used as a basis. Thus dark-skinned Hindus are classified most frequently in the same general category as white-skinned Europeans. Race is nothing more than an arbitrary statistical category based on certain superficial characteristics. "National, religious, geographic, linguistic, and cultural groups do not necessarily coincide with racial groups; and the cultural traits of such groups have no demonstrated genetic connection with racial traits" (**39**, p. 13).

"Whatever classifications the anthropologist makes of man, he never includes mental characteristics as part of the classifications" (**39**, p. 14; emphasis ours). Evidence does not bear out conclusions that "inherited genetic differences are a major factor in producing the differences between the cultures and cultural achievements of different peoples or groups" (p. 14). The genes presumed to differ from one population to another "are always few when compared to the vast number of genes common to all human beings regardless of the population to which they belong" (p. 11).

On the basis of our present knowledge, it would seem that the biological concept of race could have no conceivable utility in the study of intergroup relations. The human geneticist is interested in the classification of superficial characteristics for the possible light they might throw on other more important problems of human heredity. Certainly there is no valid basis for studying group differences in social or psychological respects as though "race" differences were being studied. The problems are kept alive in scientific circles largely because until recently many social scientists and psychologists, and even now a minority, accepted uncritically the racist norms of their own groups. For a period, it was accepted in social science that various groups differed as measured by intelligence tests and the like on a *racial basis.* There followed a period of examination of the populations studied, of the characteristics studied, and of the methods of measurement employed (**1**).

As Berry (**5**) pointed out in his recent book on "race relations," the uncritical acceptance of racist norms and belief in eventual success in measuring race differences or superiority-inferiority in various traits are clearly evident in statements by a number of scientists early in this period. For example, the anthropologist, Hooton, wrote in 1931:

> Anthropologists have not yet reached a point of an agreement upon criteria of race which will enable psychologists to isolate with any degree of facility the racial types which are to be studied. Psychologists have not yet been able to develop mental tests which anthropologists are willing to trust as fair gauges of mental measurement.
>
> *That such differences exist I have not the slightest doubt;* that with our present methods they can be summarized quantitatively so that we are justified in assigning one race a position of superiority as contrasted with another, I deny. [24, p. 597; italics ours]

At the present date, most of the material referred to in the above statements has been reëxamined and, in some cases, reanalyzed. A large number of studies, such as those by Klineberg and others, point to the factors responsible for such uncritically obtained differences in test performance of different groups. (It should be noted that the father of modern intelligence tests, Binet, was perfectly aware that such tests could not be used to test inborn differences unless the individuals or groups in question had the same opportunities and backgrounds [30]. The testing for racial differences was done chiefly by users of this and subsequent tests in the United States.) For example, it is known that test responses are affected by differences in language, educational opportunities and facilities, socioeconomic level, general cultural milieu, and many more specific factors, such as the type of test, the person doing the testing, the traditions, customs, and interests characteristic of the group, the motives aroused by the test situation, etc.

Finally, it is now realized in the field of mental testing that "intelligence" (and even "normal" or "neurotic" reactions) must be understood in terms of the culture in which it is found (1). "Cultures differ in the specific activities which they encourage, stimulate, and value. The 'higher mental processes' of one culture may be the relatively useless 'stunts' of another" (1, p. 782).

On the subject of behavioral differences traceable to "race," there is enough evidence for definite statements. On the basis of unusually careful and extensive analysis of the data, Anastasi and Foley conclude:

> It is misleading to conclude that to date investigators have merely *failed to prove* race differences in behavior. The present state of our knowledge on this question is not a complete blank; nor is the evidence perfectly balanced, with half of the data favoring a racial hypothesis and half a cultural hypothesis. It is a fact that there are *group differences in behavior*, but not that such differences are racial or biological in origin. There is a considerable body of data, both in racial studies and in other more general investigations on the origins of individual differences in behavior, to show the influence of environmental factors in behavior development. But no study has conclusively demonstrated a necessary association between behavior characteristics and race as such. [1, pp. 782–783]

NATIONAL CHARACTER AND INTERGROUP RELATIONS

Everyone who has been outside of his own immediate environment knows that there are group differences in behavior. And most peoples become aware of their own more or less distinctive features. As Fyfe said: "Almost every nation is taught to realize its own 'character,' using it as a standard by which to judge others, and assuming an attitude of superiority, which turns quickly into ill-will when dispute arises" (16, pp. 30–31).

In descriptions and assessments of national character, we are plagued with the ethnocentrisms of the writers. Certainly the large proportion of descriptions of group characteristics of nations merit greater attention for understanding the development and elaboration of national stereotypes than for understanding group differences in behavior. "The greater part of the books on the subject are . . . written under the influence of particular political situations and with a view to future policy" (18, p. 183).

Historically "national character" has been a topic of urgent concern for individuals and groups with interests and ends of a practical nature. The promulgation of differences in national character based on the Jungian approach with its guilt feelings and sadistic tendencies and the like submerged in a "collective unconscious" is too close for many social scientists to discuss the topic comfortably.

Especially since World War II, the study of national character has become more prominent. In view of the increasing daily contacts and interdependence among the various major national groups, this emergence is not surprising. It has been fostered by a concern on the part of some nations to avoid unnecessary conflict with other groups, and no doubt to facilitate diplomatic and military negotiations with them. As Klineberg notes, many sincere men of science see the study of national character as a means of correcting erroneous national stereotypes and of reducing intergroup misunderstanding and tension (29, pp. 8–9). It is possible that it may serve these purposes; but under the urgency of these problems there is a strong tendency to "deliver the goods." At the least, it is foolhardy in the present state of this area to maintain that social science or psychology has more than fragments to deliver.

At given periods, members of ethnic or national groups do exhibit more or less characteristic tendencies in the way of being more aggressive, more competitive, more coöperative, or of being more religiously, politically, financially, or aesthetically oriented, as the case may be (1, 29). Such characteristic tendencies are products of dominant factors in the mode of living and central values or norms of the group in question. These tendencies are certainly not uniformly present in all subunits of a larger group. They are not immutable. As products of the mode of living and central values or norms of the group, behavioral tendencies are subject to change as these circumstances change. At times they show considerable variation as situationally determined.

The fields of ethnology and differential and social psychology are not in a state of complete ignorance concerning the influence of such group factors. But nations today are social groups of great complexity. If the study of national character is to rise above mere reinforcement of prevailing stereotypes or the advancement of policy by this or that national group, certain pitfalls inhering in most contemporary approaches to the problem must be avoided.

At the outset, the period of observation and the major conditions and group relations at that period must be carefully studied. As Benedict pointed out, the feared, aggressive Vikings of the ninth century have become the peaceful Scandinavians of today (4). We should expect differences in the behavior of the same group in periods of, say, depression or prosperity or war. If national character is to be seriously studied, there is no obvious scientific reason for assuming that identical behavior tendencies or traits will exist after a change or shift in the social system, although they may persist for sometime thereafter. It is entirely possible that the Englishman and the American today have more in common than either has with his ancestors living under a feudal system.

The study of large and complicated national groupings cannot advance beyond a primitive state until the actual complexities of the social system in question are examined and brought into the picture in a functional way. Ginsberg (18) has suggested a few of the factors to be considered before selecting representatives of national groups for study. He includes type of political organization, degree of social differentiation and type of class structure, degree of cultural homogeneity, age or stage of maturity or growth. To these might be added other related factors, such as economic organization, degree of regional isolation or interdependence, etc. Certainly we know on the basis of concrete study that different class settings within the same country produce significant variations in values and behavior (1, chap. 23). Ginsberg suggests that: "In the more differentiated peoples it is perhaps an open question whether class characteristics are not at least as important as national characters, and it is arguable that in some cases members of the upper classes have more in common with their opposite numbers in other nations than with the lower classes in their own" (18, p. 86).

The neglect of such differentiations as class, religion, ethnic groups, and regional differences has quite accurately been described as the principal shortcoming in studies of national character (1, 16, 18, 29, 43). In countries where there is a wide gap between the rulers and the rest of the population we must, as Pear suggests, seriously consider who is to be taken as representative of the character of that nation—the nobility or the prime ministers and cabinet, or the dominated majority (43, p. 25). Studies are based too frequently "not upon the common features of the national culture, but upon an overgeneralized picture of the particular sub-group with which the investigator was most familiar" (1, p. 787). The resulting errors will become increasingly evident as more comprehensive studies are actually made.

As an example of such error, Ginsberg (18) mentions a case in which an impassive and reserved nature was attributed to Chinese character. In this case, the writer himself subsequently found that this mode of behavior was established as a standard for Chinese in governing and literary circles and was never adopted by more than a small proportion of the population.

Most studies of national character utilize techniques employed by ethnologists in small cultural groups. But even in small cultural groups it is necessary to know how representative the behavior in question is of the entire group. Very seldom are we informed of the frequency of occurrence of a particular behavior item, even in ethnological studies of small cultural groups (29). There is no immediate method for assessing whether or not conclusions based on such unspecified data are valid. Especially when this approach is extended to larger groups, the opportunity for error becomes tremendous. For example, Gorer derived the traits of neatness and tidiness among adult Japanese from the severity of toilet training for Japanese children, not specifying the prevalence of either neatness and tidiness or rigid toilet training in Japan. Subsequent research indicates that the assumption that Japanese children are more rigidly or severely toilet-trained than Western children lacks factual basis (29).

It can be argued convincingly that ethnological techniques commonly employed even in many studies of "culture patterns" of relatively small or more homogeneous social groups are at present lacking in precision, and that findings are too seldom specified as to their representativeness or source. When these techniques are applied in an unqualified and unspecified fashion to nations as large and complex as the United States, there is little justification for accepting the results as more than interesting reading. Likewise, we are cautioned against the uncritical use of psychological tests or laboratory situations in such studies. Anastasi and Foley (1) point out that some of these tests, such as the Rorschach, do not yet have established diagnostic interpretations even in our own culture. Further, it is known that the whole meaning of such tests and the types of motivations aroused in the test situation may be changed in different cultures. Obviously this conclusion does not mean that short-cut techniques may not be used for studying group differences, but it points to a different approach in both their use and their interpretation.

Another technique is the study of cultural products to tap the characteristics of a national group. Again we are faced with the problem of representativeness—*which* cultural products and *whose* cultural products are to be studied? In some countries there is a sharp delineation between the literature and art forms of the established ruling group and those of the peasants. In others powerful groups deliberately control the products which reach the people. How representative are Hollywood movies of the character of the greater part of the American people? When shown in other countries, does their selection reflect a character of those nations or tendencies of the salesmen or censors of the movies?

In short, as cogently indicated by Klineberg in his survey of these problems, the techniques used in contemporary study of national character "all suffer from the same defect, namely that their validity has never been fully established" (29, p. 90).

But the question of techniques is not divorced from the investigator's orientation to the problem at hand. We cannot expect to have adequate techniques so long as the problems are posed in such a way that the functional relationships among factors producing national differences are not organically brought into the picture: "Little attention has been given to the very important question of the *causes* of these differences" (**29**, p. 91). This does not mean that the investigators of national differences have no notion of such causes. It means rather that causes are tacitly assumed.

By far the most frequent assumption as to causation is that differences in national groups can be explained by use of concepts derived from clinical experience with individuals from a rather restricted stratum of modern Western societies. Attempts at explaining differences in national groups often explicitly or implicitly assume that such differences stem to a significant extent from variations in treatment (warmth, austerity, threat, and the like) of individuals in such areas of early childhood experiences as toilet training, weaning, swaddling, discipline, early parental relationships, etc. This theoretical approach as exemplified in psychoanalytic writings has been critically analyzed as applied to individual development by Sears, Ausubel, and others (**1, 2, 44**). On the basis of surveyed evidence, Anastasi and Foley conclude that: "The available evidence for such claims . . . is extremely meager and of dubious significance" (**1**, p. 777).

Another manifestation of this orientation is the attempt to place various national cultures into clinical categories based on *individual* behavioral deviations in Western societies. Thus a paranoid trend may be "proved" to exist in German culture. Subsequent studies of German war criminals at Nuremberg failed to reveal definite paranoid trends among most individual Nazi leaders, as would surely be expected if there was indeed a paranoid trend in the society as a whole. We are in complete agreement with Klineberg that "extension to whole nations of the categories found useful in the psychiatric classification of individuals is not justifiable without further evidence" (**29**, p. 40).

In the next section we shall have more to say about the extensions of this approach based on individual cases to explanations of group relations. Here it should be noted that analogies between individual behavior and the behavior of groups cannot advance our understanding for well-established reasons. Behavior in group situations has been shown time and again to be different from the sum total of behaviors of individuals A, B, C, etc., when they are alone. If characteristics prevalent among individuals of a group are products of group relationships and interactions, and not some essence of individual members, then the study of group differences must *begin* with analysis of these group relationships and interactions, and not with individuals in isolation. More specifically, it is difficult to foresee any value to the study of national character unless the implied group differences are related in a functional way to differences in social structure, stratification, degrees of differentiation, mode of life, and central values within the national group, and within its subgroups.

HUMAN NATURE BEING WHAT IT IS . . .

Probably no other explanation for social tensions and conflict, for strife and war, or for man's behavior generally has been so convenient and frequently called upon as "human nature." And this "human nature" is seen as predominantly selfish or altruistic, aggressive and competitive or coöperative, evil or good depending largely on the interests and values of the parties in the debate. At the height of British imperialism, Herbert Spencer emphasized the aggressive impulses of man to come out on top in the struggle for survival. Kropotkin saw fundamental human impulses toward coöperation. Today lovers of peace, builders of war, statesmen, military men, politicians, representatives of this group or that group see in human nature basic impulses in the direction of their conclusions concerning social problems.

Fundamental impulses of man in this or that direction have been the topic of discussion by many contemporary social philosophers, political scientists, and psychologists. We cannot survey them all. One approach, however, has been so fashionable and influential within and without academic circles that it is important in the whole area of group relations and is sometimes assumed without full awareness by investigators in various areas. This is the psychoanalytic approach of Freud, promulgated in a period in which explanations of human relations in terms of instincts were generally advanced by psychologists and social philosophers (e.g., McDougall, Trotter). Within psychology today, there is a healthy trend of turning to biologists for the keys to "human nature" or basic impulses of man. The wide acceptance and vogue of psychoanalytic explanation in the area of group relations is probably a by-product of its great popularity in clinical treatment of individuals caught in troublesome conflicts of modern life.

Freud, in his later writings, posited an "innate, independent, instinctual disposition in man" toward aggression (14, p. 102). In his earlier work, when his attention was concentrated more exclusively on clinical problems, Freud saw aggression as a response to frustration of impulses then conceived as still more basic. Later, and specifically when problems of group relations were coming to be of greater concern to him, Freud developed the notion of "two classes of instincts"—"Eros or the sexual instincts" and a "death instinct, the task of which is to lead organic matter back into the inorganic state" (13, p. 55).

Society was conceived by Freud as being the inevitable enemy of the individual. Conscience was conceived as essentially "dread of society" (12, p. 10). In group situations, the individual is stripped of repressions of unconscious instincts, and it is this loss of conscience which explains the difference in behavior of individuals in group situations. "From our point of view we need not attribute so much importance to the appearance of new characteristics. For us it would be enough to say that in a group the individual is brought under conditions which allow him to throw off the repressions of his unconscious instincts. The apparently new characteristics which he then displays are in fact the manifestation of this unconscious, in which all that is evil in the human mind is contained as a pre-disposition" (12, pp. 9–10).

The solidarity of a group was seen by Freud as directly traceable to the first of the two classes of instincts: "A group is clearly held together by a power of some kind; and to what power could

this feat be better ascribed than to Eros, who holds together everything in the world" (12, p. 40). But this Eros, whose powers were
considered so great as to be central in Freud's earlier work, turns
out not to be so powerful when threatened by "a powerful measure of desire for aggression . . . part of the instinctual endowment." "This aggressive cruelty usually lies in wait for some
provocation, or else it steps into the service of some other purpose,
the aim of which might as well have been achieved by milder
measures. . . . It also manifests itself spontaneously and reveals
men as savage beasts to whom the thought of sparing their own
kind is alien. . . . The existence of this tendency for aggression
. . . *makes it necessary for culture to institute its high demands.
Civilized society is perpetually menaced with disintegration
through this primary hostility of men towards one another*" (14,
pp. 85–86; italics ours).

Thus the ultimate reason for the existence of culture and its
greatest threat are seen to lie in man's innate destructiveness.
Group conflicts and war are seen as outbursts of irrepressible aggressive instincts. It is not surprising that neither Freud nor those
who follow him closely today (like Glover) can see much hope for
the elimination of group conflict or war, or, in their terminology,
for any victory of the life instinct over instincts of aggression and
death (15, 19).

It has been suggested that Freud's one-sided, pessimistic view
of society is related to his writing in a particular social setting.
Pear notes:

It is fair to speculate . . . that inferences are possible from the fact
that Freud developed his later ideas of human aggressiveness and hatred
during the most depressing time in Vienna. He never rose mentally
above the sub-culture-pattern in which he lived, and as Professor Harding suggests, Freud's ideas on government were not far removed from
Hitler's. Writers like Christopher Caudwell, Karen Horney and Erich
Fromm have made this point. It is time that social psychologists defined
their attitude toward such criticisms of what Freudians seem to regard
as axioms, and, in doing so, assessed the significance of the possibility

that at least for a short time, they may expect professional advancement in a society which puts hatred and malice before friendliness, dominance before co-operation. [43, p. 40]

Freud's notions on some more practical problems in human relations are instructive in this regard. In *Civilization and Its Discontents,* Freud wrote: "There is an advantage, not to be undervalued, in the existence of smaller communities, through which the aggressive instinct can find an outlet in enmity towards those outside the group. It is always possible to unite considerable numbers of men in love towards one another, so long as there are still some remaining as objects for aggressive manifestation. . . . One can see that it [aggression toward out-groups] is a conveniently and relatively harmless form of satisfaction for aggressive tendencies, through which cohesion amongst the members of a group is made easier" (p. 90). This is a quite logical social proposal if one assumes that aggression, being innate and instinctive, must have some outlet.

In an open letter to Einstein arranged by the International Institute of Intellectual Cooperation of the League of Nations, entitled "Why War?" Freud makes his views on the aggressive instinct and some of his notions concerning human conflict more explicit. In this letter Freud makes it quite clear that the masses of mankind are dominated by instinct. He suggests an evolutionary tendency for a "progressive displacement of instinctive aims and a restriction of instinctual impulses. . . . There are organic grounds for the changes in our ethical and aesthetic ideals" (15, p. 286). But unfortunately, he finds only a few individuals who have yet reached a stage of intellectual predominance and repudiation of war. According to Freud such individuals are obliged "to rebel against war for organic reasons"; they have a "constitutional intolerance of war." It is hardly surprising that the most positive suggestion in this letter, indeed the most positive conclusion to be drawn from it, is Freud's suggestion that the propensity to war can be combated by developing an elite group of leaders: "One instance of the innate and ineradicable inequal-

ity of men is their tendency to fall into two classes of leaders and
followers. The latter constitute the vast majority; they stand in
need of an authority which will make decisions for them and to
which they for the most part offer an unqualified submission. This
suggests that more care should be taken than hitherto to educate
an upper stratum of men with independent minds . . . whose
business it would be to give direction to the dependent masses"
(p. 284).

Throughout this letter one finds pessimism and despair. For
Freud was convinced that "there is no use in trying to get rid of
men's aggressive inclinations. We are told that in certain happy
regions of the earth, where nature provides in abundance everything that man requires, there are races whose life is passed in
tranquility and who know neither compulsion nor aggression. I
can scarcely believe it . . ." (p. 283).

Lest we believe that Freud was not really serious in his belief in the necessity for an elite group of leaders, let us hear his
warning of the dangers of group solidarity and identification
which are greater than individual identification with the leader:
". . . We are imminently threatened with the danger of a state
one may call 'la misère psychologique' of groups. This danger is
most menacing where the social forces of cohesion consist predominantly of identifications of the individuals in the group with
one another, whilst leading personalities fail to acquire the significance that should fall to them in the process of group formation. The state of civilization in America at the present day offers
a good opportunity for studying this injurious effect of civilization which we have reason to dread" (14, p. 93).

These statements are sufficient to indicate that Freud's social
psychology followed quite logically from his basic assumptions.

Now these assumptions in Freud's social psychology and in
other schemes that assume innate impulses of aggression or dominance or competition can be demonstrated to err. We will be very
brief, for the burden of proof is easily available.

In the first place, comparative ethnological evidence, such as
the studies by Mead and others (37), indicates that aggression and

competition are not found as a predominant or approved mode of response in some cultures. This evidence would tend to indicate that competitiveness, aggressiveness, rivalry, sadism are not the basic instincts Freud assumed. If they were and had simply been successfully repressed by the societies in question, Freudian theory would anticipate a host of imbalances, complexes as a consequence. Such complexes due to thwarting of aggressive impulses are not found in a consistent way.

Developmental material reveals that such impulses for competition, rivalry, and aggression in a consistent sense are not revealed until after the acquisition of some notion of the self and its more fundamental relations with other objects and persons. Further, there is wide variation in amount or degree of such behavior by children growing up in different subunits of one culture. A few examples will clarify this point. Following the studies of Leuba and Greenberg (33, 21), a series of unpublished studies at the University of Oklahoma[1] indicate clearly that competitiveness with other children is seldom found among 2-3½-year-olds and commonly found among 5-6½-year-olds. Further, while 2-3½-year-old children from different socioeconomic and ethnic backgrounds were very similar in their reactions in the situations observed, differences were found among groups of the older children. Those children from a university kindergarten were more consistently competitive than children from other, less favored backgrounds. While aggressive reactions of a sort can certainly be observed in newborn infants under certain circumstances, we can scarcely speak of their diffused responses in the same breath as those in adult social life. In this regard, we are well advised to heed the caution of Himmelweit and Pear (23, 43) not to stretch the meaning of aggression to include almost any attempts to get attention or to alter another's line of action. In terms of aggression in social groups, Lois Murphy has found that the appearance of aggressive acts in preschool groups is positively correlated with the appearance of sympathetic behavior, and this relationship is

---

[1] These studies were carried out by O. C. Elsea, K. Farwell, V. Gatch, V. T. Hill, C. Morgan, R. Jordan, M. M. Thompson, and M. K. Temerlin.

conceived in terms of development and elaboration of the self system (41). Certainly the bulk of evidence in child psychology indicates no need for positing an innate human tendency toward aggression as a basic instinct.

Second, studies of human groups and collective situations point to the fundamental error of assuming that differences in man's behavior in group situations are simply due to lifting repressions from instincts. It is a fact that in group situations qualitatively new behavioral characteristics appear. These characteristics may be evil or lofty or in between. They are directly related to the participation in or production of a group structure and are not understandable merely in terms of any one individual or all of the individuals outside of the group. They are understandable in terms of the group structure and the by-products of group interaction, such as social norms, values, or traditions. These points will be expanded throughout this book.

Third, the trend of research and experimental evidence in attitude formation, ego development, group situations is contrary to the notion of conscience as "dread of society" alone or of any sharp dichotomizing of the individual and the group. On the contrary, the central theme of what is called "conscience" is the values, imperatives, as well as prohibitions of the social groups to which the individual relates himself. In an important sense, the individual has no consistent or clear-cut personal identity apart from his ties with other persons, groups, and institutions. This development of self or ego will be considered again in Chapter 7.

Finally, society does not simply consist of a set of relations and prohibitions designed to control or inhibit instinctual impulses. It consists also of positive values which the individual acquires in the image of his society, or his group within the society, and which set new goals and aspirations for him which may not be initially in his biological make-up.

While no person in his right mind would deny the importance of hunger, sex, thirst, and other biogenic motives, or the importance of socially determined motives (sociogenic) in group relations, the explanation of social phenomena solely on the basis of either or both is bound to be one-sided. Eysenck has made this point as follows: "In their excitement about the discovery of the powers of 'emotions' over 'intellect,' many psychologists have gone to extremes, portraying the 'man in the street' as the mere plaything of uncontrollable unconscious forces which cannot in any way be influenced by reason. Such a view is no less contrary to fact than the previous over-estimation of rationalistic influences. What is needed is a more realistic appraisal of the relative importance of these two factors in each individual case" (11, p. 64).

THE LEADER AS SOLE ARBITER OF GROUP RELATIONS

Leadership and leader-follower relations are obviously important topics in the study of group relations. It is well known that the leader exerts greater influence in group interaction than any other *single* individual. But tradition has passed a view of leaders and leadership which, in proportion to its influence, dims our sight of an adequate orientation to group relations and to the role of leaders.

The era in which men on top were invested with "divine rights" is not yet ancient history. In an age where the power of a leader is still not always derived from the group, but sometimes from his relationship to the group's resources of physical, political, economic, and military power, widespread acceptance of a view like this is not startling: Leaders possess innately superior characteristics or "traits" which enable them to lead in whatever situation or epoch they may happen to be; they are ultimately the final or sole arbiter of group directions and of relations with other groups. Necessarily, the rest of the group becomes a mass of (unintelligent or inferior) followers who fundamentally differ from the leader in certain traits or in character, and who are compliant to his wishes in the degree that he successfully rouses their emotions or casts his hypnotic spell.

It follows from this traditional view that leaders can be wholly understood in terms of factors (genetic endowment, traits, or life history) *prior* to achieving the leadership position. It follows that it is the leaders who achieve harmony or foment tensions and conflict between groups. It follows that problems of group relations could be solved by bringing leaders together around a conference table.

In the days of the "divine right" of kings, there were assuredly compelling reasons to consider these assumptions as facts. In the more recent development of the long history of such views, the "Great Man" approach to history, so eloquently expressed by Thomas Carlyle and Nietzsche, represents this viewpoint. It was explicit in the work of Galton in his statistical accounts of traits of leaders. Early sociologists, who dealt with group behavior, such as Le Bon and Trotter, Sumner in the United States, Pareto, made this approach to leadership and group relations more explicit. Men in other fields, Ortega y Gasset and T. S. Eliot, have advanced a similar view. Its most infamous expression and fruition are to be found in the philosophy and acts of such political figures as Adolf Hitler.

The fruits of various psychoanalytic approaches are post-mortem accounts of the major social movements in terms of frustrations, Oedipus complexes, repressions, homosexual tendencies, pathological tendencies stored in the unconscious in early childhood. These post-mortem accounts flourish to the present day, especially to account for revolutionary leaders and such infamous figures as Hitler. Thus Clemenceau's early Jacobin affiliations are explained in terms of the Oedipus complex as rebellion against his father, and his later ascent as a political figure in France is explained by the death of his father, which permitted "identification with the father in potency." "One knows that this fresh flowering of activity and affirmation of oneself is the typical, almost universal reaction of the son to the death of his father" (32, p. 174). Robespierre's revolutionary leadership against the French aristocracy becomes a reaction against his father and fixation for his mother: "The persons against whom his hatred was chiefly directed probably were unconsciously associated with his father . . ." (7, p. 113). As for Hitler, "In his childhood a strong Oedipus complex led to reactions of resistance and spite. He wanted to remove his father and be great himself" (7, p. 207). Hitler's anti-Semitism is seen as reaction to seeing Jews in Vienna openly practicing prostitution with "blonde German girls," with whom he himself was unable to have relations because of homosexual tendencies deriving from his strong mother fixation (7, p. 209). Or, we are told, his later ruthless extermination of Jews stems from the fact that a Jewish doctor came to treat his mother for cancer of the breast. "While Hitler was consciously imbued with gratitude toward the kind doctor, unconsciously he made him the 'incestuous, poisoning murderer' of his mother, the incestuous, lascivious and aggressive father with whom he could not identify himself—and now in reality a Jew" (31, p. 30). If nothing is known about the particular leader's childhood, explanation can still be in these terms with the assumption that, if the adult leader behaves in a certain fashion, he *must* have had such conflicts in childhood. Cromwell "undoubtedly" suffered "forcible and yet insufficient repression of the Oedipus complex," although "virtually nothing" is known about his relationship with his father. "Knowing nothing of the basic conflict of childhood days we can at best imagine them" (7, p. 69).

In the dramatic terms of the psychoanalytic approach, exquisitely tortured reasoning and the most intricate logic are necessary for explaining group behavior. Take group prejudices: Members of minority groups present threats to members of the other groups because they "constitute a threat to the primal repression of the members." Specifically, "It is the repression of the incestuous drive [toward parents] which is placed in jeopardy by the presence of other group or groups" (45, p. 91). Sexual relationships within one's own group will always result in guilt because the partner is made to represent either a mother or a father figure. Members of inferior groups cannot, of course, represent the parent, so no guilt is associated with relationships with such persons. "The prejudice is derived from the feeling that the other group may jeopardize the repression of the incestuous drive" (p. 95). Or, if it pleases our fancy, we may take the explanation that

"Racial hatred is an outgrowth of an infantile relationship to parental authority" (36, p. 238).

The results of studies of leader's "traits," research on small groups, as well as historical study with serious concern for group and situational properties, will show us the errors of the general approach to leadership and group relations summarized at the beginning of this section. The study of personal traits of leaders has resulted, as Bird tells us in his *Social Psychology,* in a list of seventy-nine traits appropriate to various leaders, with very little overlapping among the traits of different leaders (6). The upshot of the traditional "trait" studies is "the general finding of wide variations in the characteristics of individuals who become leaders in similar situations, and even greater divergence in leadership behavior in different situations" (26, p. 75).

Almost every study of leadership does reveal superiority of leaders over other group members in at least one of many relevant abilities, skills, or traits (26). But the abilities and skills selected for prominence in the group seem to depend upon the values and ways of the group quite as much as on the personality of the leader. For example, in a study of school children, the first-grade leader was the boy who could spit the farthest. The fourth-grade leader (and hero) was the child who dared "sass" the teacher. So on up to high-school years, when the inconspicuous little girl of grade school became a leader in high school because of superior "dating power" (9).

Thus, as Helen Jennings concluded on the basis of her sociometric studies, the " 'why' of leadership appears . . . not to reside in any personality trait considered singly, nor even in a constellation of related traits, but in the inter-personal contribution of which the individual becomes capable in a specific setting eliciting such contribution from him" (27, p. 205).

This seems to be the main trend in the findings of the so-called "leaderless group" studies which were used in the German army and the British armed forces, by Gibb in the Australian armed services, and in the O.S.S. Division of the United States Army. In these studies, a number of men are faced with a problem situation or a task to be solved collectively, without the appointment of a leader from above or instructions as to method being given. In such situations leadership arises, although it may not always be invested in the same person throughout the group process. As Gibb has observed, the general finding is that leadership or follower traits are not exhibited in isolation. Such traits are relative to a specific social situation. The leader must excel over others in some qualities required by the problem or goal of the particular group. But he cannot be too different from others. He has to be a part of the group. "Leadership is both a function of the social situation and a function of personality, but it is a function of these two in *interaction;* no additive concept is adequate to explain the phenomenon. There is no justification for saying that personality qualities which make for leadership exist in latent form when not being exercised in a social situation" (**17**, p. 268, italics ours).

Like the studies reported by Gibb, the O.S.S. research was interested in selection of men for leadership in military service. Leadership was found to vary from situation to situation. It was not always the most "assertive" individual who dominated the group process, although many of those who rose to leadership were assertive. The leadership position sometimes shifted from one individual to another, as the demands of the situation changed. For example, a man who took the lead in discussing the problem might lose his place when attention was turned to actually carrying out the manipulations involved in solving it (**42**).

On the other hand, when groups interact over a period of time, the leadership position and follower relationships become more or less established. What happens when the individual who has achieved this position is removed? In studying groups of children in school and in camp, Toki (**46**) found that if the leader was removed while the group structure was still in formation or still unstable the developing group structure tended to disintegrate, with resulting helplessness on the part of the rest of the group. But this state of helplessness is temporary if the group continues to interact. In its place, a new structure begins to take shape. If the former leader is returned after this structure is standardized, the group members tend to continue with the now existing structure. If, however, the old leader is returned sometime afterward or assumes membership in the group again, then the more recent group structure tends to be replaced through restoration of the initial relationships within the group.

Especially sociological studies of small groups have shown us that once an individual attains the leadership position, the role, as established in group interaction, exerts certain demands on him, exacts certain obligations, arouses certain expectations. In turn, the leader exerts influence over the activities of the group. Whyte (47) found that group activities usually were initiated by individuals in the top status positions. Suggestions by low-status members, or followers, had to be sanctioned or receive the nod of those high in status. Disputes or frictions, as well as positive courses of action, pass through the leader's hands ultimately. To maintain this focal position in the group, the leader is expected to adhere more rigidly than other group members to the standards and norms of the group, to the established ways of doing things in matters of moral concern and etiquette of the group. The group has higher expectations of the leader's performance and loyalty in matters of concern to the group. A recent experimental study at the University of Oklahoma by Harvey (22) found differential expectations for leaders and lower-status members. Group members in middle and low-status positions, as well as the leader himself, had higher expectations for the leader's performance than for the performance of other group members.

From these requirements and obligations of the leadership role it follows that if the leader does not fulfill the obligations or live up to the expectations of the group in matters of importance to the group he is likely to fall down, or even to fall out of the group's hierarchy. (This is known to be the case when the leader emerges from the group in the course of interaction. It may not always hold in instances where the top man is appointed from without or imposed on the group. As we shall see presently, problems of "headship" are closely related to questions of power organization.) The important, even crucial, implication of this fact is that the leader, like everyone else in the group, is subject to regulation by the group. If he deviates from the social expectations of his fellows too widely, he simply loses his weight in group affairs. Under such circumstances leadership may change hands. The boos which Ramsay MacDonald received from his old comrades of labor in the British elections of the thirties indicate the results of such deviations. The tragic fate of Marshal Pétain, the idolized patriot of World War I, is another striking instance.

Leaders initiate, direct, manipulate group activity. But leadership in a particular group is effective *within certain limits*. While the traditional view of leadership may also point to certain limits of leadership, these limits are conceived as being imposed by blind unreasoning emotions of the masses. We may be told that leaders cannot influence group prejudices for the reason that the masses are fundamentally prejudiced and emotional and blind. But there are intelligent, educated groups having social prejudices. What, then, sets these *limits* within which leadership is effective? The source of these limits is illustrated by Merei's study of children's groups (38). Groups were allowed to interact until a *tradition* of ways of doing things, relations to one another, rituals, sequence of activities, a group jargon had developed. In short, a group structure and appropriate social norms had formed. Then individuals who had been definite leaders in other situations and who were older than the children in the particular group were brought into the situation. What happened? In all groups "the group absorbs the leader, forcing its traditions on him" (p. 25). A number of alternatives were then possible. Some "leaders" (from other groups) were completely absorbed by the established group; others were assimilated and followed group traditions but became the ones who gave the orders or made the distribution of objects in accordance with group custom. Those few "leaders" who succeeded in modifying group tradition did so by first becoming a group member, accepting the established norms, and introducing insignificant modifications. After the customs were thus weakened by slight variations, it became possible to introduce new elements, although few leaders were able to do this.

Clearly, the limits of the leadership role are set by the established social *norms* of the group. This is the finding time and again in sociological studies of small groups (Chapter 8). And leaders, because of their greater responsibility to adhere to group norms and the limits these norms impose upon variations introduced by the leader, are prone to be more aware of the social norms of the group than are other group members (8).

Once group standards or norms are established, they tend to persist in spite of inadequacies to current situations, although this condition could not continue indefinitely. This tendency may pertain to the choice of leader or the aura surrounding him. For example, in the O.S.S. study, some of the "leaderless" groups elected a leader formally at the outset. The tendency then was to maintain the leader, even though he proved to be a poor choice and others were available to replace him.

In critical situations, social norms may become weakened because of their inappropriateness to the new conditions and the compelling push-and-pull of deprivations and anxieties shared by the group. Study of times of crisis and panic indicates that they are particularly well suited for the introduction of new standards or norms. That is, the limits hitherto placed on the established leadership by the social norms are extended by their weakening or breakdown. If the established leader does not introduce new standards and solutions, he is more likely to be deposed in favor of a new leader who does, depending in part on the seriousness of the situation to the group as a whole.

The leadership role usually carries with it a primary or more weighty responsibility in contacts or dealings with other groups, and their leaders. But in such contacts or dealings he must still operate within the permissible latitude of the norms of his group, unless secrecy is possible. This is one of the reasons why the notion of solving all intergroup tensions by bringing prominent citizens around a conference table has limitations. This remark is not in the least to be construed as saying that leaders have no weight, for we have seen that they do. Under certain circumstances, when two groups and their leaders are sincerely concerned to reduce conflict between them, genuine solutions may be reached around the conference table, even though there may be wide differences between the norms of the two groups. If no other common area is found in such a crisis situation, genuine concern for survival of both groups may serve as a central theme. But such conferences are bound to fail if one or both groups are concerned only with upholding their own interests, standards, and goals and set these rigid limits upon their leaders. Under such circumstances one group or the other will be quick to see the professed desires of the other contradicted by concrete circumstances and facts. The Negroes in the South have difficulty in believing in the sincerity of expressed affection of southern white leaders when they see objective hindrances and physical force surrounding their activities in so many areas.

Among other difficulties in such practical suggestions for resolving social conflict is that pointed out by Whyte (48). Sometimes, when a group wishes to negotiate with another group, it may choose a "prominent" individual in that group who is not actually the "operational leader" of the group. Probably, Whyte suggests, he will be the individual who is closest to their own group in status and social standards. This "assumed representative" will be in no position to make a decision for his group unless he happens to have access to the leader of his own group. It is also true that some "assumed representatives" have been made into real powers in their own group by being singled out and by receiving power from another more powerful group. It has been pointed out that Booker T. Washington was a comparatively obscure teacher until his statements were seen by majority white groups as being those they desired to cultivate. Subsequently, he received grants, was influential in securing grants for others, etc., and by these means and the plaudits of the white groups became a leader in his own group.

Such observations bring us to the question of power relationships within the group. It is true that especially in informally organized small groups power ordinarily resides in the leader and other top-status individuals. But in complicated societies where no group operates alone and where groups have interests in the activities of other groups as well as their own, power is not just a question of the leadership role or the capabilities and influence of the individual who holds it. Considerable confusion concerning problems of leadership and of "headship" could be avoided if studies were made carefully tracing the sources and uses of power within the group and in relation to other groups. This confusion is also related to the lack of one-to-one correspondence between popularity and leadership. As Whyte and others have pointed out, the most popular person is not always the leader even in small play groups (48).

The emphasis on leadership and studies of leadership in inter-action terms is a valuable corrective for the traditional view, which regards leaders as sole arbiters of group relations. The finding that leadership is relative, not only to the situation, but to the group structure which develops or is standardized deserves greater emphasis. When we recover from the fascinating discovery that leadership varies tremendously in different situations and in different groups, we are led to the important problem of the limits within which leadership and other group positions operate. As Gouldner (20) has suggested, we shall probably find that these limits will be very narrow when the group is collected to tackle a highly specialized task. But when we study established groups in a variety of situations, it is possible that the limits of leadership are much broader and that common characteristics of the leadership role and the extent of its influence may emerge. Such common characteristics, we should think, would derive from social values or norms standardized in the larger society or in the particular stratum of society—in short, in the prevalent mode of living.

The O.S.S. studies found that not only the leaders but the groups themselves varied in their approaches and ways of dealing with problem situations. The study of factors making for such differences and for common features among groups and the inter-relationships of these features with the leadership position will give us a more accurate picture of leaders. In recent years there has been an unfortunate tendency to equate leadership with techniques of group manipulation. The pioneering experimental study of leadership by Lewin, Lippitt, and White (34) has been taken to mean that group process is primarily or even wholly determined by the leadership techniques employed. Although this was not the concern of the study, it gives us some indication that the structure and traditions (norms) established in the group also exerted some influence. It is not possible to specify the exact nature of this influence, but had the investigators been concerned with this problem they would have certainly specified more fully the aggressive reactions of one group with an "autocratic" leader and the apathetic behavior of another in these terms.

Sociological studies of small groups indicate the error of equating the character of group structure and organization (as "democratic" or "autocratic" or the like) only with the technique of the leader in initiating, directing, organizing group activity. Conceivably, if the group structure and its norms were so standardized, a leader could give orders in a very high-handed autocratic manner to carry out a group decision in which all group members participated democratically. It is not inconceivable that a group can be led by most democratic methods to give the leader life or death power over other members, to indulge as a group in murder, or to fight another group.

In assessing the weight of leadership in determining the directions of the group, we have to consider seriously the structure of the group, including the power structure, its norms and major objectives, which tend to set limits for the permissible latitude or range in which changes can be effected without bringing about various kinds of internal frictions. It will be well worth the effort if leadership study along interaction lines concentrates on the rest of the group as well to determine under what conditions and by what means the group's latitude of change can be increased to include within its limits a greater number of alternatives.

REFERENCES

1. Anastasi, A., and Foley, J. P., Jr. *Differential Psychology*. New York: Macmillan, 1949.

2. Ausubel, D. *Ego Development and the Personality Disorders.* New York: Grune & Stratton, 1952.

3. Benedict, R. *Race: Science and Politics.* New York: Modern Age Books, 1940.

4. Benedict, R. *Race and Cultural Relations,* Problems in American Life, No. 5. Washington: National Education Association, 1942.

5. Berry, B. *Race Relations.* Boston: Houghton Mifflin, 1951.

6. Bird, C. *Social Psychology.* New York: Appleton-Century-Crofts, 1940.

7. Bychowski, C. *Dictators and Disciples.* New York: International Universities Press, 1948.

8. Chowdhry, K.   Leaders and their ability to evaluate group opinion. Dissertation, University of Michigan, 1948; see T. M. Newcomb, *Social Psychology.* New York: Dryden, 1950, 658–659.

9. Cunningham, R., and Associates. *Leadership and the Group.* Reprinted from *Group Dynamics and Education.* Washington: National Educational Association, Division of Adult Education, 1948.

10. Dunn, L. C., and Dobzhansky, Th. *Heredity, Race, and Society.* New York: Mentor Books, rev. ed., 1952.

11. Eysenck, H. J.   War and aggressiveness: A survey of social attitude studies, chap. 3 in T. H. Pear (ed.), *Psychological Factors of Peace and War.* New York: Philosophical Library, 1950.

12. Freud, S. *Group Psychology and the Analysis of the Ego.* London: Hogarth, 1922.

13. Freud, S. *The Ego and the Id.* London: Hogarth, 1927.

14. Freud, S. *Civilization and Its Discontents.* London: Hogarth, 1930.

15. Freud, S. *Collected Papers.* London: Hogarth, 1950, chap. 25.

16. Fyfe, Hamilton. *The Illusion of National Character.* London: Watts, 1940.

17. Gibb, C. H.   The principles and traits of leadership, *J. abn. & soc. Psychol.,* 1947, *42,* 267–284.

18. Ginsberg, M.   National character, *Brit. J. Psychol.,* 1942, *32,* 183–205.

19. Glover, E. *War, Sadism and Pacificism.* London: Allen & Unwin, 1947.

20. Gouldner, A. W.   Introduction, in A. W. Gouldner (ed.), *Studies in Leadership.* New York: Harper, 1950.

21. Greenberg, P. J.   Competition in children, *Amer. J. Psychol.*, 1932, *44*, 221–248.

22. Harvey, O. J.   Status relations and expectations in informal groups. Unpublished manuscript, University of Oklahoma, 1952.

23. Himmelweit, H.   Frustration and aggression: A review of recent experimental work, chap. 8 in T. H. Pear (ed.), *Psychological Factors of Peace and War*. New York: Philosophical Library, 1950.

24. Hooton, E. A.   *Up from the Ape*. New York: Macmillan, 1931.

25. Huxley, J. S., and Haddon, A. C.   *We Europeans: A Survey of "Racial" Problems*. New York: Harper, 1936.

26. Jenkins, W. O.   A review of leadership studies with particular reference to military problems, *Psychol. Bull.*, 1947, *44*, 54–87.

27. Jennings, Helen H.   *Leadership and Isolation*. New York: Longmans, Green, 2nd ed., 1950.

28. Klineberg, O.   *Race Differences*. New York: Harper, 1935.

29. Klineberg, O.   *Tensions Affecting International Understanding, A Survey of Research*. New York: Social Science Research Council, Bull. 62, 1950.

30. Klineberg, O.   *Race and Psychology*. Paris: UNESCO, 1951.

31. Kurth, G. M.   The Jew and Adolf Hitler, *Psychoanal. Quart.*, 1947, *16*, 11–32.

32. Lacombe, P.   The enigma of Clemenceau, *Psychoanal. Rev.*, 1946, *33*, 165–176.

33. Leuba, C. J.   An experimental study of rivalry in young children, *J. comp. Psychol.*, 1933, *16*, 376–378.

34. Lewin, K., Lippitt, R., and White, R. K.   Patterns of aggressive behavior in experimentally created "social climates," *J. soc. Psychol.*, 1939, *10*, 271–300.

35. MacCrone, I. D.   *Race Attitudes in South Africa*. London: Oxford University Press, 1937.

36. Maloney, J. C.   Authoritarianism and intolerance, *Internat. J. Psychoanal.*, 1948, *29*, 236–239.

37. Mead, M. (ed.).   *Cooperation and Competition Among Primitive Peoples*. New York: McGraw-Hill, 1937.

38. Merei, F.   Group leadership and institutionalization, *Human Relations*, 1949, *2*, 23–39.

39. Montagu, Ashley.   *Statement on Race*. New York: Schuman, 1951.

40. Murphy, G.   *Personality*. New York: Harper, 1947, chap. 31.

41. Murphy, L. B.   *Social Behavior and Child Personality*. New York: Columbia University Press, 1937.

42. O.S.S. Assessment Staff. *Assessment of Men.* New York: Rinehart, 1948.

43. Pear, T. H. Peace, war, and culture patterns, chap. 2, in T. H. Pear (ed.), *Psychological Factors of Peace and War.* New York: Philosophical Library, 1950.

44. Sears, R. R. *Survey of Objective Studies of Psychoanalytic Concepts.* New York: Social Science Research Council, 1943.

45. Seidenberg, R. The sexual basis of social prejudice, *Psychoanal. Rev.,* 1952, *39,* 90–95.

46. Toki, K. The leader-follower structure in the school-class, *Japanese J. Psychol.,* 1935, *10,* 27–56; English summary in E. L. Hartley and R. E. Hartley, *Fundamentals of Social Psychology.* New York: Knopf, 1952.

47. Whyte, W. F. *Street Corner Society.* Chicago: University of Chicago Press, 1943.

48. Whyte, W. F. Small groups and large organizations, chap. 12, in J. Rohrer and M. Sherif (eds.), *Social Psychology at the Crossroads.* New York: Harper, 1951.

CHAPTER 3

Л ЛЛ ЛЛ ЛЛ ЛЛ ЛЛ ЛЛ ЛЛ ЛЛ ЛЛ ЛЛ ЛЛ ЛЛ

Animal Behavior and
Human Relations

In the last chapter certain traditional approaches to group relations were critically surveyed. A currently influential trend in psychology is based on the notion that human social behavior and human relations can be understood through an understanding of the behavior of subhuman animals. The idea is offered as, and indeed has the appeal of, a methodological advantage, in that complex phenomena could be observed and experimented upon more effectively if they were studied first in their simpler forms. If *reductionism* from human social relations to insect, rodent, canine, or subhuman primate relations implied in this notion were indeed possible, it would certainly ease the scope and difficulty of our task.

The great strides in the biological sciences during the last century, in particular the developments in evolutionary theory, have correctly led to interest in similarities and continuities in phylogenetic development. In earlier days, students of animal behavior were warned of the dangers of anthropomorphism—attributing human characteristics to animal behavior on the basis of anecdotes. The student of human behavior who finds hope in reductionist solutions may as cogently be cautioned of the pitfalls of "zoömorphism"—uncritically attributing infrahuman characteristics to human behavior.

Many of the cruder analogies have fallen under critical examination. At least it becomes more difficult to gain a scientific audience for some of the lurid pictures which were focal near the century's end of human society as a biological jungle dominated by animal aggressions, with war a biological necessity. Alluring and colorful as analogies between subhuman and human relationships may be, they have fundamental weaknesses which, as Professor Schneirla elaborates in this chapter, render them inadequate for their task. Analogies between animal and human social responses especially on complicated topics such as intergroup relations are based most frequently upon superficial similarities rather than significant common processes. Believing that comparative study aids in gaining insight into all kinds and types of social behavior, Schneirla notes that genuine understanding of the principles and processes underlying various types of social organization requires insight into *differences* among them as well as common features.

In the area of human relations that is our primary concern in this book, viz., intergroup relations, some of the crucial influences are factors which represent differences between the human type of social relations and those of subhuman animals. Among these distinctly human influences are the cultural heritage of every ingroup, a codified system of symbols constituting the language of the group, and accumulating technology, which give the unique structure to the group's social organization. All of these—culture, language, accumulating technology and the mass mediums of communication it makes possible, the unique social organization of the group—are transmitted, not biologically, but culturally. Cultural transmission is made possible through capacities and processes which, if not unique, are most highly developed in the human species. These vastly increased capacities of the human organism make possible the development of a whole system of new wants and desires formed in relation to the culture and social organization of the group. Far from being reducible to basic biological impulses, these impulses are uniquely human, socially derived motives.

Throughout this book, it is stressed that the kind of social structure and the norm system, which are transmitted and propagated primarily through language, are crucial in the formation of positive or negative relations between human groups. Without these distinctly human institutions it is inconceivable to comprehend *modern* group tensions and *modern* warfare, as Pear has stressed so cogently in *Psychological Factors of Peace and War* (14). In view of these vital consequences of the psychological equipment of man, it is unrealistic to gloss over inter-specie differences as though they were a question of slight degree, of shades merging into one another. The notion that we can learn the processes and principles of behavior of subhuman species and arrive at principles of human behavior by adding another quantity in the equation is truly enticing. But it obscures the fact that the differences between the highest subhuman primates and the human species result in the differences between primitive communication and a codified language system, between no-culture and culture.

To do justice to these differences, as well as to similarities, the positive approach is not through reductionism or analogies but rather through the concept of *levels* of organization. In view of the vogue for using simple models and reducing inter-specie differences to matters of shading or quantities to be added, Professor Schneirla gives us an authoritative account of the concept of levels with some of its implications for the study of human relations.

THE CONCEPT OF LEVELS IN THE STUDY OF
SOCIAL PHENOMENA

T. C. Schneirla
American Museum of Natural History, New York

There are many types of animal aggregations typically formed under natural conditions, from groups of the protozoan organism, Paramecium, to human organizations (15). How are we to understand them? Despite their apparent diversity, all such groups have in common a "togetherness" of individuals. In every such aggregation, unity is evident to some extent, suggesting properties more or less different from those of the separate, unassembled individuals. The nature of the properties of group unity is by no means immediately apparent in any case. More than one writer has conceived it mystically, as an intangible agency and even a kind of collective mentality, exemplified in Maeterlinck's concept "spirit of the hive" for an insect colony, (12) and Le Bon's "crowd mind" for human groups (10). However appealing they may be, such ideas serve only to emphasize the existence of a unified group, and make no substantial contribution toward explaining the question of its nature. More recently, a realistic method has developed which promises to correct such difficulties.

Modern scientific investigations have sharpened the realization that there are numerous types of aggregations typically formed by different animals, similar to one another in certain respects and different in other respects. Understanding what holds various types of groups together and what principles underlie their organizations derives from insight not only into their common features but also into their differences.

The concept of "levels" has developed as a means of organizing our evidence concerning the types of collective behavior exhibited in the animal series. In this approach, various kinds of aggregation are ranked "higher" or "lower" in a scale, according to our evaluation of these groups in terms of criteria of tested validity. Of course it is not a simple matter to determine what clues in the evidence are most valid as indicators of relative superiority or inferiority in group function. In the scientific study of varied types of aggregations, however, it is understood first of all that the principles whereby higher groups are considered superior to lower-level types can be worked out dependably only through actual investigations of groups to learn their real characteristics. In this chapter the point will be discussed principally in terms of some comparisons of human and insect aggregations.

The primary purpose of the *levels concept* is to understand the relationships of varied natural phenomena in general, and not social phenomena alone. Although all types of animals are basically regarded as having had a common ancestry, animals now living may be considered the representatives of different stages attained through evolution. The *levels* concept represents the different types of individual organisms as differing in stage of organization, from the viruses, considered at a lower level than the Protozoa, to various multicellular organisms, considered respectively higher. With justification we may consider the viruses a simpler type of organism than a multicellular animal, but differences in organization other than relative complexity must be taken into account as well, in the study of organismic levels. In what respects, finally, is a bird considered an organism on a higher level than a starfish, a monkey on a higher level than a bird? Further and more elaborate difficulties arise when we pass beyond the comparison of types of individual organisms to compare *groups* of organisms in regard to their respective levels.

First of all, social levels are not to be distinguished in terms of how successful various types of groups have been in meeting (i.e., how well they are adapted to) the conditions of their environments (1), because environmental conditions are not the same for various types of organisms, but differ greatly according to the different capacities of their members—their sensory equipment, for example. A large group of "tent caterpillars," reassembled each night within its enclosure of silken threads spun on a tree, may be as relatively successful at surviving in its environment as human inhabitants of a nearby settlement are in theirs, notwithstanding the far greater total and greater variety of sensory impressions received by members of the human group from their surroundings. For the rise of all animal species has occurred through natural-selection processes in the course of which poorly adjusted animal types are "weeded out." These varied events in evolution have led to the survival of animals which acquire (through mutation and related biological processes) adequate adaptive resources and to the elimination of those acquiring inadequate adaptive resources. Thus a species so constituted that its members were always attracted to intense stimulus changes would risk extinction through an unusual frequency of serious injury to member individuals. Surviving species, animals now existing, may be ranked high or low with respect to social characteristics but do not have *corresponding* ranks with respect to adaptive success. Colonies of the swimming protozoan, Paramecium, colonies of a social insect, and communities of mankind are not clearly different in this respect. For present purposes we may assume that all meet their respective environmental conditions reasonably well, although these conditions are very different in complexity and other respects more important for the psychologist. The differences crucial for social levels depend upon the *ways* in which various types of animal groups adjust to their typical surroundings.

In other words, differences in "levels" depend upon *what kinds of processes and capacities are available* to an animal and its species mates in adapting to their environments. Because of their sensorimotor capacities in particular, social insects such as ants and bees in their colony settings may be ranked higher in the group-level array than the sponge, a colonial organism very deficient in such capacities. Furthermore, a higher status in this respect depends more upon advantages in the *kind* of capacities available in the group than upon complexity. Thus the pattern of community life in social insects evidently is influenced only in limited ways through learning—ways which may be considered meager in group potentialities compared with the relatively vast functions of learning in the socialized life of man. This is the case despite the fact that the social life of insects tends to be very complex. This point bears further study.

It seems also true that animal aggregations of the most different types (and levels) exhibit certain basic similarities (1, 19). A point that soon impresses even casual observers is that very different aggregations often attain recognizably similar end results. Thus, for example, man builds huts or grand skyscrapers, termites simple ball-nests of mud or impressive rock-hard spire nests; human cities are complexly organized, but insect communities also show an amazing complexity in their daily affairs. However, in the internal and basic processes whereby these assemblages function, maintain their organization, and attain their characteristic results, the social phenomena are very different.

We must discard both the notion that sheer complexity is the most dependable guide to the level of a social phenomenon and the corollary idea that the kind of result achieved through group action is a necessary guide to the level of a society. On the contrary, the problem is not that simple, for as suggested above, the key of social levels must be sought in underlying processes. Let us consider one of many possible examples in which great functional complexity exists in a group which, qualitatively considered, is relatively low in level.

In certain species of army ants living in tropical forests, mass or swarm raids are organized anew each day by the colonies (16). These forays are amazingly complex as to both numbers of participants and the variety and organization of their behavior. They are also highly successful (i.e., very adaptive) in their tangible outcome, which is great quantities of living prey delivered as booty to the temporary nest of the colony. The swarms of one common species often grow larger than fifteen yards in width each forenoon and then may contain more than 30,000 individuals. The intricacy of internal organization is suggested by the fact that, although such a body becomes very large, it continues to sweep along as a growing unified group moving roughly in a single direction away from the temporary nest. The movement of the body is not strictly linear but is complicated by alternate wheeling or "flanking" movements, first right and then left in rhythmic fashion, whereby more ground is covered and more booty captured. The size of a swarm and the complexity of its internal organization develop from the first beginnings after dawn, until near midday a maximum is reached in size and complexity, whereupon the sections of the main body interfere with one another and unity decreases. Here a process of swarm division occurs, through which two or more sub-swarms arise. These influence one another through indirect connections with the nest far in the rear. Actually, the study of swarm-division processes throws valuable light upon the nature of organization in the unitary swarm which first develops.

Such highly complex and adaptive collective maneuvers might well encourage exaggerated notions of both individual capacities and group processes involved. To a casual observer the effective strategy seems to depend upon a central officership of some kind, carried out "as if by word of command," as one writer puts it. However, a systematic investigation of this seemingly very intelligent social strategy shows that it rests not upon humanlike processes of leadership and group communication but on the complex interaction of very simple behavioral processes (17).

By studying how these complex raids develop through the day, and how oversize swarms divide, one basis for understanding their organization and function is provided. Another is provided by studying the behavior of groups comparatively, in laboratory and field. The individual army ant, psychologically considered, is very simple—indeed, much simpler than many other ants. No worker ant in the swarm ever adds more than a very limited and uncomplicated contribution to proceedings. The swarm advance involves a "relay" process carried out through simple responses of successive myriads of individuals when they encounter new (chemically unsaturated) ground ahead of the swarm. Organization within the mass is attained through an interplay of columns and masses among the sections of the whole, based upon individual reactions to chemical and tactual stimulation. Observations and appropriate tests of individual workers in these species reveal a small repertoire of reaction capacities which may lead to results which are complex and variable or simple and stereotyped according to the complexity of the prevalent environment. In the heterogeneous forest environment, a swarm raid builds up after dawn each day; but under the simplified conditions of a large enclosed space in the laboratory the ants will run for days in an endless circular column, unladen or carrying their brood (18). In the forest environment, where the complex phenomenon of the raid can build up, stage upon stage, only humanized (i.e., anthropomorphic) terms might seem adequate for the group action. But such terms are not adequate for the student of animal societies, comparing group patterns.

Insect and mammalian societies are a well-known source of analogies. For example, the terms "king" and "queen" are commonly used for the male and fertile female of the termite colony, or "royal pair" for them both. The terms certainly are descriptive in a literary sense, but their use is not always free of the implication that a mysterious overlordship beyond biological functions may be exerted by reproductive individuals over the colony. To discuss the queen seriously as "ruler" over her colony is plain nonsense. More seriously, analogies are frequently drawn between conditions such as a government or social pattern in man and a type of colony organization in insects, or between communication in man and social coördination in insects. Let no one dismiss such analogies on the plea that they are generally intended figuratively or for literary purposes, and not seriously and meaningfully. They are used too frequently and relied upon too heavily by writers and speakers to be lightly cast aside.

Analogies between human and insect behavior are frequently encountered in serious discussions with often impressive but usually not very sound reasons given. The patterns of insect society seem to resemble some of those in human society—why should we not use the same terms and apply conclusions from the insect situation directly to man?

A book by Friedrich Christian Lesser (*Insecto-Theologia*, 1738) served as one of the principal sources for the many English writers in the following century who used insects as examples for worthy human moral conduct. One such writer, the Reverend W. Farren White (*Ants and Their Ways*, 1884) endeavored to make clear how many important lessons could be derived from ants, with

. . . their industry, their well-regulated government, the *devotion of the queen for the commonwealth, loyalty of her subjects,* their affection for their youthful charges . . . *their public works and national enterprises, planned and executed with the most surprising promptitude, uncontrolled by parliamentary committees, orders in council, and circumlocuous offices* . . . their social institutions, their provident clubs, and savings banks . . . their habits of early rising, of cleanliness, of moderation, of economy, of temperance, their love of fresh air . . . their skill in industry in many trades . . . their language, which though more difficult to acquire than Chinese, yet is to them so intelligible that there are no misunderstandings, all speaking it fluently . . .

In a sentence from which these few portions are taken, the Reverend Mr. White draws many lessons for mankind from the ants, not the least of which is the one (indicated by our italics) which implies that human monarchial systems might do well to follow those of ants in dispensing with trammeling parliamentary procedures.

Social groups of insects commonly share food among all members of the colony, without regard to labor or other social contributions—is this not equivalent to socialism or communism in human society? Do not both insect societies and human societies have their "social parasites"? Have not many insects "worked out" a form of warmaking state which resembles a human pattern such as fascism rather closely in many respects? If striking similarities such as these appear, why should we not use illustrations from insect societies in a *direct* application to man?

Such writers seem not to have been sufficiently industrious or careful to have read the writings of scientific students of ant life such as R. Réaumur, *Mémoires pour Servire à l'Histoire des Insectes,* T. VI, 1742, who expressed himself as follows: ". . . But writers have not been content to admire what the ants permit us to see. They have sought to interpret to their advantage all their actions, even those whose motives are most obscure. . . . A government has been said to exist among them which ours might take as a model; they have been made to appear as civilized as ourselves. . . . They have endeavored 'to convert the ants into little men.' " (From R. Réaumur, *The Natural History of Ants,* tr. W. M. Wheeler, 1926.)

Because general analogies of this type usually depend upon superficial similarities rather than evidence for significant common processes, they cannot be tested readily; hence they may be turned whichever way may suit the purposes of the user. A particular value judgment is determinative, rather than the validity of a comparison. Such arguments therefore are likely to be not only specious but hazardous to truth when the analogy is used to force home an important point. For example, in social insects there are many forms of social parasitism and dependency, of predation and pillaging, of food-sharing and mutual relationships, but their adaptive importance in the respective insect social patterns has no direct or necessary bearing upon the advantages or disadvantages of roughly similar patterns in man. For insect social patterns have developed through the processes of biological evolution, and have persisted with minimal and slow change through more than sixty million years. In man, however, we may look to tradition and institutional factors for the elaboration and continuance of existing social patterns. Any human pattern must be evaluated as desirable or undesirable in terms of its psychological bases, its meaning, and its consequences for human society, and no argument from the biological processes underlying an insect pattern can have an immediate and decisive bearing upon the human issue. The point here is that conclusions taken from apparent similarities alone are questionable, *not* that a comparative study of animal societies can fail to increase our insight into *all levels* of social behavior.

The analogy between human and insect communication is a subtle one, likely to depend upon the application of similar names rather than how insects on the one hand and men on the other hand actually influence one another in social situations. Insect communication frequently is complex and difficult to understand—witness in particular the dances of the returning honey bee forager on the comb, as Von Frisch has described them (**7, 8**). This investigator has reported that hive mates are somehow influenced by the finder's dance, so that they are able to locate the food place sooner than by chance, not only in its direction but also in its distance. *How* this particular effect occurs is still unclear although its occurrence is factual. Those who are inclined to regard it as symbolic, in the human sense, should consider the really nonsymbolic nature of other social interactions which are well known in bees. From other research of Von Frisch we know that a returning finder bee, through the stimulative effect of a perfume carried back on her body from the flower she has visited, may arouse other bees somehow to a specific "set" for the odor of this type of flower. This effect is produced even when the experimental perfume is a different one from that of her own nectar source, dusted incidentally upon her body as she feeds.

Types of insect communication are known in which the community is aroused through the rapid propagation of excitement from individual to individual, often by antennal contact with or without an accompanying odor effect. In other cases, an effect is transmitted through the air from specialized vibratory (stridulatory) organs set into action when the insect becomes excited, affecting specialized receptors (chordotonal organs) in other individuals within range. These types are well known in many species of ants and other social insects. A cruder form is effective when vibrations are transmitted through the ground or nest structure, as when the "sender" is an excited ant or termite striking its head or abdomen repeatedly against the wooden walls of the nest galleries. Although perhaps tempting, it is very unsafe to conclude that these interchanges are qualitatively like human symbolic forms in which one man calls a command or an appeal to others, or beats a drum to them in code.

The known insect interchanges appear to have in common an important limitation, that if the behavior of the finder insect not only arouses others but also guides them to some extent the latter effect is an incidental product of the finder's behavior and not the cause of it (13). Experiments by Eidmann and others show this fact clearly for various species of ants. For example, in a standard laboratory test with certain ant species, one ant finds food while wandering about, then returns across an area to the place where her nestmates are confined. Her behavior on entering arouses them, many of them soon leave by the now open door, and some of these soon find the food place. They find the food sooner than by chance, but is this because the finder has directed them to it? She has, but incidentally and *not by code*. If, after the finder has returned, the paper floor across which she ran is replaced with a fresh one, the newcomers (aroused by her) wander about and find the food place only by accident. The excited finder during her feeding and return has released a glandular secretion which the others can follow so long as its traces remain on the floor. However, she does this by virtue of reflex responses, and not intentionally any more than a man sweats under certain atmospheric conditions *in order to* furnish a social cue to others that he is uncomfortably warm.

Only in its general adaptive function as social transmission does insect "communication" resemble human language. When men speak to one another, the following criteria are satisfied: (1) The words are used more or less intentionally, with respect to anticipated social consequences; (2) the words are typically symbolic, in that they have learned, meaningful connections with objects and situations; (3) the words are directive, in that they influence others as well as the speaker in characteristic ways; and (4) the words may be patterned and rearranged according to the motivation of the speaker and his perception of situation and listeners. Human language is a symbolic discourse, mastered through long experience. There is no evidence that the social transmission of insects in the typical pattern of the species is learned, or that it is symbolic in the sense that human words are symbolic. Rather, the insect forms are derived through biological processes characteristic of the species and are fixed in nature rather than culturally changeable and socially versatile, as are those of man. Since the insect colony can exhibit only rigid forms of social transmission produced through the predominant influence of species heredity, they stand in sharp contrast with those of a human culture, which are psychologically very different in their origin, character, and social potentialities.

Symbolic transmission in social groups is not, however, confined to the human level alone. For example, in experiments at the Yerkes Laboratories of Primate Biology, chimpanzees were able to learn a gestural form of communication and use it symbolically. When a food box was made too heavy for one chimpanzee alone to pull it within reach, chimpanzees which had previously pulled alone learned to pull together. Then, with further experience, they became able to summon one another by means of self-initiated gestures such as gentle taps on the shoulder (6). These were truly symbolic, and not merely signals to action. The chimpanzee who tapped was presenting, in anticipation of its social effect, a special cue which had come to symbolize, that is, to stand for meaningfully, the expected social result. The symbolic, anticipative, and directive nature of this gestural cue was indicated by the fact that when shoulder taps were insufficient, or slow in producing coöperation, the active animal would turn to pulling alone, or might act forcibly and directly to get the second animal involved in pulling. Although it is not known how far and in what ways such gestural devices may be involved in chimpanzee group communication under natural conditions, their use is probably very limited.

In lower primates, it is probable that there is virtually no symbolic communication outside of gestural procedures. Although the sounds produced by chimpanzees have an excitatory function in various settings, they are evidently uttered interjectionally as parts of excited behavior, to which the responses of other animals become conditioned according to the social situation in which the different types of sounds are usually heard. In lower primates, it is doubtful that vocal communication can attain the status of a symbolic language, much less a conventionalized language, as in human society. Here is an important difference in levels, resulting from the limited capacities of lower primates for the processes of learning, perception, and reasoning—inferiorities which account for their meager social training as well as their low social heritage and institutionalized behavior, as compared with man.

How are we to recognize a true "social" group in a lower animal, since these groups appear to differ widely in their organizations? First of all, let us recognize that not all groups are necessarily social; unless the aggregation is grounded upon the interdependence of individual members, upon their responsiveness to one another, it is not a social group. There are invertebrate assemblages in which such intragroup relationships are lacking;

these are termed "associations" rather than social groups. Thus in many species of flies, individuals gather together because all of them approach the same environmental stimulus and remain within the area of its effect. At twilight or dawn, large clouds of male mosquitoes may form on a basis of common response to environmental features such as light and temperature. In contrast, the members of a clan of monkeys remain in a group by virtue of an interindividual attraction within the group and not merely because there happens to be an independent individual attraction to the same area. What is common to all "social" groups is this responsiveness to other individuals as having definite attractive properties of their own apart from those of the physical environment.

Nothing is gained except obscurity when we say that some animals are social because they are "gregarious." This term means simply that they tend to come together; it merely describes what we already know but does not suggest an explanation for it. Progress is made in these problems only when students become impatient with impressive but really hollow terms such as "gregarious instinct" and look behind them for the real meanings. A promising approach has been made through the study of "trophallaxis" processes in a social group, that is, processes based upon the interchange of mutually attractive stimuli in the group. As Wheeler (20) developed the term for social insects, it signified food exchange; however, we may extend it to mean all stimuli which are equivalent to food in their organic effects, and all which come to elicit approach to other individuals. Thus a newborn sheep is licked by its mother, then nurses and is soothed by cuddling with her; soon it is following her about, and later follows other sheep. On the basis of reflex processes which are at first limited and rather random in their influence upon general behavior, organized group responses appear through learning and the young lamb becomes socialized. After such early socialization it is disturbed and restless when it is away from the group for very long. By virtue of the initial crude reflex processes (e.g., nursing upon finding the nipple) the young individual experiences tension relief in the presence of another individual (its mother), thus learns to approach the other and finally the group. Bottle-raised lambs kept apart from the flock do not approach the group or mix with it on later tests, except after special training. Thus gregarious behavior does not appear automatically but requires an initial ontogenetic process, characteristic of the species, for its development.

The attraction of a young mammal to the mother develops as a part of a mutual bond, for the mother also obtains tension relief in various ways from the young, relief from mammary-gland tension, for example. The group-adjustment process of course differs considerably in its form according to the condition of the young at birth, their sensitivity, and other developmental features characteristic of the species. In insects, the bond seems assured by the presence of physiological equipment such as body-surface secretions of the larvae which attract adults, arouse licking, and thereby open the way for feeding of larvae by adults. The process of a conditioned approach to the colony chemical and to individuals bearing it may really begin with larval feeding. Unity in the colony thus depends upon trophallactic effects which insure that each individual is attracted by and is attractive to all others.

Although we may postulate a fundamentally similar biological basis for the trophallactic processes through which gregariousness develops on different social levels, there are of course marked differences in the final social patterns. These depend especially upon how far adjustments to other individuals may develop psychologically, and what other individuals come to mean to the responder, that is, upon processes limited by the psychological capacities of the species. Thus, the limitations of social interactions in insects are suggested by the predominance of *present* chemotactual stimulative effects from *present* individuals. Even crudely daubing an ant of species A with the body fluids of species B may lead to her acceptance for a time in a colony of species B, although normally A is attacked by B. The partially stimulated B-colony odor is her badge, so to speak, and she is accepted more or less as a nestmate until the chemical has dissipated; then she becomes a "stranger." This social process must not be likened to human recognition of a fellow group member and friend; for we have no evidence that social interactions in insects involve the meaningful properties of human social perception. To be sure, somewhat similar results are achieved in the group affiliations of ant and man, but through processes which may differ very radically in their psychological nature. Not only does a *present* social stimulus such as his mother's "frown" come to have an increased perceptual meaning for an infant, but its meanings become more subtle and indirect in time, as when he perceives the frown according to his anticipation of what an *absent* individual (his father) may do when he enters the situation.

Even in insects, a responsiveness to species mates, however simple and apparently automatic it may appear to be, depends to an appreciable extent upon the conditions of early experience. Thus mixed colonies of ants may be created by putting individuals of different species together from the time they are removed from their cocoons. This type of evidence suggests that normally a conditioned responsiveness to the prevalent nest-colony chemical arises in ontogeny. After an infant chimpanzee had been raised to the age of nine months in a human household but away from chimpanzees (other than itself), when placed with an infant chimpanzee of similar age it was first disturbed and noticeably aggressive. These two young chimpanzees require a few weeks of experience together for relationships of acceptance and companionship to develop (9). Their behavior reminds us of the characteristics of "unsociability" and "shyness" which may appear in an only child deprived of early experience with other children. Whether on a lower or a higher social level, interpersonal relationships do not develop automatically or "instinctively" into a pattern; rather, they arise through a socialization process of progressive interrelationships between an organism and surrounding conditions.

The contributions of the social environment and of group history to the socialization process are very different according to the species, as we have said. In insects they are narrow and rigid; in man they are both wide and plastic. Although insects are capable of learning, so far as our evidence goes this capacity seems to be secondary in the early adjustments of new individuals to the social group. Its function may be largely held to a generalized conditioned approach to the colony chemical, established through early feeding. Such processes are dominated by hereditary properties of the species, for example, by the relatively automatic character of certain insect feeding reflexes. On the other hand, the wide and predominant role of learning in the socialization of a human individual cannot be disputed. Some specific organic processes such as the sucking reflex are prominent, of course; however, their social function and their significance change greatly in the course of time. The predominance of biological factors in the insect social pattern may be emphasized by terming such a pattern *biosocial;* that of psychological factors in the human pattern by terming it *psychosocial.*

These differences may be illustrated in another way by asking what influences may be exerted by the past upon animals at different social levels. In insects, through genetic factors underlying growth, the evolutionary past of the species is rather directly dominant over the development of social behavior and thus accounts for the persistence of such behavior in an insect group. Hence, as we have mentioned, the principal social insects have had their characteristic group patterns for many millions of years. Furthermore, because these patterns are dominated by organic, hereditary factors developed through evolution, as behavior systems they are typically very stable. In contrast, human social patterns are changeable, plastic, and often unstable. Man has a cultural pattern characteristic of the social climate in which he lives, since he acquires it through learning under the conditions of that social setting. In his individual acquisition of language, ways of dressing, attitudes toward books, and judgments of the beautiful, the process is profoundly influenced by group circumstances and by the conditions of individual social experience from start to finish. Continuity in this process is maintained through a cultural heritage, transmitted from generation to generation through psychological functions such as learning, understanding, and symbolic communication. In this sense, insects have only a very negligible culture: their social heritage is limited to the general influence of a spatial odor-pattern and various physical properties of a nest built up by earlier generations. In a comparable sense, chimpanzees in the wild have their established group territories, their regular feeding and nesting places, to which the young learn to conform as an inevitable part of their socialization. Their gesture language doubtlessly is involved in aiding the transmission of such effects to further generations. Wide psychological differences are represented here. The insect level is very stereotyped and limited in comparison with the primates', yet that of chimpanzees like other lower primates is vastly below the representative social level of man (21).

We have considered some of the concepts derived through analogy which tend to obscure differences among social levels in the animal series. A further one, originally developed in studies of group behavior in domestic fowl, is that of "dominance hierarchy" (5). As illustrated with a flock of chickens in the barnyard, the dominance hierarchy constitutes a so-called peck order, or a series of different aggression-submission relationships in the group. In the simplest case, approximated in small groups of chickens placed together experimentally, a linear dominance ranking develops in which superior members dominate all those lower in the group but are dominated by all those of higher dominance rank. With chickens these relationships at first involve actual aggression by pecking, with A pecking B and all others, but not being pecked by them; B pecking C and all others except A; C pecking D and all others except A and B; and so on. Through learned discriminations depending upon the consequences of initial encounters in the group situation, the amount of overt pecking of others steadily decreases, especially in the most dominant members, and a mere beginning of such behavior or the mere approach of a socially dominant member becomes sufficient to obtain withdrawal or other submissive behavior. Of course, social situations may be described in which rats, dogs, chimpanzees, and people seem to behave in a way closely approximating the peck-order situation of the henyard. However, it would be a serious fallacy to assume that all of these group situations are adequately covered by the peck-order outlines described for hens in the yard.

This type of behavior situation is readily recognized in many animal groups; however, the idea can easily be carried too far. Even in birds, with their characteristically stereotyped group relationships, prominence of the peck-order feature of group behavior differs greatly according to the limitations of space, food, and other basic conditions. Moreover, its prominence differs greatly among species, and its form varies considerably in groups under natural conditions. For example, the dominance-hierarchy aspect is not easy to recognize among the score or more of individuals in a clan of Central American howler monkeys (4); on the other hand, rather sharp differences in dominance with frequent overt aggressive interchanges characterize the group behavior of Old World monkeys such as the rhesus. Leadership in the former group is mainly a matter of ascendance and other non-conflict relationships, but in the latter it is more clearly a result of aggression and conflict interactions. It is also to be noted, with respect to the rhesus as example, that the dominance pattern of primate groups seems much more complex in its origin and variations than that characteristic of birds.

Social patterns such as aggression-dominance relationships, as would be expected, are most involved and most variable in form and degree in human groups. Here the relative prominence of such aspects of social life varies most widely according to differences in the conditions of early socialization. Investigations in the United States have shown that hostile and aggressive social attitudes and behavior are prominent or are minimal in the group adjustments of children according to earlier experiences in groups (11) and the extent of unfriendly or aggressive relationships with adults (3). It is an elementary principle of social psychology that human group patterns may differ widely in their nature according to the background of the groups and their members. To say that this statement holds relatively less for social patterns in lower animals obviously does not mean that early family adjustments and socialization can be ignored in their case.

Social organization on any level must be studied first of all in terms of factors responsible for group unity. A condition such as dominance is really a secondary part of this question, since instead it opposes group unity. More properly, trophallactic relationships in the early life of individuals in the social group may be postulated as furnishing group-approach tendencies opposing aggression and withdrawal tendencies underlying dominance relationships. Aggression-dominance adjustments arise through conflict and friction among group members, as in sharp competition over limited food or space; hence they have to do with "social distance" rather than with group unity directly. In the more solitary lower vertebrates such as many birds, male dominance and aggressiveness in the breeding season tend to ward off all species members save one, keeping neighboring mated pairs at their distance (2). When aggression-dominance and intragroup conflict reach a high point, a weakening or even a disappearance of group unity may be expected. Group organization depends first of all upon the strength of social-approach tendencies. Modifications and limitations in group organization then may be understood in terms of the function of such basic factors in relation to the strength of aggression-dominance and other modifying influences.

On the whole, social levels are relatively, but not absolutely, different. We have noticed indications of a basic similarity in the biological factors underlying trophallactic relationships and determining group unity in a variety of animal societies. Yet the social patterns which can develop on this general basis in different species must be referred in their specific nature to the psychological capacities (and particularly learning capacities) of the different animal types. Differences in psychological endowment account for qualitative social differences which are very striking in widely separated groups. Thus, while insects, chimpanzees, and man all communicate after their fashions, in insects this function is stereotyped and nonsymbolic, and in chimpanzees although symbolic it is tremendously limited in its social scope in comparison with the symbolic systems of man. Thus, change is possible in insect social patterns only as it is enforced to limited extents through environmental alterations or through exceedingly slow processes of biological evolution. In man, on the other hand, social patterns change through psychological processes which are not at all directly dependent upon evolution since their relationship to a biological basis (e.g., function of cerebral cortex) does not determine or limit their pattern in any direct way. This means that, in an animal capable of greatly extended learning and mastery of symbolic processes, important qualitative differences in social pattern may arise and develop rapidly in a short succession of generations.

Unfortunately, the processes of psychosocial evolution, like those of biosocial evolution, have their negative as well as their positive aspects. An insect species, by and large, can rid itself of maladaptive social behavior only through appropriate changes in the organic characteristics promoting such behavior, by virtue of natural selection in evolution. Man, on the other hand, has far more efficient ways of correcting maladaptive social behavior through use of his psychological facilities. However, to say that human social patterns occupy a "higher" level than those of lower animals does not mean that man's social procedures are always better adapted to his needs than are those of lower animals to theirs. When man attempts to settle his social difficulties by resorting to physical combat, no analogy with lower animals can adequately explain his failure to use the maximal psychological facilities at his disposal. For man's patterns of social misconduct are as characteristic of him under the conditions, and as different from any to be found in lower animals, as are his more desirable social processes. Sufficient emphasis on the human conditions which characteristically produce human social disasters may finally teach man how to improve his group procedures.

REFERENCES

1. Allee, W. C. *The Social Life of Animals.* New York: Norton, 1938.

2. Allee, W. C. Social dominance and subordination among vertebrates, in R. Redfield (ed.), *Biological Symposia,* 1942, *8,* 139–162.

3. Anderson, H. H. Domination and social integration in the behavior of kindergarten children and teachers, *Genet. Psychol. Monogr.,* 1946, *21,* 287–385.

4. Carpenter, C. R. A field study of the behavior and social relations of howling monkeys, *Comp. Psychol. Monogr.,* 1934, *10,* 1–168.

5. Collias, N. Aggressive behavior among vertebrate animals, *Physiol. Zool.,* 1944, *17,* 83–123.

6. Crawford, M. P. The cooperative solving of problems by young chimpanzees, *Comp. Psychol. Monogr.,* 1937, *14,* 1–88.

7. Frisch, K. von. The dances of the honey bee, *Bull. Animal Behavior,* 1947, No. 5, 1–32.

8. Frisch, K. von. *Bees, Their Vision, Chemical Senses, and Language.* Ithaca: Cornell University Press, 1950.

9. Jacobsen, C. F. and M. M., and Yoshioka, J. G. The development of an infant chimpanzee during her first year, *Comp. Psychol. Monogr.,* 1932, *9,* 1–94.

10. Le Bon, G. *The Crowd: A Study of the Popular Mind.* London: Fisher Unwin, 1920.

11. Lewin, K., Lippitt, R., and White, R. K. Patterns of aggressive behavior in experimentally graded "social climates," *J. soc. Psychol.,* 1939, *10,* 271–299.

12. Maeterlinck, M. *The Life of the Bee.* New York: Dodd, Mead, 1903.

13. Maier, N. R. F., and Schneirla, T. C. *Principles of Animal Psychology.* New York: McGraw-Hill, 1935, chap. 6.

14. Pear, T. H. Peace, war, and culture patterns, chap. 2 in T. H. Pear (ed.), *Psychological Factors of Peace and War.* New York: Philosophical Library, 1950.

15. Redfield, R. (ed.). *Biological Symposia,* Vol. 8, Lancaster: Cattell Press, 1942; especially articles by Jennings, Allee, and Carpenter.

16. Schneirla, T. C. Further studies in the army-ant behavior pattern—Mass organization in the swarm raiders, *J. comp. Psychol.,* 1940, *29,* 401–460.

17. Schneirla, T. C.   Social organization in insects, as related to individual function, *Psychol. Rev.*, 1941, *48*, 465–486.
18. Schneirla, T. C.   A unique case of circular milling in ants, *Amer. Museum Novitiates*, 1944, No. 1253, 1–26.
19. Schneirla, T. C.   Problems in the biopsychology of social organization, *J. abn. & soc. Psychol.*, 1946, *41*, 385–402.
20. Wheeler, W. M.   *The Social Insects*.   New York: Harcourt, Brace, 1928.
21. Yerkes, R. M., and Yerkes, A. W.   Social behavior in infrahuman primates, in C. Murchison (ed.), *Handbook of Social Psychology*, Worcester: Clark University Press, 1935.

CHAPTER 4

ЛЛЛЛЛЛЛЛЛЛЛЛЛЛЛЛЛЛЛЛЛЛЛЛЛЛ

Implications of Present-Day
Prejudice Studies

During the last few decades, one of the areas in which active research has been carried out is that of prejudice (social distance). A good many psychologists and sociologists have contributed to the mounting list of literature under the general titles of prejudice (social distance) and "race relations."

These studies were presented in terms of various theoretical approaches, some of which we discussed in the last two chapters. On the whole, the prejudice or social-distance studies were conceived and carried out as if the prejudice shown by the groups in question and the particular groups against which it is directed constitute a problem area independent of the general area of intergroup relations. As emphasized in Chapter 1, prejudice studies will gain much in perspective and validity if they are carried out, not with the finality of a unique or distinct area, but as an important part of the general problem of intergroup relations.

In the intricate and interdependent state of intergroup relations in the world today, observed behavior is increasingly showing variances from behavior predicted from expressed attitudes of prejudice (social distance). There are cases, for example, in which individuals actually behave in an inconsistent way when it is compared with their expressed attitudes of prejudices. We shall deal with such cases in the last section of Chapter 7 when we discuss the effects of multiple reference groups. Also there are observed cases of discrepancy between expressed opinion and behavior due to the impact of *situational* factors—a significant point which is being well emphasized by some investigators currently engaged in research in this area. In the world today, we cannot help noticing some line-ups or alliances among groups against other groups which would be inconceivable if the classifying of these groupings were being made on the basis of preferences and avoidances derived from social-distance or prejudice scales (Chapter 8).

Nevertheless, the standardized social-distance scales of various groups still do count among the important factors in the scheme of intergroup relations. The effects of social-distance scales are especially potent in societies with a relatively slow rate of transition, in which there are relatively fewer situational demands and pressures on the individual at variance with behavior prescribed by the social-distance scale, and in which individuals are not caught between contradictory group affiliations pulling them in different directions.

The empirical findings in the rich literature of prejudice studies do have serious implications for building up a more generalized theory of intergroup relations. In this and the next chapters our task is to point to these implications. We shall not attempt to give a survey of prejudice studies as such.

SOCIAL DISTANCE

In dealing with prejudice here, we refer specifically to *group prejudice,* that is, prejudice shown by members of a group toward other groups and their individual members. Since it is shared in some degree by members of a group, group prejudice may be distinguished from interpersonal likes and dislikes which may be unique to particular individuals. Group prejudice may be characterized as the negative attitude of members of one group, derived from the group's established norms, toward another group and its members.

Like many other terms, "prejudice" has been lifted from its more colloquial uses by social scientists. Consequently, some confusion surrounds it. For example, in daily life we may speak of being prejudiced *in favor* of a group (usually but not necessarily our own). We mean, of course, that we are personally involved with the group, whether or not we are actual members. The use of prejudice as a *negative* attitude toward other groups is amply justified by the results of prejudice studies. They demonstrate clearly the different consequence of being prejudiced or having a negative attitude toward a group in contrast to being involved or identified with a group. It goes without saying that the intensity and content of attitudes of prejudice toward various groups vary. The negative characteristic of attitudes of prejudice is revealed in the *social distance* at which the members of a prejudiced group hold another group and its members. We use prejudice in this sense.

With the use of the Bogardus social-distance scale and variations of it, the social distance or degree of prejudice one social group has against others is indicated satisfactorily (7). For example, subjects are asked to express their willingness to accept various groups on a scale like the following:

1. To close kinship by marriage.
2. To my club as personal chums.
3. To my street as neighbors.
4. To employment in my occupation in my country.
5. To citizenship in my country.
6. As visitors only to my country.
7. Would exclude from my country.

When various groups are thus rated, we find that the social distance at which different groups are held varies. By arranging these groups in descending order, a fairly accurate picture of the scale of social distances for the particular group making the ratings is gained.

In the United States, social scientists have been checking the established scales of social distance for various groups by such means for over twenty years. Although we have fewer test results from other countries, there are a number of studies which make possible some comparisons with social distances in other countries. Scales of social distance are not the exclusive property of any one country.

Social Distance in Different Countries

Merely glancing at social-distance scales gives us a static picture of group relations. But such a glance at the relative rankings of various groups in a country and some of the characteristics of the resulting scale must precede adequate understanding of the processes of change (Chapter 8). These social distances are established social norms. In relation to the single individual they are first external: they are first stimuli embodied in practice, example, or word.

The general picture of social distance for various national and ethnic groups in the United States is remarkably consistent. In Table 1 we see two lists of groups, the first obtained by Bogardus in 1926 and the second after a twenty-year interval in 1946 (8). Both lists are based on the rankings of a "roughly defined" stratified sample. In short, various population groups were represented in about the proportion they are found in the total population. There were somewhat larger proportions of persons from 18–35 years old, with at least a high-school education, and from skilled and professional groups, than in the total population. There are some shifts in the positions of a few groups in these two lists. These shifts offer leads for problems of change and will be referred to again in Chapter 8. But the most striking feature of the two lists is their remarkable correspondence. In Bogardus' words: "The population groups to which the greatest nearness was expressed in 1926 . . . maintained this role for the most part in 1946. . . . Likewise the groups which were placed at the greatest distance in 1926 maintained this position with only one major exception, the Chinese, in 1946. It is likewise true that the groups which occupied middle positions on the scale in 1926 were accorded similar positions in 1946. These observations lead to the first major conclusion. That racial distance as a rule changes very slowly" (p. 56).

TABLE 1. Racial Distance in the United States in 1926 and 1946[1]

Groups	Rank 1926	Groups	Rank 1946
English	1	Amer. (nat. white)	1
Amer. (nat. white)	2	Canadians	2
Canadians	3	English	3
Scotch	4	Irish	4
Irish	5	Scotch	5
French	6	French	6
Germans	7	Norwegians	7
Swedes	8	Hollanders	8
Hollanders	9	Swedes	9
Norwegians	10	Danes	10
Danes	11	Germans	11
Spanish	12	Finns	12
Finns	13	Czechs	13
Russians	14	Russians	14
Italians	15	Poles	15
Portuguese	16	Spanish	16
Poles	17	Romanians	17
Romanians	18	Bulgarian	18
Armenians	19	Italians	19
Czechs	20	Armenians	20
Indians (Amer.)	21	Greeks	21
Jews	22	Portuguese	22
Bulgarians	23	Jews	23
Greeks	24	Indians (Amer.)	24
Syrians	25	Chinese	25
Mexican Amer.	—	Mexican Amer.	26
Mexicans	27	Syrians	27
Japanese Amer.	—	Filipinos	28
Japanese	29	Mexicans	29
Filipinos	30	Turks	30
Negroes	31	Japanese Amer.	31
Turks	32	Koreans	32
Chinese	33	Mulattoes	33
Mulattoes	34	Indians (East)	34
Koreans	35	Negroes	35
Indians (East)	36	Japanese	36

[1] Reprinted from Bogardus (8), p. 58.

In 1938, college students at such different colleges and universities as Bennington, Columbia, Howard (a Negro university), Princeton, and the City College of New York ranked various groups in much the same way (17).

Such a social-distance scale has been found in diverse parts of the country—Florida, New York, Illinois, Kansas, Nebraska, and Washington (16). Very high relationships have been noted between the social-distance scales of school children in low, middle, and upper social classes in St. Louis, of different religious groups, and even of Negro and white college groups (17, 35, 41).

Of course, the social-distance scale varies somewhat from region to region in the United States. But the variations are relative, with few if any reversals from the lower and upper parts of the scale by members of majority groups.

The social-distance scales of minority ethnic group members in the United States are on the whole strikingly similar to those of the majority group members. There is one important difference. The minority group in the United States retains the established scale, but moves its own group from its lower position up to or near the top of the scale. Implications of this fact will be mentioned later in appropriate context.

In short, there is a scale of social distances in the United States which is established throughout the country. The technique by which it has been studied permits the individual to record degrees of acceptance or rejection of various groups. There are individual differences in the placement of various groups and the general level of social distance. But only a small proportion will be found willing to accept members of all groups to intimate relationships. Such individuals reject the existing social-distance scale and probably the concept of such a scale. But by and large, the established social distances in the United States are accepted in some degree by the overwhelming majority of people. It will be clear later that this rather consistent picture of social distance within a country over a period of years does not imply that all people are equally responsible for the maintenance of the established scale, or that it is unchangeable.

Once a group accepts a social-distance scale, putting itself at the top and ranging other groups downward, prejudice becomes generalized to include even groups about which absolutely nothing is known. In the list of groups to be rated, Hartley (17) included the names of three groups which he simply made up: Danirean, Pirenean, Wallonian. These groups do not exist in actual life. But people who tended to hold groups other than their own at considerable distance also placed these nonexistent groups low on their scale. People in less prejudiced groups accepted them in rather close proximity—closer than implied in the statement "To my school as classmates."

Though established, the social-distance scale in the United States cannot be taken to represent any final verdict of the relative standing of different groups along any dimension or of "natural" preferences or aversions. In other countries different preferences and aversions are established as "natural." In 1928, LaPiere (27) reported very little prejudice against Negroes among the French middle and lower classes. American Negro soldiers in Italy during World War II were not discriminated against, according to newspaper reports.

In Brazil, the native Indians, Portuguese settlers, and Negroes intermarried to an extent such that "racial" identification is difficult. However, the upper class is predominantly light in color and the lower class predominantly black (36). The social-distance scale is apparently based on class lines to a greater extent than on ethnic or color lines. Willems (40) and Freyre (13), both Brazilians, report that, while prejudice toward persons of darker coloring exists, the degree is much less than in the United States. Public opinion and legal sanctions in Brazil are against discrimination on such basis. There is evidence of social distance in reactions of Brazilians to other national groups, for example, the Japanese. It is interesting that while the social distance in relation to Germans is probably greater than in the United States, Italians (who are rather low on the United States scale) are assimilated into Brazilian life (25).

The population of the Hawaiian Islands includes persons of

American, British, Norwegian, German, Spanish, Puerto Rican, Portuguese, Negro, Chinese, Korean, Japanese, Filipino, Hindu, Danish, Micronesian, and Polynesian derivation and about every possible combination of these. Intermarriage has been the rule for the largest segments of the population (1). The upper class is chiefly white. A premium is put on the lighter complexion in such matters as employment offering good status and income. Part-Hawaiians find themselves in some advantage in this respect. Orientals (Japanese and Chinese) are ranked somewhat higher than in, say, California. The Japanese group, which is one of the larger minorities, tends to rank the other various groups in about the same order as does the dominant white group, with the exception that its own group is ranked first above the white groups and greater preference is expressed for fellow Orientals (33). In general, because of the greater variety of groups in a relatively small area and their history of intermarriage, the level of prejudice is probably considerably lower than in the United States. Because there has been so much assimilation of the various ethnic groups, the use of "racial" weapons against one particular group by the white upper classes would result in alienating friendly minority groups whose coöperation is necessary in the life of the islands.

Still differing pictures of social distances among groups are found in the Near East and in Panama and other South American countries. By way of contrast, in countries such as South Africa, ethnic delineations and class lines coincide more closely, and social distance between ethnic groups is probably at its maximum (30). In colonial countries, some individuals of the subordinate ethnic groups may be allowed to rise in status, but exclusively within their own groups. Lower-class groups (usually dark or yellow skinned) are kept at the utmost social distance. Economic, political, and legal barriers are rigid, though by no means unchanging, as we are seeing in several parts of the world today.

In summary, various countries of the world have different social-distance scales. These divergent patterns of social distance can be accounted for only by exploration of the particular historical circumstances and the functional relations between groups at their establishment and throughout their history. We shall attempt to gain some historical perspective in this problem in the following chapter.

Stereotypes Used as Justifications for Prevailing Social Distances

Allport tells us the following incident:

"Once during a session of summer school a lady in my class came to me and in alarmed tone of voice said, 'I think there is a student with some Negro blood in this class'—and pointed out a dark brunette to me. To my non-committal 'Really?' she persisted, 'But you wouldn't want a nigger in the class, would you?' Next day she returned and firmly informed me, 'I know she's colored because I dropped a paper on the floor and said to her, 'Pick that up.' She did so, and that proves she's just a darky servant trying to get above her station' " (2, p. 8). The behavior of the brunette in question was seen as *proof* of her being a Negro because the lady believed in the subordinate nature of all Negroes. This essential characteristic would, as she saw it, show up no matter how much it might be "covered over."

Stereotypes of the essential nature of a group and its members always accompany a social-distance scale. In fact, stereotypes can be taken as one index of the social distance at which groups are held. In the United States, those peoples high on the scale, the English, for example, are stereotyped in terms acceptable to American tradition, even though some critical traits are included. The natures of peoples low on the scale (Chinese, Negro, Turk) are taken to be completely alien to characteristics Americans admire (15). Even seemingly desirable traits may, in a context of unfavorable characteristics, take on unfavorable connotation. Thus, while both Japanese and Americans considered the Japanese "suave" in 1936, we would expect that "suave" meant something less complimentary to the Americans, who placed the Japanese fairly low on the social-distance scale even at that time (26). The relative favorableness or unfavorableness of stereotypes toward various national and ethnic groups varies in terms of the position of those groups on the social-distance scale.

Once established, stereotypes tend to persist, though they are not unchanging. In 1932, Katz and Braly (23) found that Princeton students assigned stereotypes with a high degree of consistency, even in the case of groups personally unknown to them. A repetition of this study in 1950 showed that the characteristics most frequently checked in 1932 were those most frequently checked in 1950 (14). As might be expected from the Bogardus findings reported in the previous section, stereotypes of Germans and Japanese had changed in a negative direction.

Like the social-distance scale, the accompanying stereotypes of various groups are shared even by members of groups who suffer discrimination in the name of these stereotypes. The stereotypes of Negro and white college students in relation to various groups are closely similar (5, 34). Some minority group members may completely reject the traits attributed to their group. But in the United States many accept even the unfavorable traits assigned them by the majority group. Negro college students by and large accept the generally unfavorable stereotypes of the Negro (e.g., "superstitious, happy-go-lucky, loud, lazy"), according to a study carried out in 1935 and repeated in 1942 (34).

It is a general characteristic of categorical thinking that contrary cases are taken, not to break down the category, but as accidental exceptions. Thus most white Americans regard such individuals as Marian Anderson, Ralph Bunche, or Jackie Robinson as exceptions to one or more of the traits traditionally assigned to Negroes. In the study of stereotypes of Negro college students, these young people said that these stereotypes applied to "Negroes in general," but not to themselves. Being serious minded and hard working, they could not picture themselves as superstitious or lazy; but since they had accepted the prevailing stereotypes about their group, they could only regard themselves as exceptional.

The acceptance of the major social-distance scale and the ac-•

companying stereotypes has important consequences for the individual member and for the minority group as a whole. Acceptance of the majority's scale of social distance, even with one's own group moved near the top, contributes to the maintenance of this scale. In the tragic instances in history when minority groups by and large came to accept the places and negative traits assigned them, they have regarded their plight as "natural" and inevitable. To a lesser degree, some minority group members in the United States today substantially adopt the majority's views of the way relationships should be established between the groups, even though they ask for alleviation of discriminations and hardships suffered (24).

The psychological consequences of the minority group member's acceptance of the stereotypes and "place" assigned him are not limited to his relationships with other groups. They pervade even such "private" areas of life as the goals the individual strives toward, the sort of person he wants to become. The cruel, but sometimes realistic, limits which are placed on the individual's aspirations are illustrated by the following interview with a teenage Negro girl in a northern state:

Interviewer: What do you want to be, when you grow up?
Girl: Oh . . . I guess I'm going to be a cleaning lady.
Girl's mother (also in room): Oh, don't tell the lady that! Tell her something *nice*—like working in an office.
Girl: Okay. I guess I'll clean offices, then.[2]

Some members of minority groups who have achieved success in climbing up the established scales of American life reveal the conflict between acceptance of the standards and stereotypes of the majority and relating themselves to their own group by thinking of their own unusual success as applicable to the whole minority group. "The boaster often reveals that he, himself, is not unaware of the self-deception that he has made into a 'race philosophy' by showing in one way or another that he actually considers

---

[2] Personally communicated by Professor John Dean of Cornell University. This observation was obtained during the Elmira Intergroup Relations Study.

himself as a great exception while common Negroes are classed as inferiors" (38, p. 249). As we shall see in discussing reference groups in Chapters 7 and 8, it is this essential acceptance of the unfavorable position and traits attributed by the majority group which leads to the phenomena of self-hatred by some minority group members, as well as hatred of one's own group.

Like the social-distance scale, stereotypes of national and ethnic groups are widely accepted by most people in the United States, from the east to the west coast (25). A comparable study in England by Eysenck and Crown (12) has revealed similar results, with important exceptions which we shall mention later.

Of course, the stereotypes assigned Americans are not identical to those maintained in this country. The British stereotype of Americans centers around the conception of a person who does not "grow up" (32). Almost every day we are learning more about contemporary concepts of Americans, not only from research, but from newspaper reports coming back from various parts of the world.

Are group stereotypes true or false? The traditional view of stereotypes was that they represented characteristics which the group actually possessed, or possessed at one time. Such an unqualified stand by itself merely justifies existing stereotypes, at least with minor corrections to bring them up to date, and serves to rationalize the social distance at which various groups are held. The opposite view, held by many people of good will who desired to see group prejudice and stereotypes eliminated, holds that stereotypes are always totally false, that any correspondence between stereotypes and characteristics which may be observed in some members of the group in question is accidental.

Now it would seem likely that putting the problem in this two-sided form actually hinders our understanding of the rise of stereotypes. As we found in examining race doctrines and studies of national character, the personal and emotional characteristics usually included in stereotypes are so widely distributed that we can almost be sure of finding them in some degree in all groups. Individuals in any one group will vary sufficiently so that it is not meaningful from a scientific point of view to characterize all individuals of a group as being good, bad, cruel, kind, etc. On the other hand, the structure of relations within a group, the ways of life, the social values or norms, treatments of other groups, etc., certainly do have consequences for individual members. As Klineberg suggests (25), we do need more studies of these consequences for various groups and their members. We know that the relations and values of some groups, such as those in the United States, emphasize competition and acquisitiveness, and that these relations and norms inevitably affect the lives of individuals in these groups. We suspect that the most valuable data of this kind are those concerning the value dimensions prevailing in different groups and the ranges of acceptance and rejection by individual members. But we must not think that we are explaining the origin of stereotypes by doing such studies. We might find, for example, that many Negroes in the South are apathetic toward work (because of the restrictions imposed on them in getting work, because of scarce, low-paying, difficult jobs. Are they lazy?). While at a given time certain specific stereotypes are demonstrably false (28), and others seem to hold a "kernel of truth," a more fruitful line of inquiry would seem to lie in finding why certain characteristics are selected to the exclusion of others. Studies of characteristics more or less predominant in a group can help to give us some idea of the range of objective stimuli which may or may not be crystallized in stereotypes. But such inquiries cannot teach us why stereotypes develop, why they are maintained, why certain characteristics are chosen while others are excluded, or explain their pertinence to more basic relationships implied in the social-distance scales.

Whenever the economic, political, and cultural interests and institutions of national or ethnic groups clash, a set of negative traits is attributed by one group to the other and is standardized as a result of the conflict. When the interests, goals, and directions of interacting groups are in harmony or supplement one another, more favorable traits are attributed. Avigdor (4) has proposed that when groups come into conflict certain traits which are observable

in at least some members of the group in question are selected
for emphasis precisely because these traits serve the interests of the
other group in the conflict situation. On the other hand, when
groups are engaged in harmonious or coöperative interaction,
certain other traits are selected which serve to further the cooperative relationship between the groups. Her ingenious experiment using comparable groups of children, some in conflict situations and others in coöperative situations, substantiates this view.
We shall return to this experiment in detail in Chapter 10.

Group stereotypes can be fruitfully regarded as labels for an
out-group which are standardized within an in-group in harmony
with the relationships between the groups in question. It is these
relationships between groups, and not primarily the truth or false-
ness, which gives stereotypes their functional significance. Once
established, stereotypes tend to persist so long as the relationship
between the groups in question remains functionally similar.

Some Psychological Bases of Stereotyping. To people who accept group stereotypes, the "traits" attributed to various groups
seem a part of their "nature." The process is as natural as "calling a spade a spade." To those who are distressed at the deleteri-
ous effects of stereotypes in social life and who reject them,
stereotyping is an unnatural, abnormal affair. Neither view can
help us much in understanding stereotyping.

Our first step is in understanding the conditions in which stereotypes develop and the way these conditions influence selection of
traits to be attributed to an out-group. We have said that unfavorable stereotypes arise when groups come into conflict. By analyz-
ing literature, songs, cartoons of the times, Goldstein (15) has
shown us how unfavorable stereotypes have varied and been
adapted during the course of Negro-white relations in the United
States. The stereotype of the happy Negro slave grew after 1820,
when slavery began to feel some real opposition. Among other
channels, this belief was spread through the popular minstrel
shows, in which sadness was confined to personal losses, such as
that of "My Darling Nelly Gray," and "political" themes were
abolished through ridicule. Of course, some slaveholders could

point to their own slaves, who had learned that a broad smile and a bow were fairly good ways to please the master and to avoid any conflict. As a matter of fact, prior to the Civil War there were many more slave revolts and uprisings than is commonly presumed, and runaway slaves presented such a severe problem that lawsuits and legal rulings on the question were not uncommon (15). The picture of· the contented slave, who readily served his master and spent his spare time singing, is not preserved intact; but it is probably related to the notion of the Negro as a "second-rate human, of little intelligence, few needs, great religious fervor, and a congenital incapacity for the appreciation of the white man's civilization."

It was not until after the Civil War that the stereotype of the "brute Negro" emerged full blown. Until he was freed, the Negro was pictured as a gentle fellow to the public, for it would not do to have stories of uprisings and rebellions spread about the "contented slave." This concept of an animal-like creature whose passions could not be controlled has been reinforced to the present day by the policies of many news sources in playing up stories of crimes committed by Negroes. (This can be done effectively enough by printing all crime stories and minimizing other types of news.)

After the slaves were freed, the Negro in stereotypes became also a comical figure who tried to emulate "white folks" and desired above all else to wear flashy clothes and have gold teeth. Today, the appearance of a Negro individual in a recent-make car is enough to activate this stereotype for some people.

It would seem that these stereotypes are understandable in terms of selective attribution of traits as determined by the motive of the white group which created and perpetuated them in specific circumstances. In terms of a slave-owning group somewhat wary of the future of slavery, it would suit their purpose if slaves were thought to be simple people, happy and content with their lot. In terms of a defeated slave-owning group, what could be better than that all, including the victors, become convinced that they had unleashed a monster, and that the very notion of a Negro slave's becoming like one of them was absurd?

It would seem that careful tracing of historical situations and group interests will reveal that negative group stereotypes are selected as specific justifications for the position and practices of the attributing group in a conflict relationship. (Once such stereotypes are established for a number of subordinate groups, it seems possible that some of the traits may be generalized from one group to apply to others in a subordinate position as well. Such generalizations would not be surprising in view of the tendency for prejudiced individuals to maintain prejudice even toward unknown groups.)

Our second step toward understanding group stereotypes is an examination of some characteristics of language and concepts. Words in a language consist to a large extent of labels or categories within which objects, events, experience are grouped. When persons, objects, situations, etc., are subsumed under a common label, they are perceived and responded to in a similar way. When we view the objective world, labels serve to accentuate aspects of this world to which they refer. This characteristic holds for language concepts less laden with emotional value than group stereotypes. It is hardly surprising, then, that individuals prejudiced against Jews *see* more Jews than less prejudiced individuals (3). When Negro students were admitted to the summer session of a southern college for the first time, the remark was heard, "Have you been to the campus? There are Negroes all over the place!" Actually there were fifty Negro students in a student population of several thousand. Allport (2) reports that people taking a public service examination in South Africa estimated that the Jews constituted 20 percent of the population, while the actual proportion was 1 percent.

There is good reason to believe that concepts of a language, even simple names like those for animals, are not such intellectual affairs as they are often supposed to be. It seems that the vocabulary of a group, hence its classification of things, reflects also the practical activities of the group in dealing with life processes (31, 39). Classifications of objects found in certain less developed societies are different from those in our own society. They stem from differences in the vital activities carried on by the group in specific environments. They are standardized by the group to deal with these vital activities. This observation does not mean that concepts are just subjective affairs. They usually refer to actual objects or characteristics, but they also refer to the functions of these objects. For example, objects which are built out of material strong enough to hold an average person, with a seat and back raised off the ground by suitable support, are classified as chairs. Such an object made of a fragile substance like paper would not be consistently classified as a chair because one could not sit on it.

Children's concepts of familiar objects are generally defined in terms of their *use* (an orange is what we have for breakfast). From the point of view of the psychological processes involved, there is little justification for taking "value" concepts and "fact" concepts as entirely separate and different (39). The evidence indicates that all concepts are connotative in some degree. We should expect that the concepts used by scientists in their work would be determined more by measurable characteristics and relationships of the objective world than are many concepts in colloquial use. But we must note that science has discarded some concepts for the very reason that they are largely a reflection of the motives of the users and not applicable to the objective world. It is for this reason that social scientists today insist that "race" is a concept of possible utility only for the biologists or physical anthropologists. Science advances through the attainment of concepts which refer to measurable events in the objective world—physical or social. At the other pole are concepts like group stereotypes which, though they may have referred to characteristics observable in at least a part of the group in question, are so burdened with the emotions, values, and purposes of those who standardized them that they are understandable only in those terms.

As an antidote to stereotyping effects, it has been suggested that the abstract nature of concepts be stressed and that reactions be based on observable events and cues. Semanticists especially have emphasized that there is no such entity as the generalized cow or tree. What actually exists is Cow_1, Cow_2, etc. Likewise, there is no such entity as the generalized Negro. There are $Negro_1$, $Negro_2$, etc., each different, as is the case in any group. In the case of group stereotypes, the effort to get people to consider individuals of a group as individuals is a laudable one. Since scientists have found such overlapping of the personal characteristics of members of various groups, there is factual basis for this orientation. But the semantic antidote overlooks a psychological tendency that seems basic. Individuals think and react in terms of generalized standards—of concepts. Especially when individuals face situations which are vague, indefinite, unstructured, it is painful to postpone judgments and wait for all the relevant facts. Certainly in some situations, breakdowns would occur if experience were not categorized in a way permitting some course of action. The categorizing tendencies of man have made possible some of his greatest achievements. Man is not wholly stimulus-bound. On the other hand, those categorizing tendencies also produce blinding effects when the resulting concepts have little relation to real events to which they purport to refer. It is the task of science to provide valid concepts in social areas too.

We do not mean to imply by any means that group stereotypes will inevitably arise and be perpetuated. In studies done in England, a number of people either refused to attribute "traits" to other groups or indicated that they were aware that the only basis they had for doing so was group stereotypes (12). A tendency in this direction was also found in a recent study in the United States (14). Of course we cannot assume that all of those individuals who indicated awareness of group stereotypes do not fall back on them in their daily social relations. At least some may simply be expressing sophistication derived from lectures or reading which is not reflected in their day-to-day behavior.

Group stereotypes refer to qualities which are presumed to inhere in this or that group. The tendency to account for or describe events in terms of their *essence* or *nature* may be described as a "substantive mode of mentality." Men and women are presumed to have fundamentally and immutably different *natures,* even though these *natures* have changed a good deal in the last fifty years, especially the nature of women. Italians are, in this substantive mentality, just naturally a bunch of easygoing, talkative individuals, and this characterization will explain the behavior of Italians. But all problems are not dealt with in this fashion in our society today. Very few people in the United States would seriously suggest that it was in the essence or the nature of their car to backfire. We want to know what causes the defect. We take the car to a mechanic or work on it ourselves to find out. This represents a "process analysis" of events. Certain factors contribute in a related fashion to produce a certain effect. The concepts arrived at by process analysis are not taken as essences. No physicist today would propose that it was the *nature* of the atom to behave in a certain way. He aims at knowing what factors are responsible for this activity. When groups accept such a process analysis in dealing with their social problems too, we should think that the blinding effects of group stereotypes would be considerably reduced and eventually eliminated.

THE FORMATION OF CHILDREN'S PREJUDICES

A popular legend concerning the wisdom of children holds that a baby will cry if he sees a colored face, thus demonstrating instinctive repugnance. It is true that some babies at a certain period of their development will cry when they see *any* strange face, including that of the father just back after a long absence. This legend could not be taken seriously in the South, where nurses of colored complexion have often gained the first attachment of a child.

Today all factual evidence points to one conclusion: Attitudes toward members of other groups, as well as attitudes toward one's own group, are learned. But attitudes toward members of other groups are not determined so much by experiences while in contact with the groups in question as by contact with the attitudes toward these groups prevailing among the older members of the groups in which they develop (19, 29). This is the reason that attitudes of children toward Negroes in the South and in the North are so similar, and also that children of individuals who reject the social-distance scale, who do not conform to the major norms of the society in which it exists, show no apparent prejudice toward Negroes (19). Herein lies the explanation of MacCrone's finding in his extensive studies in South Africa in 1937 that the most important factor determining individual variations in social-distance attitudes was *group membership* (30, p. 232). Although contact among certain ethnic and color groups varied in different regions of South Africa, these environmental differences were considerably less significant than the group affiliations of the individual.

These findings, which are representative of a rather substantial body of related observations and results, run counter to accounts of prejudice as a direct consequence of unpleasant or unfavorable individual contacts with members of the group toward which prejudice is directed. Prejudices of some individuals may be built on the basis of such unpleasant experiences as the individual grows up. But as a general rule, the scale of social distance is handed down by adults through example and short-cut dicta. In this sense, the "cognitive maps" relating to other groups are ready-made for the individual group member, of course to be altered, adapted, and in some exceptional cases even changed by him in the course of his life experiences.

But so crucial is the group in determining the individual member's "cognitive maps" that if the individual's group prejudices, built up in the course of his personal dealings with members of out-groups, should violate lines drawn in the standardized "maps" of his group, he would be asked to be "reasonable" and not to give free reign to his personal dislikes.

Another account of the formation of group prejudices which is currently influential will be considered at greater length in the next chapter, viz., displacement theories. According to these theories, any frustrations which the individual suffers in the course of development, even though not related to the groups in question, may result in aggression which can be displaced to out-groups.

Either unpleasant experiences with out-group members or frustrations suffered in the course of development may enter into the formation of attitudes of group prejudice. However, as we shall see, they cannot account for the existence of a social-distance scale. Such factors may be important in determining the degree or intensity with which the individual upholds or practices the social-distance scale of his group. But the "cognitive maps" regulating the behavior of individuals in relation to members of given groups are products of the interaction of the groups in question. They become standardized in the interaction process in time. If the individual is to remain a member with any standing in his group, he has to share in some degree these standardized cognitive maps with other members of his group.

The formation of attitudes toward groups, as toward other stimulus objects and situations, is made infinitely simpler by the acquisition of language. If the child had to wait to come into contact with the groups in question, he would develop attitudes toward them in a more specific way, and he might never form attitudes toward certain groups for the simple reason that he has not known them. Language telescopes this process. As soon as the child learns and accepts the instrumental use of language, he is equipped to form attitudes toward other groups, even though he has never seen members of some, through short-cut dicta, concepts, or stereotypes of adults. As we have seen, a chief characteristic of such concepts is their classificatory nature. Once concepts of social distance are learned in the adult sense, one has only to fit various individuals into the appropriate categories.

All research on the appearance of prejudice points to its beginnings at an early age. For most children in the United States, it begins during the preschool age. Of course before this children are able to discriminate between various skin colors. This ability is shown by the different degrees of awareness of skin color, before social definitions of this color have been elaborated, by young Negro children of different complexions (light, medium, and dark) (9). But the mere fact of recognizing color differences has no special significance for very young children.

The social definition and significance is not long in coming. The child learns group labels even before he can identify members of the group in question, and he senses their emotional and affective value (18, 37). At this stage, roughly school age and under, children's attitudes toward various groups tend to be somewhat unintegrated aspects of their psychological make-up. Young children are often highly "inconsistent" in their reactions. For example, one child was told by her mother to call older women "ladies." One day, the little girl answered the door and then ran to her mother, saying that a lady wanted to see her. Her mother went to the door and when she returned she said, "That wasn't a lady, dear. That was a Negro. You mustn't call Negroes 'ladies.' "

This observation gives us a clue concerning one of the most important sources of prejudice. It was found that young children under about the third grade freely acknowledge that they choose white children as playmates because their parents have told them not to play with Negro children. Older children are more aware of pressures from their own groups of age-mates (21). As one boy said: "I represent a room in safety council which has many Negroes. They say their safety laws to me. When I meet them in the hall I say hello to them. All the other children look at me like it would be a crime to be sociable with them" (42).

The younger child ordinarily reacts toward other persons in the ways which please his grownups, and naturally seeks to avoid their punishments. In one southern community the most frequent cause of punishment was playing with Negro children (21). Even once children "get the idea," their attitudes and stereotypes are not identical with those of the adults. They tend to take things in an absolutistic way. One study in a southern community showed that the children in the fourth and fifth grades were inclined to attribute all unfavorable traits to Negroes, without the more favorable traits ("musical") commonly found in adult stereotypes (6). These children had learned that nothing good could be found in this group. This would perhaps not be the case in all localities. Elsewhere the generality and the urgency of the lesson might be less emphasized. Among younger children we sometimes see very specific items, learned just as well, concerning an out-group. A preschool child who had been exposed to the cowboy and Indian game, the "ten little Indians," and the popular pictures conceived of Indians as people who wore feathers and were bare to the waist. When a small gathering of Oklahoma citizens of Indian descent was pointed out to her, she completely rejected the possibility that these were Indians: "They couldn't be. They have shirts on!"

By the time they reach high school, children tend to have the established adult stereotypes intact. Older children are inclined to forget the role of parents and other persons in transmitting the social-distance norms and claim them as their own. The high-school student or the adult feels that his attitudes toward other groups have always been his own. He feels, for example, his desire to associate with white friends and not colored people as a purely *personal* preference.

In order to account for this phenomenon, we must return to the child as he is forming his prejudices. The preschool child is just learning "what he is." His sense of identity is more fluctuating, more variable or inconsistent, and more specific to the situations he has encountered. He is a "big boy," a "good girl," etc. If a four-year-old is asked, "What are you?" he is not very likely to answer in terms of ethnic or religious group membership (18). But the child comes to learn that he belongs to the Smith family, that as a child of the Smith family he does not play with "bad children," with "dirty children," with "Negro children." He finds he belongs to a Sunday School or church. He goes to a certain school, etc. It is from achieving such group identifications that the child begins to be aware of his self with certain appropriate "places" and standards of conduct in life. This developing self or ego consists of both "what I am" and "what I am not"—"how I act among my kind" and "how I act toward *others.*" By the time the child is in about the sixth grade, we find, even in New York City, that the "cleavages" between white and Negro children in terms of preferences are clear cut. Personal preference, satisfaction, interest, and prestige in group activities then lie in one's own color group (11). Children are increasingly able to invest the developing self with group memberships. This increasing ability is closely related to the functional development of language and its concepts. Such concepts are largely responsible for the development of a consistent pattern of self-identity and awareness found in adults.

Children who grow up as members of a discriminated-against minority may acquire clear-cut identification with their group even earlier than children of the majority group (22). The evidence points to the tragic fact that along with learning that they belong to a color group or (later) a "Negro" group, very young Negro children are aware of the low evaluation placed on their color and on their group (10). In one study, well over half of the three-year-old Negro children called brown children "bad" and said that white was a "nice" color.

In short, attitudes of prejudice, learned chiefly through contact with the norms of social distance prevailing in the group, impressed by the approval of grownups (including parents) for "proper" behavior along with punishment or disapproval for "improper" or "naughty" behavior as well as by the sanctions of age-mate groups, come to constitute a part of the individual's very self-identity, of his ego. Once a part of the ego constellation, attitudes of prejudice are factors regulating behavior in situations related to out-groups and their members. It is small wonder that they come to be experienced as a "natural" part of oneself—almost as "natural" as one's name.

In anticipation of later chapters, it should be pointed out that to understand the behavior of any single individual in a prejudice-related situation one must know something of his other attitudes and identifications, their organization in his ego system, as well as the demands of the situation. Even grownups do not always behave in a consistent way, if consistency is taken to mean behaving only in terms of one's attitudes of social distance toward other groups.

REFERENCES

1. Adams, Romanzo. *Interracial Marriage in Hawaii*. New York: Macmillan, 1937.
2. Allport, G. W. Prejudice: a problem in psychological and social causation, *J. soc. Issues*, Supplement Series, No. 4, Nov., 1950.
3. Allport, G. W., and Kramer, B. M. Some roots of prejudice, *J. Psychol.*, 1946, *22*, 9–39.
4. Avigdor, R. The development of stereotypes as a result of group interaction. Doctor's dissertation, Graduate School of Arts and Sciences, New York University, 1952.
5. Bayton, J. A. The racial stereotypes of Negro college students, *J. abn. & soc. Psychol.*, 1941, *36*, 97–102.
6. Blake, R., and Dennis, W. The development of stereotypes concerning the Negro, *J. abn. & soc. Psychol.*, 1943, *38*, 525–531.
7. Bogardus, E. S. A social distance scale, *Sociol. & soc. Res.*, 1933, *17*, 265–271.
8. Bogardus, E. S. Changes in racial distances, *Internat. J. Opin. & Attit. Res.*, 1947, *1*, 55–62.
9. Clark, K. B., and Clark, M. K. Skin color as a factor in racial identification of Negro pre-school children, *J. soc. Psychol.*, 1940, *11*, 159–169.
10. Clark, K. B., and Clark, M. K. Racial identification and preference in Negro children, in T. M. Newcomb and E. L. Hartley (eds.), *Readings in Social Psychology*. New York: Holt, 1947, 169–178.
11. Crisswell, J. H. A sociometric study of race cleavages in the classroom, *Arch. Psychol.*, 1939, No. 235.
12. Eysenck, H. J., and Crown, S. National stereotypes: an experimental and methodological study, *Internat. J. Opin. & Attit. Res.*, 1948, *2*, 26–49.
13. Freyre, G. Reported in O. Klineberg, *Tensions Affecting International Understanding*. New York: Social Science Research Council, Bull. 62, 1950, 192–193.
14. Gilbert, G. M. Stereotype persistence and change among college students, *J. abn. & soc. Psychol.*, 1951, *46*, 245–254.
15. Goldstein, N. F. *The Roots of Prejudice Against the Negro in the United States*. Boston: Boston University Press, 1948.
16. Guilford, J. P. Racial preferences of a thousand American university students, *J. soc. Psychol.*, 1931, *2*, 179–204.

17. Hartley, E. L. *Problems in Prejudice*. New York: Kings Crown Press, 1946.

18. Hartley, E. L., Rosenbaum, M., and Schwartz, S. Children's use of ethnic frames of reference: An exploratory study of children's conceptualizations of multiple ethnic group membership, *J. Psychol.*, 1948, *26*, 367–386; Children's perceptions of ethnic group membership, *ibid.*, 387–398; Note on children's role perception, *ibid.*, 399–405.

19. Horowitz, E. L. The development of attitudes toward Negroes, *Arch. Psychol.*, 1936, No. 194.

20. Horowitz, E. L. "Race" attitudes, Part IV in O. Klineberg (ed.), *Characteristics of the American Negro*. New York: Harper, 1944.

21. Horowitz, E. L., and Horowitz, R. E. Development of social attitudes in children, *Sociometry*, 1937, *1*, 301–338.

22. Horowitz, R. E. Racial aspects of self-identification in nursery school children, *J. Psychol.*, 1939, *7*, 91–99.

23. Katz, D., and Braly, K. Racial stereotypes of one-hundred college students, *J. abn. & soc. Psychol.*, 1933, *28*, 280–290.

24. Kay, L. W. Frame of reference in "pro" and "anti" evaluations of test items, *J. soc. Psychol.*, 1947, *25*, 63–68.

25. Klineberg, O. *Tensions Affecting International Understanding*. New York: Social Science Research Council, Bull. 62, 1950.

26. Kusunoki, K. Mental characteristics of the Japanese race as seen by Japanese and American students, *Jap. J. appl. Psychol.*, 1936, *4*, 232–237; reported by O. Klineberg (25).

27. LaPiere, R. T. Race prejudice: France and England, *Soc. Forces*, 1928, *7*, 102–111.

28. LaPiere, R. T. Type-rationalization of group antipathy, *Soc. Forces*, 1936–37, *15*, 232–237.

29. Lasker, B. *Race Attitudes in Children*. New York: Holt, 1929.

30. MacCrone, I. D. *Race Attitudes in South Africa*. London: Oxford University Press, 1937.

31. Malinowski, B. The problem of meaning, Supplement I in C. K. Ogden and I. A. Richards, *The Meaning of Meaning*. New York: Harcourt, Brace, 1930.

32. Mass-observation, Portrait of an American? *Internat. J. Opin. & Attit. Res.*, 1947, *1*, 96–98.

33. Masuoka, J. Race preference in Hawaii, *Amer. J. Sociol.*, 1936, *41*, 635–641.

34. Meenes, M. A. A comparison of racial stereotypes of 1935 and 1942, *J. soc. Psychol.*, SPSSI Bull., 1943, *17*, 327–336.

35. Meltzer, H. Group differences in nationality and race preferences of children, *Sociometry*, 1939, *2*, 86–105.

36. Pierson, D. *Negroes in Brazil*, Chicago: University of Chicago Press, 1942.

37. Radke, M., Trager, H. G., and Davis, H. Children's perceptions and attitudes of children, *Genet. Psychol. Monogr.*, 1949, *40*, 327–447.

38. Rose, Arnold. *The Negro in America (A Condensation of An American Dilemma)*. New York: Harper, 1948.

39. Sherif, M. Some social psychological aspects of conceptual functioning, in *The Nature of Concepts, Their Inter-relation and Role in Social Structure*, Proceedings of the Stillwater Conference, New York Foundation of Integrated Education, 1950.

40. Willems, Emilio. Racial attitudes in Brazil, *Amer. J. Sociol.*, 1949, *54*, 402–408.

41. Zeligs, R., and Hendrickson, G. Racial attitudes of 200 sixth-grade children, *Sociol. & soc. Res.*, 1933–34, *18*, 26–36.

42. Zeligs, R., and Hendrickson, G. Checking the social distance technique through the personal interview, *Sociol. & soc. Res.*, 1933–34, *18*, 420–430.

CHAPTER 5

ᒫᒣᒫᒣᒫᒣᒫᒣᒫᒣᒫᒣᒫᒣᒫᒣᒫᒣᒫᒣᒫᒣᒫᒣᒫᒣᒫ

Social-Distance Scales in Formation

Each new member of a group acquires in time a conception of his place in the existing scheme of things. Through precept, example, praise, blame, satisfaction, punishment, and the like, he learns where he stands in relation to other people and how he should behave toward them. He learns where his group stands in relation to other groups and how he, as a member of his group, should act toward members of those out-groups. Thus, in becoming a member of his own group, he acquires the prevailing social-distance scale on which other groups are ranged. He learns stereotypes which make these social distances seem "reasonable" and "sound." These form the main content of his attitudes toward other groups and their members.

Standardized scales of social distance and accompanying stereotypes are found in differing forms in different societies. To find out why these social-distance scales differ and how they came into being, to be passed on to new generations, it is necessary to look back as best we can to the events and settings that gave rise to them.

Some contemporary psychologists have emphasized that every individual carries with him those aspects of his background which affect his behavior at a given moment. This "here-and-now" approach, which correctly emphasizes that in psychology background factors must be handled in terms of psychological concepts, has had the unfortunate effect of deterring some psychologists from intensive study of the background. Others, discouraged by confusions and bias, which are found in history as well as in

103

other social sciences, have thrown up their hands exclaiming "History doesn't give us the answers to these problems."

Of course history does not give direct answers to many problems of social psychology. But we cannot hope to understand background factors of the formation of group products unless we study the events and processes from which they arise. This is one of the underlying tenets of this book.

As Allport says, the gap between psychology and history is regrettably wide (4). (Probably the reasons for this gap would prove a fascinating study.) The gap cannot be closed by prefacing psychological studies with historical accounts which have little functional relevance to the psychology which follows. Attempts to psychologize history have, on the whole, been unrewarding for both disciplines.

Perhaps, in the area of our concern, we may be in a position to utilize historical findings profitably if we limit our aims to singling out only those factors and those conditions which have been *necessary* for the rise of the group products in question, namely, social-distance scales and group stereotypes. This investigation will provide background in terms of which we may deal with careful observations of events in real life. Further, it is possible to create situations embodying the essential conditions found, and to study for ourselves, here and now, the effects of these conditions on groups and on individual members in a *longitudinal* way (see experiments, Chapters 9 and 10).

If this is our aim, it follows that historical examples will not be used to explain psychological phenomena of prejudice and social distance, but rather to elucidate weighty *background* factors in the rise of standardized scales of social distance. If there are common characteristics in the conditions of contact between groups which foster the standardization of social-distance scales, we will gain a basis for understanding the variations in social-distance scales and their complications in various groups. But such findings will not give a complete account of prejudice or social distance even for the period in question. For this, we would have to study as well factors in each situation which might be unique to that situation.

Our aim in the following section is more limited in scope. Through examination of periods in which social-distance scales developed, attention will be focused on common features in the conditions of contact which led to standardized social-distance scales. Since group customs, values, moral systems followed by the groups in question at the time varied considerably from one contact situation to another, such features are necessarily neglected in this attempt. We do not imply in the least that such factors are not important. They do have importance in the total picture. In some cases of intergroup contact they may be the weighty factors. In the next section, we shall try to achieve some insight into factors which seem common to the background conditions under which social-distance scales are standardized. Throughout the remainder of the book, the main effort will be directed toward an adequate approach to intergroup relations in which all of the various background factors, factors in the immediate situation, values, strivings, personal involvements, attitudes, and goals of individuals relevant to intergroup relations may be studied in their functional interrelationships.

SOME BACKGROUND EXAMPLES

Social distances between groups are found in all periods of recorded history. When a society is relatively homogeneous with minimum functional differentiation, like a small tribe subsisting on some cultivation and hunting, social distances are not found within the society. There are different statuses within every human grouping; but status differences within an in-group do not usually imply social distance as the term is used. Such relatively small, homogeneous societies do develop social distances toward other groups with which they come in contact.

As Allport (4) has noted, social distances within a society are found only in heterogeneous or differentiated societies, in which different groups of people have differing and even conflicting interests and functions. The rigid class lines of feudal periods are excellent examples of the coincidence of functional delineations within a society and social distances maintained. The great masses of people worked for a relatively small ruling class (e.g., feudal lords, clergy). The trades and artisan group, though developing, was small. Degree of social intimacy and, conversely, of social distance was determined on the basis of class membership. Social distances based on class membership have not disappeared. In the United States, where occasionally a beautiful laborer's daughter marries a millionaire amid much publicity, we are not so conscious of these bases. We are reminded by the authors of the *American Dilemma* that "Upper-class people in all countries are accustomed to look down upon poor people as born to be inferior" (34, p. 70). They found that many ideas current about Negroes in America ("Higher wages will make the nigger lazy and morally degraded") were comparable to ideas about laboring classes developed by some European writers of the seventeenth and eighteenth centuries. In some communities, a Negro who gets a car draws unfavorable comment, as did a maid who "dressed like a lady." These observations should not be taken to indicate that class lines and social-distance delineations always coincide. In a highly complicated and changing society like that of the United States, for example, we find a few members of ethnic groups placed fairly low on the scale of social distances as members of the upper class, while a sizable proportion of the lower class is made up of members of ethnic groups placed high on the social-distance scale.

The point to be emphasized is that social distances have not always been based on ethnic delineations supported by racist doctrines of the inherent biological superiority of one group over another. As indicated in Chapter 2, it seems that racist doctrines supporting social distances flourished at a time when the Old World was expanding through the resources, work, and exploitation of men of different complexions (7, 8, 24).

A more traditional explanation of the origin of social distances and group conflicts suggests that group conflict develops from the ethnocentrisms of culturally different groups in contact with one another. There is a tendency for members of in-groups to evaluate other groups in terms of the scale of values developed within their own group; however, social-distance scales and intergroup conflicts cannot be accounted for solely on this basis. There are instances of groups with different cultures existing peacefully side by side with comparatively little social distance. Lindgren (20) tells of two groups in western Manchuria with quite different cultures. Members of these cultures prefer their own group but accept members of the other group. There were no recorded cases of conflict between them at the time of the study. One of these groups is the Tungus, an illiterate, nomadic group of Mongoloid ancestry. The other is a farming group of Cossacks descended from seventeenth-century settlers. They trade with the Tungus, buying their furs and selling them produce. There has been no attempt by the culturally more developed Cossack group to dominate the Tungus. The somewhat greater dependency of the Tungus in this relationship is revealed by the fact that while they know both their own and the Cossack language, the Cossacks know only their own language. Lindgren notes that there was no competition between the groups for land or resources; rather their economies supplemented one another. In this case, there was no clash, in spite of cultural differences, because it was to the interest of each group for the group efforts of both to thrive.

Cultural differences alone certainly cannot explain some of the clashes between groups today. The Negroes in the United States are not culturally distinct from white Americans, while certain immigrant groups, higher on the social-distance scale, have carried on a good many aspects of the ways brought from Europe. The leaders of some of the most militant nationalist movements in colonial countries have been individuals who have been educated and have lived in the lands of their rulers. Men like Gandhi or Nehru, for example, knew and understood British ways well indeed, perhaps better than some Englishmen. Had they chosen, they could have been successful and prosperous functionaries in the British scheme of things. Their understanding of British culture strengthened, rather than weakened, their nationalism.

Personal documents and journalistic accounts in the American colonies prior to and during the Revolutionary War testify to the hostility and bitterness which can develop between groups of the same culture, one in the motherland and one across the sea. When the clash of vital interests and goals of the colonies and of England finally led Britain to attempt to maintain her dominant position by force of arms, "the mother country began to appear in American eyes as a foreign, despotic and 'Papist' power" (27, p. 374).

When examining conditions of contact and the rise of standardized ways of seeing and dealing with culturally different outgroups, a common finding is that one group initially had or attempted to gain cultural, socioeconomic, and military tools enabling it to control the other (7). To understand the nature of relations established, we must look on the one hand at the interests and characteristics of the more developed or developing group, and on the other hand at the vital interests and established ways of the less developed group (8). In the earlier days of Indian-white contact on the American continent, the initial relations between groups seem to have been more than casually related to the aims of the white group. When white men came as traders, it was more to their interest that the Indian hunting, trapping, and ways of life be continued, for the welfare of their trade. When white men came with families as settlers, their interests in acquiring land came into direct conflict with the interests of Indian groups, especially those whose existence depended on large areas in which to hunt and trap (8). Tribes more dependent on stable agricultural existence might be, at least for a time, less exposed to the overwhelming pressure of the expanding interests of the settlers.

Of course, some Indian groups, like the Fox, had already developed in their way of life warlike and aggressive ways of dealing with out-groups. Other Indian groups, like the Blackfoot and Ute, became aggressive and warlike after white contact had effectively altered the basis of their old way of life (22).

For reasons such as these, initial contacts between Indian and white groups varied considerably in degree of hostility or friendliness. However, as the westward expansion of the growing and more powerful groups of white settlers swept on supported by the arms of the United States, a more uniform, less specific pattern of relationships between Indian and white groups took shape. While the Indian groups were being forcibly displaced and constricted, the increasingly dominant white groups came to regard them with considerable unanimity as troublesome savages in the way of their progress—"A good Indian is a dead Indian." Although the aims of expansion were achieved, the American Indian has been kept at considerable social distance except in areas where his educational and financial advantages have enabled him to participate in the main stream of American life.

Brazil, which has a somewhat different social-distance scale, presents a contrast in Indian-white relations. Initial white and Indian contacts were marked with bloody conflict, and many Indian groups were driven from their land. But the Portuguese settlers were predominantly males, rather than families, with the result that Indian-Portuguese intermarriage was not infrequent. As sugar became the principal crop and the plantation system the chief method of production, the white group became dependent upon the labor of Indians (8, 18). The intermixing of Portuguese and Indians produced a sizable *mestizo* population. As additional supply of labor, Negro slaves were brought into the country. After the Civil War in the United States, the Negro slaves in Brazil were liberated by government proclamation. The probable effect of this was comparatively less resentment, bitterness, and self-justification by the slaveholding group than in the United States where the process was achieved by military force (18).

The Portuguese had been exposed in earlier times to darker-skinned Moorish conquerors, which fact may, as Brazilian writers have suggested, have made some differences in their initial attitudes toward darker-skinned peoples. But as Klineberg has pointed out, the Spaniards also lived under a Moorish conquest, yet in the Argentine today attitudes toward dark-skinned people are much less favorable (18, p. 193). Social distances in Brazil, therefore, must have been chiefly the product of interaction between a relatively small, dominant, but not self-sufficient white group and subordinated Indian and, later, Negro groups. The insufficiency of the white group led to intermixing with the Indian group. But the bulk of the Indian and Negro groups served as laborers on plantations. Social distances in Brazil, as we have seen, tend to follow these class lines. When the dominant white group is relatively small, somewhat blended with other groups through intermarriage, and dependent upon other groups for a labor supply, it does not seem to be to its interests to emphasize ethnic or racial backgrounds. Apparently such emphasis has been more frequent in Brazil in areas where large-scale European immigration has occurred more recently (8).

The background of intergroup relations in Hawaii is not completely dissimilar. Initial contacts in Hawaii were between white traders and the native groups (8). In general, this trade was found mutually profitable. Early white traders intermarried with native women of high status, and the children of these unions were recognized by native groups as persons of superior status. In about 1850, sugar came as a large-scale commercial possibility. After this time a succession of immigrations of many different peoples occurred. The multiplicity of sources for laborers was not entirely accidental. "Toward the end of the nineteenth century the residents began to fear that Hawaii would become a Chinese colony, and a different source of supply was sought. . . . Then it was that attention was directed to Japan. . . . The Japanese government shrewdly insisted that each shipment include a sufficient number of women. The fear then arose that Hawaii would become a Japanese community, and still other sources of labor were explored" (8, p. 143). It seems that the dominant, but relatively small, group of whites rather deliberately created a working population of many different ethnic groups in Hawaii.

In the United States, Negro slaves were brought in as the demand for plantation workers exceeded the available supply of indentured white and Indian slaves (14, p. 105). "Under slavery the Negro was owned, bought, and sold as property. In general the Negro slave had no 'rights' which his owner was bound to respect. While most states inaugurated statutes to protect the slave from unnecessary sufferings, to the extent that these regulations were not sanctioned by the master's own economic interests and his feelings for his human property or by community sentiment, they seem not to have been enforced" (34, p. 173). The justification for this system was in terms of racial stereotypes of biological inferiority.

On the part of the Negro slaves, there was hostility which between 1826 and 1860 resulted in 200 slave revolts or uprisings on relatively small scales, in addition to sabotage, escape, malingering, etc. (34). The possibility of uprisings was dreaded by white owners. While contacts and intimacy between slave and owner were restricted, the total segregation of Negroes from all white people was not seen as the pressing necessity which it became later. In an instance reported in Georgia in 1842, Negro and white workers toiled side by side in a cotton mill without conflict (14). In fact, as the struggle which led to civil war crystallized, the Negro in the South was not seen simply as a plantation worker but also as a valuable "buffer" between the owners of industry, which had begun to expand in the South, and free white working people. Governor Adams of South Carolina made this argument explicit, noting that white workers could not be made to work as cheaply as Negroes, and that if compelled to do so they would rise against the owners. The Negro labor supply could effectively minimize such a possibility (14, pp. 71–72).

After emancipation of slaves and the Civil War, attempts were made by at least a part of the victorious group to help the Negroes become independent, to rise above their recent slave status. But defeated and embittered slave owners were not unsuccessful in convincing northern business interests and the general public as well that all this was a mistake. In the 1870's and 1880's, a series of moves and decisions by the federal government and the courts turned the question of Negro rights back to the southern states (25). The dominant white groups in the South, to whose interest it was to keep the Negro in a position as nearly like that of a slave as possible, effectively disfranchised Negroes (as well as many poor white people) in the South by a series of laws requiring property ownership, payment of poll tax, literary tests, good character, and the like as voting qualifications. Segregation laws governing almost every possible area of contact were passed (34, pp. 143–144). The advantages accruing from a restricted and subordinated Negro group had been foretold. Wages for Negro workers were low or, in the case of sharecroppers, based on the sale of crops, exchange of goods, and accounts all executed by the white owner (34, p. 88). Correspondingly the wages of white workers and farmers were kept low. It is not surprising that poor white groups in the South have easily been led to see the Negro as their greatest threat. It would seem that upper-class whites in the South consisting chiefly of "big landowners, the industrialists, the bankers, and the merchants" along with "Northern corporate business with big investments in the region" (34, p. 147) would have little to lose from this type of relationship. Although the functional differentiations in the North differed from those in the South, the availability of a low-paid labor supply of Negroes was not found entirely without advantage in the North. (Wages of Negro and white workers in the North have been equalized comparatively recently.)

Such factors and relationships as these are not the only ones determining the nature of relations between groups or the attitudes of whites to Negroes in the United States. But the social distance at which Negroes are kept in the United States cannot be understood unless such facts as these are taken as ordinates in the picture (14, 34).

The people who came to the United States were not free of prejudices to start with. They came with stereotypes toward various groups, e.g., the Jews, already formed. But the social-distance scale prevailing in the United States today is not wholly explainable in these terms. Immigrant groups who came early in the history of the United States as independent colonists have by and large become integrated into a majority group. In the waves of immigration of the nineteenth century, much of the reaction to the various groups seems to have depended upon the class of people represented and the type of livelihood they were able to find on arrival. Peoples with some skill as farmers or as independent tradesmen were in general in an advantageous position. The great bulk of immigrants especially late in this period came as unskilled or semiskilled workers. It is suggested that there is some tendency for the ranking of groups to follow their cultural level on arrival and the length of stay. For example, in both respects, the German immigrants, by and large, held some advantage over the Italian and Greek immigrants. There was a tendency, of course, for these immigrant groups to cling to old ways in a new and lonely land. But the dominant culture was admired and they strove for acceptance in it. In this striving, the major classifications and social distances of the dominant groups were accepted. The criteria of these classifications are those of the dominant groups. In a New England community, for example, it has been found that the "Old Settlers" are more aware of these criteria and of ethnic origins than other groups (6, p. 24).

It does not always happen that an ethnic or national group came to the United States, improved its position, and rose above the next group of arrivals. The position of the various ethnic groups seems to depend also on their role in the life activities of the country and their functional relations to other groups. The importance of these factors is illustrated in Klineberg's summary of the changing stereotypes toward Chinese on the west coast over a period of time:

When the Chinese were needed in California—when the white migrants from other parts of the United States were so anxious to get rich quickly that they had no patience with domestic labor or with work in cigar factories—the Chinese were welcome. During that period newspapers and journals referred to them as among "the most worthy of our newly-adopted citizens," "the best immigrants in California"; they were spoken of as thrifty, sober, tractable, inoffensive, law-abiding. They showed an "all-round ability" and an "adaptability beyond praise." This flattering picture prevailed during a considerable period. Then around the 1860's, when the economic situation had changed and other groups were competing with the Chinese for the positions which they were occupying, there was a corresponding change in the stereotype of the Chinese. In the elections of 1867 both political parties introduced into their platforms legislation "protecting" Californians against Mongolian competition. The phrases now applied to the Chinese included: "a distinct people," "unassimilable," "their presence lowered the plane of living," "they shut out white labor." They were spoken of as clannish, criminal, debased and servile, deceitful and vicious; they smuggled opium; Chinatowns were full of prostitution and gambling; the Chinese were filthy and loathsome in their habits, undesirable as workers and residents in the country.

This startling change in the "characteristics" of the Chinese can hardly be accounted for by any change in the nature of the Chinese population of California. The only acceptable explanation is that the change in economic conditions there made it advantageous for the whites to eliminate the Chinese from economic competition as far as possible, and the stereotype was altered in a direction which would help to justify such action. [18, pp. 114–115]

As social psychologists interested in intergroup relations, we cannot take facts such as those cited in this section as complete explanations of social distance or prejudice between differing ethnic, color, or national groups as it exists today. The concern of this section has been limited to certain factors which are insufficient in themselves to explain psychological phenomena of prejudice or social distance, but are basic to doing so. These factors are background factors. The study of the background indicates that social-distance scales did not arise only through haphazard individual encounters between members of the groups in question. Social-distance scales are products of interaction between groups in which vital interests, goals, values of the groups come into conflict. All sorts of complicating factors are produced by or are brought into these relationships.

As changes occur in the society at large, the relationships between groups may change and social-distance norms may not keep pace. Or different factors may come to facilitate their perpetuation. Before stating the major factors making for maintenance of social-distance norms which seem to be wholly carry-overs from earlier periods, we should have to study the changing functional relationships of groups within the society.

The main point of emphasis here is that scales of social distance emerge from interaction between functionally related groups with conflicting vital interests, values, ways of life, etc. The value of studying such background factors and their relevance to understanding social-distance scales is demonstrated in MacCrone's intensive historical study of race relations in South Africa and his experiments on social-distance attitudes among various groups in South Africa in 1937 (24). His examination of the attitudes of the original European traders and settlers in South Africa and those of subsequent generations revealed "radical alteration" of original attitudes. In brief, he traced these alterations to the relationships of white settlers to less culturally developed native groups who resisted the encroachments and exploitations of the white settlers, with ensuing violence; to the importations of more docile colored labor as slaves; to the effects of the isolated life on an expanding frontier on these relations, etc. By the end of the eighteenth century, even the content of the original attitudes of white settlers had undergone revision. Less emphasis was laid on the Christian-heathen dichotomy. Baptism was no longer the chief basis for inclusion in the Christian European community. Although the content further changed after this period toward contemporary emphasis on "the white man and his 'civilization,'" the attitudes of social distance "as they existed towards the end of the eighteenth and at the beginning of the nineteenth century are very similar to those which we find displayed on all sides at the present time" (24, p. 135). In the experiments he conducted, MacCrone found that the social-distance scale was remarkably similar to the findings of his historical studies, and that prejudice and race stereotypes were held in varying degrees by English-speaking students, Afrikaans, Jews, and even certain Bantu (native) subjects who were trying to "reach and maintain themselves at a higher level of civilization" (p. 166).

When we speak of a social-distance scale or of prejudice over a time span, it can be seen that *the classifications and definitions which come to prevail are those of the majority, and not those of minority groups.* Initially scales of social distance, stereotypes, attitudes of prejudice flow from powerful dominant groups and are defined in terms of their particular status and point of view, not upward from weaker, subordinate groups. Subordinate groups may, in their strivings to become accepted by the dominant groups, even come to adopt the social-distance scale of the more powerful group. As objects of low placement and discrimination, individuals may carry hidden hostilities toward the dominant group. But such hostilities, hidden in the face of overwhelming odds against their expression, cannot prevail in society at large, and not even in the subordinate group in question until they are experienced by members of that group as a cause for *group* concern. The implication is that in-group organization of oppressed peoples is prerequisite to militancy.

Ignorance or neglect of such background factors in the formation of social-distance scales and norms of prejudice has led to numerous pitfalls. Among these is the widely prevalent notion that attitudes of prejudice can be satisfactorily explained *solely* in terms of the individual and his development.

SOCIAL DISTANCE AND DISPLACEMENT THEORY

In Chapter 2 some traditional theories which make factors coming from within the individual the sole or chief determinant of social distances and hostilities between social groups were surveyed. Modern versions of such theories are flourishing today, variously called "displacement theories," "scapegoat theories," frustration-aggression theories, and the like. All these theories deal with the role of individual frustrations in creating aggressions, hostility, and conflict in relation to various groups. Since frustrations are important factors, these theories require our serious consideration. No attempt will be made to outline specific versions. The sources are readily available (for example, 1, 2, 3, 9, 11). Himmelweit has made a comprehensive critical summary of some research relating to these theories (15). The theories all stem in various ways from the work of Freud.

In simplest form, stripped of some variations and qualifications, modern versions of displacement theories of prejudice run like this: When an individual is frustrated (by external conditions or internal conflicts), he reacts with aggression, which may or may not be manifested at the time. There is a tendency for aggression so generated to be directed against the source of frustration, if it is readily available. Thus when an object in our path prevents us from going on our way, we may kick at it, even though the kick may not clear the path. But if the source of frustration is not available, is hidden, or is too powerful, then the aggression tends to accumulate. It may not be directed toward any specific object or person but may be unattached or "free floating." The aggressive tendencies can then become *displaced* to almost any object, person, or group, preferably something or someone who cannot retaliate, who is too dependent or too weak to punish the person. The husband who "takes it out" on his wife after an altercation with the boss, the child who tears up a toy after being prevented by his parents from following his desires of the moment are examples of such displacement.

No matter what the causes of the original frustration, this theory holds that minority groups, ethnic groups low on the social-distance scale may serve as such objects for displaced aggression. Hostility against other groups serves as an outlet or discharge for the pent-up aggression generated through frustration. It is suggested that out-groups are more desirable objects of aggression than the in-group, since most in-groups have effective ways of dealing with aggressors within the group.

The individual is not aware of this process of displacement. In order to square himself with his conscience (superego), he invents good reasons for his hostility. These rationalizations consist largely of attributing his own troubles to the object of his aggression and, possibly, projecting his own undesirable traits and guilt feelings on him. From these processes of rationalization and projection, stereotypes of the out-groups emerge. The modern versions of displacement theories usually state that certain ready-made "scapegoats" are provided by society and that stereotypes are available for suitable rationalization.

If this sequence can be taken as valid, it would follow that individuals who had suffered unusual frustrations, perhaps in childhood at the hands of authoritative parents, would have unusual degrees of pent-up aggression available for direction against minority groups.

In order to evaluate the present status of these displacement theories, the evidence supporting them must be critically evaluated. Necessarily, only a few main points can be mentioned here that relate especially to the role of individual frustrations in determining intergroup antagonisms. The consequences of individual frustrations in relationships of a strictly personal nature need not be our chief concern, for we are interested in this theory as applied to intergroup relations. Nevertheless, it is necessary to glance briefly at the sort of evidence on which the major assumptions of this theory are based.

In the experiments performed, the frustrating experience has almost always been one of brief duration produced in most instances by obstacles in the environment. The frustrating circumstances, as Himmelweit notes, have all been frustration "without hope" (15). It has been suggested that many aggressive responses to such situations are reactions to an "unreasonable" situation (30). In short, as Sargent pointed out, we may say that the role of the individual's perception of the frustrating situation has been largely neglected (35).

Unfortunately, what is meant by "aggression" has been and is still loosely defined. The term is used somewhat indiscriminately. "Apparently, for some psychologists, if A does anything which modifies what B was doing or intending to do . . . his action is aggressive" (31, p. 38). The matter of delineating just what constitutes aggressive behavior under given conditions is certainly important, especially when experimental results are being evaluated.

It is established that frustrating experiences lead to responses other than aggression. Himmelweit (15) lists the following responses which have followed frustrating situations in different studies: aggression, regression or lowering of the level of performance, evading the situation by leaving it or "going out of the field," apathy and resignation (especially for prolonged frustration), repression or "forgetting." Ordinarily several of these responses occur in the same situation and there is considerable variation in the *degree* of their manifestation by various individuals.

The experimental evidence concerning the relation between individual frustration and aggression leaves much to be desired. For example, a survey of these experiments reveals that "the degree of aggression shown is in part a function of the strength of the frustration experience, and in part affected by situational factors. Added security given by the presence of friends may enable aggression to be expressed more freely" (15, p. 177). One study reviewed by Himmelweit found considerable in-group aggression, especially within a well-organized group. Perhaps a less one-sided approach to the study of individual frustrations and their consequences, which includes the role of perception of the situation and of situational factors, may prove fruitful. These experiments do indicate that under some circumstances experiences which are frustrating for the individual may lead to some sort of aggressive response. Himmelweit's conclusions concerning displacement of aggression are based chiefly on well-known studies by Lewin, Lippitt, and White and by French. They are somewhat contrary to a displacement theory of prejudice. "Aggression tends to be inhibited by a feeling of insecurity and by anticipation of punishment. In these circumstances, it tends to be displaced on to *some individual or group of a status more nearly equal to the subject's,* and from whom no retaliation is expected" (15, p. 177). It would appear that punishment for aggression toward members of in-groups or groups of similar status is not always so prohibitive as might be expected. However, in these studies no groups of low status were readily available for displacement purposes. Himmelweit cautions: "The absence of experimental knowledge of what precisely constitutes aggression makes it well-nigh impossible to draw parallels between the detailed kind of aggression displayed in these experiments, and the aggression exhibited by groups in their attitudes and subsequent behavior to one another. An example of the difficulty is the finding of several investigators that individuals who displayed aggression freely in the form of aggressive comments, tended at the same time to be less neurotic and to be more amenable and co-operative in their actual behaviour than those who were verbally less aggressive" (15, pp. 186–187).

In evaluating evidence in support of displacement theories of prejudice, one of the crucial considerations is that comparisons in these studies have not been made between *prejudiced* individuals and *non*-prejudiced individuals. The people studied have been *more* prejudiced or *less* prejudiced. The procedure has consisted of taking those individuals with scores at one extreme on tests of prejudice as "prejudiced" individuals and those at the other extreme in terms of test scores as "unprejudiced" (4, 23). For example, in a study of veterans of World War II, even those individuals labeled as most tolerant toward Jews expressed stereotypes from time to time; and many of these were revealed to be anti-Negro (9).

A recent experimental study by Lindzey (21) indicated that while displacement of aggression followed the various frustrating procedures used, highly prejudiced individuals showed no greater tendency to displace aggression or to direct aggression outward than did those individuals with relatively less prejudice. These findings are not in harmony with displacement theories. They indicate that in a situation where restraints upon direct aggression toward the experimental situation (including the experimenter) exist, aggression is displaced by highly prejudiced individuals and less prejudiced individuals alike.

Recent large-scale studies have reported close relationships between high scores on tests of personal rigidity and ethnocentrism and high scores on tests of prejudice. An attempt is made to relate high scores on these measures to prolonged frustrations suffered in earlier life, especially in the family situation. There are indications that this relationship between a polar personality "type" and prejudice does not hold independently for groups from the "low education stratum" of society. The evidence gives reason to suspect that these measures are related to other factors which may vary in different social strata of society (36). Another study of prejudice and ethnocentrism in two different regions in the United States (California and a southwestern city) has indicated

that these two factors may vary even within the same socioeconomic classes (10). Higher scores in both ethnocentrism and prejudice were found for subjects in the southwest city. The authors
concluded: "Insofar as the matched samples equate socioeconomic
factors which are known to be related to child-rearing practices
. . . and both samples are composed of primarily urban, middle-class residents, it would seem such differential early experiences as age at weaning, early toilet training and so forth are
highly suspect as explanatory concepts for the significant disparity
in acceptance of F scale items" (pp. 477–478). The differences
found can be attributed, the authors believe, to differential exposure to a variety of "ideological stimulation." California students were "exposed to a wider range of relatively liberal social
viewpoints," while the southwest city students were exposed to a
"narrower range of expressed ideology which was fairly conservative by nature." It is possible that when situational, class, and
status factors, group identifications, and the like are systematically
included in studies of individual or "personality" factors in prejudice, some interesting relations may be found between such factors and *degree* of prejudice.

But the crucial test of displacement theories of prejudice must
demonstrate that those individuals who have prejudices have endured greater frustrations, have greater pent-up aggressions than
do *non*-prejudiced individuals. This crucial test has not been
made.

Considerable evidence suggests that attempts at such a test are
likely to fail. This line of evidence concerns the role of conformity to the groups in which the individual moves and to which
he relates himself psychologically in the acquisition and maintenance of prejudice. Briefly, in a society in which groups are held
at various social distances, the individual who conforms to the
major norms of the majority group will, of course, be prejudiced.
It is the individual who is rebellious against at least some of the
major norms of the larger society (including those of social distance)—the nonconformist—who tends to be unprejudiced toward various out-groups (4, 16, 29, 38).

We find high degrees of prejudice associated with close con-

formity to the major institutions in the society. Thus greater prejudice is manifested by regular churchgoers than by those who attend irregularly or not at all (5, 17). Greater prejudice is found
among individuals with higher degrees of patriotism (28). As
Horowitz (16) has pointed out, the individual who is a "dissenter"
or nonconformist to the wider society is not a rebellious spirit at
loose ends. His rejection of the social-distance scale prevalent in
the larger society may represent conformity to a smaller group
within the society.

It seems highly unlikely that individuals who are nonconformists in relation to the larger social units in which they grew up
and must move have been less frustrated than those who have conformed to society's major tenets. Studies in the United States have
revealed a tendency for dissenters to be antagonistic toward or at
least keep some distance from their parents. In evaluating these
results, Eysenck suggests:

> Thus it might be inviting to speculate that radical attitudes towards
> social issues are founded on parent antagonism, but it must be remem-
> bered that the correlations apparently supporting such a belief were
> obtained in a society in which radical beliefs are ostracized. . . . Where
> the great majority of parents of all classes, and particularly of college
> students, share a capitalistic outlook, the rising generation's disagree-
> ment with their parents on emotional grounds may easily make them
> critical of social and political beliefs held by the parents, thus inevitably
> leading them to the only alternative social and political outlook. . . .
> The crucial test would be a repetition of the experiment in a socialist
> country; would children of socialist parents, who are antagonistic to
> these parents, develop a conservative outlook? If so, the alleged affinity
> between childhood antagonism and radical attitudes would be shown
> to be merely an instance of a more embracing generalization of the
> linking up of emotional antagonisms with cognitive disagreements, a
> generalization which in other circumstances would lead to a correla-
> tion between childhood antagonisms to parents and conservative politi-
> cal attitudes. [12, pp. 51–52]

We may find a relationship between eventual nonconformity
and frustrations and deprivations in the family situation; but this

relationship is not likely to be a one-to-one sort of thing. Some individuals may become estranged from their families precisely because they have accepted nonconformist ideologies derived from other groups. At any rate, evidence such as this would not tend to support the displacement theories of group prejudice and aggression. It would indicate rather that nonconformists might have endured greater frustrations in their family situations than conformists to larger society. It would seem that once one becomes nonconformist, the obstacles in the path of achieving one's goals are likely to be greater than those the conformist faces. The way of nonconformity is not ordinarily thought to be an easy way.

On the other hand, it may be possible to relate *degrees* of prejudice (in contrast to prejudice or nonprejudice) to frustrations, insecurities, status changes, and the like within the conforming bulk of society. It should be noted that in present-day complicated societies it is possible to deviate from many of society's norms without being a social outcast. Some groups, while nonconformist in relation to certain values in American society, conform strongly or even violently to other major tenets, including the norms of social distance. The Christian Front movement might be cited as an example. We shall see later that there is good evidence that insecurity in one's status within the in-group may lead to more intense manifestations of the group norms as a way of "proving" one's support and contribution to the group.

The relationship between prejudice and conformity to the larger social setting indicates that, even in considering internal factors and motives, displacement theories have been one-sided. The chief defect of displacement theories in accounting for the facts of social distance and prejudice is not that they give a major role to frustrations. There seems little doubt that frustrations are important factors in intergroup relations as well as in personal relations. The chief defect of displacement theories is, rather, that they are *monistic* or one-sided. The cause of prejudice is sought in factors coming from within the individual, and further only in *certain* factors from within the individual (43). For this reason, there are many facts concerning social distance which displacement theories cannot handle adequately, and there are several questions such theories cannot answer.

One question we have referred to above: Why are some individuals prejudiced against members of certain groups, while some individuals are not prejudiced against such groups? A reply that non-prejudiced individuals have found other ways of ridding themselves of aggression could not be considered an adequate answer to this question without valid evidence.

Zawadski has posed four questions concerning prejudice which displacement theories cannot answer:

1. Why, sometimes, a certain minority is selected to pick on where there are several to choose from.
2. Why there is sometimes a striking difference in intensity of dislike toward different minorities.
3. Why certan minorities are respected, if not liked, while others are disliked and despised.
4. Why it is that not only do majorities have their prejudices against minorities, but minorities also have their prejudices against majorities. [43, p. 132]

These may be increased and illustrated with concrete facts and examples. Why is it that some of the more victimized groups in a society may have less prejudice? As a group, Jews in the United States have been found relatively less prejudiced than other religious groups (5, 26). They have been found less militaristic than other religious groups (37). Yet Jews are more frequently victims of intergroup aggressions than Catholics or Protestants (5). Certain interracial groups, labor unions, and radical groups whose norms are contrary to the established social-distance scale also come in for a large share of hostility and aggression directed against their members.

If aggression against minority groups is explained entirely in terms of aggressive impulses developed within the individual as a consequence of his frustrations, how can we explain the fact that in certain other countries where the citizens are at least as frustrated as those in the United States acts of violence against minority groups do not occur in the same way? For example, Klineberg notes:

> White Brazilians are, on the whole, much more economically frustrated than white Americans. The economic standards of the former are definitely much lower, and relatively many more of them live near or at a bare subsistence level. There are fluctuations in economic conditions in Brazil, just as in the United States. However, there are no lynchings of Brazilian Negroes. . . . This fact makes it clearly inadequate to explain aggression against the Negro or, in more general terms, hostility against other groups (which may take the form of war in extreme cases) entirely in terms of the aggressive impulses developed within the individual as a result of his frustrations. [18, p. 198]

Klineberg asks another penetrating question in relation to displacement theories of group aggression: "Why, if war is due to these factors within the individual, are the majority of individuals opposed to war? Why must they be made to fight? Why must every country, in seeking to build its army, have recourse to conscription?" (18, p. 199)

Certainly aggression and vindictiveness were not characteristic of the American armies in World War II. Studies of the American soldier conducted during World War II found that a majority of soldiers fought to get the job done, or because they didn't want to let their outfit down. Only 2 percent said they fought out of anger, revenge, or "fighting spirit." Another 3 percent gave "making a better world; crushing aggressor; belief in what I'm fighting for" as reasons for fighting, and some of these replies might be interpreted as aggressive (39, p. 109). It must be remembered that these answers were obtained from soldiers actually doing the fighting—men in situations where aggression toward the enemy was perfectly permissible. It could hardly be argued that aggression was repressed, suppressed, or denied expression in these war situations.

Such critical facts constitute plausible evidence against the validity of an "aggression theory of war." Modern warfare is conflict between modern states, which have very definite organizational structures and norms. As Pear says:

It fails to distinguish between the aggressiveness of the warmakers, which can be very real indeed (though frequently personal greed, still socially disapproved if found out, masquerades as socially approved aggressiveness) and the attitudes of the general population, many of whom may not know of the impending war, of the combatant, semi-combatant, and non-combatant soldiers, and of the victims. In a war involving more than half the population of the world, a vast number of people who had nothing to do with declaring war suffered passively. Often aggressiveness had to be stirred up and intensified even in the fighters (we have recently read about the experimental army "hate school," abolished as a result of psychiatrists' reports), in the uniformed sections many people of both sexes lived an unaggressive life and yet helped to win the war, "backroom boys" and scientists are unlikely to have done their best thinking if viscerally stirred; "beating the enemy" cannot have been a constant day-and-night goal giving incentive to all non-combatants, as the excellent book *War Factory* among others, showed. [31, pp. 40–41]

Statistics of the number of wars engaged in by the major nations of the world from 1850 to 1941 (33) reveal that Britain heads the list with twenty wars—more than the Japanese (nine), the Germans (eight), or the United States (seven). Can these statistics be explained in terms of the individual frustrations and resulting aggressive tendencies of the British people channeled into war against other nations? The warlike tendencies of modern Germany are often attributed to pent-up aggressions of the populace resulting from the authoritarian character of the German family, social, and political life which imposes severe frustrations on individuals. But if this analysis is valid, then it should be true that the British people are more frustrated than the German people. It seems reasonable to pose a question, which historians can help us answer: Doesn't having an empire with far-flung interests to be defended and expanded have anything to do with this frequency of wars?

One of the more important evidences which has been used to support displacement theories of intergroup prejudice and hostility concerns the relative role of poor whites and upper-class whites in the South in participating in group aggressions particularly against the Negroes. Participants of lynching parties, of race riots, of active and brutal aggression against Negroes are often members of the frustrated "poor white" class. Probably the frustrations of the poor whites are directly related to their participations in these instances of group aggression. These "poor whites" are led to believe that their frustrations, which are not merely individual frustrations but frustrations common to all members, are attributable to Negro groups, and that these frustrations will increase if Negroes are allowed to change their low place in the scheme of social life.

On the other hand, it is not true that upper- and middle-class white people do not have anything to do with prejudice, hostility, and violence against the Negroes. Raper's study of lynchings in the United States of the early 1930's showed that, while most lynchers were propertyless people with low education, middle- and upper-class people were by no means apart or above the lynchings (32). In Scooba, Mississippi, a lynching was organized and "engineered from start to finish" by men prominent in church, school, and other community activities (p. 10).

Intensive study of such acts of violence has revealed that: "The actual participants usually belong to the frustrated lower classes of Southern whites. Occasionally, however, the people of the middle and upper classes take part, and *generally they condone the deed*. Women and children are not absent from lynching mobs; indeed, women sometimes incite the mob to action" (34, p. 186, italics ours).

They "generally condone the deed"—this is what displacement theories neglect in evaluating these facts. "Plantation owners and employers, who use Negro labor as cheaper and more docile, have at times been observed to tolerate, or even co-operate in, the periodic aggressions of poor whites against Negroes" (34, p. 200).

Poor whites, frustrated as they are, are dependent upon this condoning, this tolerance, even coöperation, from more powerful groups. They know that members of lynching mobs are "practically never" brought to court, and that there is even less likelihood of being punished (34, p. 181). The names of participants

"This is her first lynching." By Reginald Marsh. Reproduced by permission. Copr. 1934, The New Yorker Magazine, Inc.

in lynchings are usually not too difficult to secure and they may even be given nation-wide publicity, as was the case in a South Carolina lynching in 1947. But they really have little to fear from the local courts (34). (Federal intervention of any effectiveness has been recent.) In most cases they have the support of the law enforcement officers, either tacit or active (32). But law enforcement officers are not answerable only to the mob. In terms of the political structure, they could not give in to the lynchers without the tacit support of politicians and political supporters in superior positions.

These poor whites hear their distinguished United States senator say that "every red-blooded, Anglo-Saxon man in Mississippi must resort to any means to keep hundreds of Negroes from the polls." Such statements by men in high places are to be found in the daily papers. We read too of incidents like the following: "In Rupert District of South Georgia's Taylor County, Macie Snipes was the only Negro to vote. The day after election four white men called him out from supper. Macie Snipes staggered back into the house with blood gushing from the bullet wounds in his belly. A coroner's jury solemnly reported that he had been killed by one of his visitors in self-defense" (40).

Of course, by and large, upper- and middle-class people might find it quite contrary to their stations, quite below their dignity, even repugnant to participate in such brutal crimes. Perhaps the *extent* of the brutality against Negroes, which includes murder, torture, and dismemberment of victims, may be directly traceable to pent-up aggressions of the poor whites.

In some cases, violence against Negroes is occasioned by the orders of powerful persons who control law enforcement agencies. This is the implication of a survey of riots in Columbia, Tennessee. It was found that "The people of Columbia are not responsible for this outrage. . . . It was the state forces sent in from outside that organized the armed invasion and pillaging of the Negro business section. Even the killing in the jail was done by state officers" (13). Negro deaths in jails are by no means unusual (34). The actions of police, especially state police, can hardly be explained solely on the basis of individual frustrations. Such men are occupying an institutional role. This role is defined *for* them, not by them. If they were to deviate too far from this definition, they would no longer be state officers.

In any accounting for the aggressive actions of frustrated poor whites, it is not enough to deal simply with their frustrations and aggressions. These frustrations and aggressions must be seen in relation to a social setting and power structure which condone and even support or encourage the aggressions. Williams writes: "In some areas, especially in rural portions of the deep South, tension and conflict arise largely from the efforts of the white population to maintain castelike controls and privileges. . . . Myrdal's thesis of an 'American dilemma' in which the white person is torn between his creeds and his specific operating practices would not apply to the case in which the dominant whites feel little value-conflict in supporting inequalitarian, discriminatory patterns" (42, p. 365). The social scientist is forced to the reluctant conclusion that violence toward Negroes in some areas is an acceptable pattern of social behavior not just for poor whites but for organized society. The range of tolerable behavior sanctioned by social values or norms includes possible violence to Negroes.

The Negroes of the South—the victims of these aggressions— are surely even more frustrated than the poor whites. Negroes in the South do not at present attempt to lynch or otherwise violate or terrorize "poor whites." Those who do are quickly put in jail and are punished. In a setting in which out-group aggressiveness was both formally and informally outlawed and this norm was enforced all along the line, frustrated individuals and groups would not find it necessary to release their aggressions on members of minority groups.

Displacement theories of prejudice cannot answer many urgent questions, cannot adequately account for many facts of intergroup relations. They cannot because they dwell on certain factors to the exclusion of others equally or more important. No amount of patching up or adding to theories which seek to explain prejudice and intergroup hostility through displacement of pent-up aggressions resulting from individual frustrations with bits from sociology or anthropology will make the assumptions of these theories adequate for the task. Nor is this the course of scientific progress. A theory which does not account for the facts it seeks to encompass is not retained just because it deals with an important factor. *Rather we must work to develop new theories which do integrate the facts, including those handled by the old.*

In making this attempt, frustrations will be included among important factors. It is probable that *degree* of manifestation of prejudice may be related, among other factors, to frustration. It seems likely that frustrations become crucial in producing intergroup hostilities when the frustrating experiences and situations interfere with the course of vital activities and directions of the group, when they interfere with the attainment of *group* goals. In such cases, frustrations are shared by members of a group, in the sense that the individual member experiences the frustration as impediment to attainment by the group and by himself as a group member. To lead to intergroup hostility, common frustrations of a group and its members must be *seen* by the group members as attributable to another specific group. But even in such instances, the frustration in itself cannot be taken as the sole explanation for hostility between groups.

We have referred to the frustrations of oppressed peoples who are victims of group prejudice and hostility. It is significant that such frustrations do not seem to lead to militancy or aggression toward out-groups until some in-group feeling has developed. Then individuals become aware that their individual frustrations are reflections of obstacles imposed upon all members of their group by another group. It is probably for this reason that the most militant minority groups have not necessarily come from the most oppressed, most frustrated sections of humanity (41, p. 61). Militancy is associated with the attainment of some in-group structure by the oppressed group. Individual members experience belongingness in the minority group and see their plight as related to its plight. As Berry notes, the rising tide of resentment and the militancy of the Negro people of South Africa has followed oppression by the whites, communication between the smaller in-groups, and urbanization of many of their members brought on by the way of life of the white group (8). These conditions fostered the rise of an in-group to which Negro individuals related themselves, and the rise of aggressive tendencies toward whites as the dominant group in response to the oppressions and frustrations imposed on them as black people. Cultural differences helped the accentuation of this conflict.

In a society in which minority groups are allowed to participate in some degree, even if unequally and separately, and where the values and achievements of the dominant (majority) group are held out for attainment, members of minority groups accept the norms of the majority to the extent that they are related to the majority group psychologically and seek their satisfactions and successes on its terms. This incorporation of the norms of the majority group, including norms of social distance, by members of the minority divides the group among itself. The incorporation of the majority's values of norms also deters the formation of in-groups composed of other peoples sharing similar frustrations as members of groups also placed low on the social-distance scale.

REFERENCES

1. Ackerman, N. W., and Jahoda, M. *Anti-Semitism and Emotional Disorder.* New York: Harper, 1950.

2. Adorno, T. W., *et al. The Authoritarian Personality.* New York: Harper, 1950.

3. Allport, G. W. *ABC's of Scapegoating.* Chicago: Anti-Defamation League of B'nai B'rith, rev. ed., 1948.

4. Allport, G. W. Prejudice: a problem in psychological and social causation, *J. soc. Issues,* Supplement Series, No. 4, Nov., 1950.

5. Allport, G. W., and Kramer, B. M. Some roots of prejudice, *J. Psychol.,* 1946, *22,* 9–39.

6. Anderson, E. L. *We Americans: A Study of Cleavage in an American City.* Cambridge: Harvard University Press, 1937.

7. Benedict, R. *Race and Cultural Relations,* Problems in American Life, No. 5. Washington: National Education Association, 1942.

8. Berry, B. *Race Relations.* Boston: Houghton Mifflin, 1951.

9. Bettleheim, B., and Janowitz, M. *Dynamics of Prejudice.* New York: Harper, 1950.

10. Christie, R., and Garcia, J. Subcultural variation in authoritarian personality, *J. abn. & soc. Psychol.,* 1951, *46,* 457–469.

11. Dollard, J., et al. *Frustration and Aggression.* New Haven: Yale University Press, 1939.

12. Eysenck, H. J. War and aggressiveness: a survey of social attitude studies, in T. H. Pear (ed.), *Psychological Factors of Peace and War.* New York: Philosophical Library, 1950.

13. Foreman, Clark H. Statement, in report, Southern Conference of Human Welfare, *The Truth about Columbia, Tennessee,* 1946.

14. Goldstein, N. F. *The Roots of Prejudice Against the Negro in the United States.* Boston: Boston University Press, 1948.

15. Himmelweit, H. Frustration and aggression: a review of recent experimental work, in T. H. Pear (ed.), *Psychological Factors of Peace and War.* New York: Philosophical Library, 1950.

16. Horowitz, E. L. "Race" attitudes, Part IV, in O. Klineberg (ed.), *Characteristics of the American Negro.* New York: Harper, 1944.

17. Information Control Division, American Military Government in Germany. Survey reported in New York *Herald Tribune,* May 4, 1947.

18. Klineberg, O. *Tensions Affecting International Understanding.* New York: Social Science Research Council, Bull. 62, 1950.

19. Lewis, O. The effects of white contact upon Blackfoot culture, *Monogr. Amer. Ethnolog. Soc.,* 1942, 6.

20. Lindgren, E. J. An example of culture contact without conflict, *Amer. Anthropologist,* 1938, *40,* 605–621.

21. Lindzey, G. An experimental examination of the scapegoat theory of prejudice, *J. abn. & soc. Psychol.,* 1950, *45,* 296–309.

22. Linton, R. (ed.). *Acculturation in Seven American Indian Tribes.* New York: Appleton-Century-Crofts, 1940.

23. Luchins, A. S. Rigidity and ethnocentrism: a critique, *J. Personal.,* 1948–49, *17,* 449–466.

24. MacCrone, I. D. *Race Attitudes in South Africa.* London: Oxford University Press, 1937.

25. McWilliams, Carey. The Negro problem: a case history, in B. Moon (ed.), *Primer for White Folks*. New York: Doubleday, Doran, 1945, pp. 137–169.

26. Merton, R. Fact and factitiousness in ethnic opinionnaires. *Amer. Sociol. Rev.*, 1940, 5, 13–28.

27. Miller, J. C. *Origins of the American Revolution*. Boston: Little, Brown, 1943.

28. Morse, N. C. Unpublished study summarized in G. W. Allport, Prejudice: a problem in psychological and social causation, *J. soc. Issues*, Supplement Series, No. 4, 1950.

29. Murphy, G., and Likert, R. *Public Opinion and the Individual*. New York: Harper, 1938.

30. Pastore, N. A neglected factor in the frustration-aggression hypothesis: a comment, *J. Psychol.*, 1950, 29, 271–279.

31. Pear, T. H. Peace, war, and culture patterns, in T. H. Pear (ed.), *Psychological Factors of Peace and War*. New York: Philosophical Library, 1950.

32. Raper, A. *The Tragedy of Lynching*. Chapel Hill: University of North Carolina Press, 1933.

33. Richardson, L. F. Statistics of deadly quarrels, in T. H. Pear (ed.), *Psychological Factors of Peace and War*. New York: Philosophical Library, 1950.

34. Rose, Arnold. *The Negro in America (A Condensation of An American Dilemma)*. New York: Harper, 1948.

35. Sargent, S. S. Reaction to frustration: a critique and hypothesis, *Psychol. Rev.*, 1948, 55, 108–113.

36. Srole, L. Social dysfunction, personality, and social distance attitudes. Paper read before American Sociological Society meetings, Chicago, 1951.

37. Stagner, R. Some factors related to attitudes toward war, *J. soc. Psychol.*, 1942, 16, 131–142.

38. Stagner, R. Studies of aggressive social attitudes: I. Measurement and interrelation of selected attitudes, *J. soc. Psychol.*, 1944, 20, 109–120; II. Changes from peace to war, *ibid.*, 121–128; III. The role of personal and family scores, *ibid.*, 129–140.

39. Stouffer, S. A., *et al.* *The American Soldier: Combat and Its Aftermath*. Princeton: Princeton University Press, 1949.

40. *Time*, August 5, 1946.

41. Williams, R. M., Jr. *The Reduction of Intergroup Tensions: A Survey of Research on Problems of Ethnic, Racial and Religious Group Relations.* New York: Social Science Research Council, Bull. 57, 1947.

42. Williams, R. M., Jr. *American Society.* New York: Knopf, 1951.

43. Zawadski, B. Limitations of the scapegoat theory of prejudice, *J. abn. & soc. Psychol.*, 1948, *43*, 127–141.

ௗௗௗௗௗௗௗௗௗௗௗௗௗௗௗௗௗௗௗௗ

The Need for a Comprehensive Approach to Intergroup Relations

It becomes evident that social psychological theories of intergroup relations which base the whole edifice *primarily* on a universal instinct (e.g., aggression), on displacements of aggressions always as the product of frustrations in personal life history, on a leadership principle, on situational factors, on culture, on national character, or, in a direct and mechanical way, on economic conditions result in one-sided pictures. These theories deal, however, with factors that do enter into determining the character of relations between groups. These factors jointly enter in various degrees in the shaping of the final product each with a *relative weight*. And the relative weights are not fixed quantities consistent for all historical circumstances. Compilations of these factors side by side in the form of a syllabus with enumeration of unrelated hypotheses concerning them have not led to a clear functional picture.

What is needed in the formulation of an adequate social psychology of intergroup relations is the psychological principles which will enable us to handle all these factors within a unified conceptual scheme. In this conceptual scheme, relevant factors will be functional parts of an interdependent process. While exclusive preoccupation with one set of factors leads to blind alleys, our emphasis on the functional interdependence of factors should not obliterate but rather accentuate the relative weights of various factors operative at a given time. In a functioning system, everything is related to everything else; but certain parts exert greater influence in determining the character of the outcome than others. Changes in these parts result in changes in the character of the whole product. Here, we shall take time to give only the high points in brief outline of the psychological principles from which we proceed. In our previous works we spelled them out in greater detail with the historical sources of these principles and ample evidence from psychological literature, experimental and otherwise.

Such a unified scheme should start with the assertion of *the unity of experience and behavior*. This assertion becomes necessary because of a contrary tendency encouraged in recent years by findings of discrepancies between what people say about their attitude on an issue and how they act in concrete situations. Some authors discussed such discrepancies under the title of "objective" approach vs. "phenomenological" approach. Advocating divorce of experience and behavior is like saying that the muscles function independently of the central integrative processes. In cases of discrepancy, which are not infrequently found in the complicated setting of modern life, we suspect one of the following: either the individual did not give his attitude originally owing to the way or the setting in which it was obtained, or other factors entered the actual behavioral situation which were weightier at the time. In either case, there is no question of divorce of experience and action in such findings. Either case can be explained on the basis of new factors entering into the situation—new factors which the psychologist was not set to take into account. But, when we look closely, we find that the effect of new factors is not on experience alone, or behavior alone, but on both as they are organically related to one another. We shall give illustrations of this point in the last section of Chapter 7.

Behavior is the consequence of *central structuring or patterning*. Hence the unity of perception and action. The dissociation of perception and action in extreme pathological cases is not typical in group relations of consequence in human affairs.

The psychologist's data consist of items of observed behavior (verbal or nonverbal) and external stimulus situations. Perceptions, motives, attitudes, etc., are *inferred* from observed behavior. The unity of experience and action is implied in this scheme.

Perceptual structuring is not only a "cognitive" affair. It is jointly determined by the totality of functionally related external factors and internal factors coming into the structuring process at a given time. These interrelated factors—external and internal —constitute the *frame of reference* of the ensuing reaction. Observed behavior (verbal or nonverbal) can be adequately understood and evaluated only when studied within its appropriate frame of reference or system of relations. (See accompanying figure.) The concept—frame of reference—does not denote a specific psychological item. It does not refer to a judgment, an attitude, a social norm. Rather the concept denotes a system of relations operative at a given time which determine perceptual structuring and hence behavior. Here perceptual structuring is taken as the prototype of all psychological processes (judging, learning, remembering, imagining, decision making).

The *external factors* are stimulating situations outside of the individual (objects, persons, events, etc.). The *internal factors* are motives (needs), attitudes, emotions, general state of the organism, effects of past experience, etc. The limit between the two is the skin of the individual—the skin being on the side of the organism.

The psychological tendency is toward structuring of perceptions. Perception is taken as the prototype of all experience. We tend to see definite forms, definite patterns, definite sequences and structure in events. Experimental evidence has shown that this is not an additive matter. Different parts in a structure have properties different from those they have in a different structure, and different from their properties when studied alone or in isolation. This characteristic is referred to as *"membership character"* in literature on the subject. The implications of this fact for group relations will become evident in the chapters that follow.

The physical world around us consists of objects, streets, buildings, contours in space with definite structures of their own. In such cases the structure of perception corresponds on the whole to the physical structures. The world is not just what I make of it at will. The shape of steps and their sequence on the staircase are compellingly perceived as such. Very few people will recklessly tumble down a staircase. Such situations are referred to as *structured situations.*

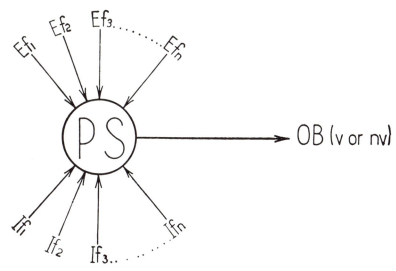

OB (v or nv): Observed Behavior (verbal or nonverbal)
Ef: External factors (objects, persons, groups, etc., in the external stimulus situation)
If: Internal factors (motives, attitudes, emotions, various states of organism, effects of past experience, etc.)
PS: Perceptual Structuring

There are stimulus situations, however, which lack objective structure in various degrees. The contours, beginning and end points in space or time, the sequence of characteristics or the objects or events are not sharply defined. As such they are subject to various alternatives in the structuring on the part of the perceiving individual. The simplest illustrations of such a stimulus object are the reversible pictures which are constructed so that two or more different objects can be perceived in them. The

Rubin reversible picture, which can be seen either as a goblet or as two profiles facing one another, is an example. If the individual is instructed to expect two profiles, he will be likely to see two profiles first. If set to expect the goblet through instructions or some other influence, he will see the picture first as a goblet. The objective properties of this picture allow only two perceptual alternatives. As the objective structure, the pattern of the stimulus situation, decreases, as it becomes more ambiguous, more complicated, as the demarcation lines of the situation or event become more uncertain, the *alternatives* for its perceptual structuring increase. Such stimulus situations are referred to as *unstructured* stimulus situations.

The more unstructured the stimulus situation is, the greater the contribution of internal factors (motives, emotions, attitudes, identifications of the person, etc.) to the ensuing perceptual structure. Accumulating laboratory evidence substantiates this fact. To the frightened person in the dark there are many hostile moving things in the shrubbery.

The more unstructured, the more uncertain the stimulus situation, the greater are the effects of social influences (personal suggestion, information, group demands, etc.) in perceptual structuring. In studying the effect of social factors, the motives, the attitude of the individual in relation to the stimulus situation, which includes the social influences at hand, have to be brought into the picture. Otherwise, some important internal factors operative as parts of the frame of reference at the time will be neglected.

If our aim is not simply to give a general picture of the psychological tendency revealed in perception and behavior, the mere citation of the external and internal factors operative within the frame of reference at the given time to give rise to particular perceptual structuring is not sufficient. If our aim is the prediction and eventual control of events, then we have to go further and discover the *relative weights* of various external and internal factors in a given framework by systematically varying this factor now, that factor then.

Even though all of the various factors that constitute parts within a frame of reference influence other parts, certain factors, or a certain factor, are operative as limiting influences in the determination of the main character of the structure. If the limiting factor or factors are changed or eliminated, the whole character of the structure and of other parts will change or be transformed. These limiting, these weighty factors will be referred to as the main *anchorages* in the frame of reference. Recent work in judgment dealing with the effects of experimentally introduced anchoring stimuli demonstrates the importance of such weighty factors in determining the character of the structure and of other parts. The implications of these features of main anchorages for attitude formation and resistance to change will be examined in Chapters 7 and 8.

The concept of main anchorages will be crucial in the discussion of reference groups in Chapter 7. Change in the major group identification, or even intense aspiration for such a change, brings about alteration in many other attitudes which were not specifically challenged by the individual himself or by appropriate communication.

In laboratory situations, the individual's stimulus field is circumscribed to the specified items meticulously prepared and delimited by the experimenter. The more exclusively delimited the external field to the experimental variable—the more others are excluded—the more successful the experiment. Consequently, the subject is forced to attend only to the stimuli intended for him by the experimenter. The structured or unstructured nature of the stimuli determines the organization of judgment or perception along the lines outlined above.

However, in actual life situations, on a street, in a department store, on a college campus, in a concert hall, there are, in addition to the most compelling features which are likely to be noticed by most people, literally hundreds of objects which are well structured and which, if noticed, would arouse perceptions that would correspond, on the whole, to the objective structure of those objects. Only a small proportion of these structured objects are perceived during the period in question. Those objects or persons which are perceived are likely to be the ones related to our motives, attitudes, preoccupations at the time, in addition to the ones whose objective characteristics are sufficiently compelling that they "hit" most of us in the eye.

Take a young man whose flow of energy is flooding the banks of his existence, take a social climber restless in his upward moves, a pretender to the title of best-dressed lady in town, a person deeply concerned with human affairs. As they come from the lecture hall, from the address of an invited celebrity, ask them to jot down all the items they perceived in the hall. Classify the items in terms of the frequency of relevance to major personal goals. There will be significant differences in the frequency of items under each classification for these persons, in line with their major goals. This rather trite example shows a psychological tendency well known for decades. It embodies the major principle of *perceptual selectivity,* brought to the foreground by almost dramatic demonstrations that "we do not see with our eyes alone," "hear with our ears alone," but see and hear as well with all the person we are at the time, with our desires, attitudes, and ambitions.

In short, of all the potentially "perceivable" objects, those are likely to stand out as *figures* with distinct contours which have relevance to our preoccupations, desires, attitudes, or ambitions operative at the time. Other objects or persons, which are potentially just as "perceivable" as structured objects but which have little relevance to interests or motives at the time, are likely to stay in the perceptually rather indistinct *background.*

The above facts point to certain limitations in the work practice of psychologists who deliberately reduce the stimulus world of the subject to experimentally introduced items. This is the only feasible way to study "cognitive" processes and their physical correlates. But the natural psychological tendency is to perceive *selectively* not so much as determined by the restricted nature of the stimulus field but as determined by internal factors. The starry sky above with its constellations of rather definite grouping was always there, but man did not always attend to its distinctive features. Man's vision was not any different then, but he attended rather to the distinctiveness of other structures. Certain structures had little or no relevance in terms of the preoccupation of the human groups living at a given place at a given time. But with the change of preoccupation of the group, at times some generations later, these stimulus structures figured in the foreground with all parts keenly perceived, sharply differentiated.

Perception, being jointly determined by external and internal factors operative at a given time, is not only a cognitive affair. Ordinarily both cognitive and motivational factors contribute to its organization. In actual life conditions the motivational factor is *implicitly* there even in cases of perceptions whose structures correspond closely to the structure of stimulus objects. This implicit participation of motivational factors becomes clear, as we have noted, when we ask: Why the perception of this object at this time rather than the perception of other possible objects in the situation which are equally well structured? The answer lies in the perceptual selectivity determined by desire, attitude, passion, and the like, operative at the time.

One of the remarkable developments in psychology in recent times has been the study of human motives and attitudes through perceptual variations, the underlying assumption being the joint determination of perception by external and internal (motivational) factors. In the study of motives or attitudes through perceptual reactions, the usual device has been the use of various sorts of unstructured stimulus situations, which are conducive to the greater contribution of internal factors in the structuring of perception. Because of the facts of perceptual selectivity, it is feasible to study motivation through the perception of structured stimulus objects as well. Of course, in this case it will be necessary to present a larger, but specified, number of structured stimulus objects, preferably presented over an appropriate time span or with too many objects presented to be all perceived in the short time available.

When perception, taken as a prototype of experience, is conceived as jointly determined by external and internal factors and the implications of perceptual selectivity are realized, the use of special "defense mechanisms" (projection, introjection, and the like) becomes unnecessary. The conception outlined above gives us a dynamic approach to the study of motives, attitudes, etc., through perceptual variations and the ups and downs of these variations in time. In handling the demonstrated facts of perceptual variations, perceptual distortions, judgmental deflections, the approach outlined briefly above corresponds to the interdependent nature of psychological functioning more closely than to the use of separate "mechanisms." The abstraction of different mechanisms, even though they are recognized as mere labels, tends *to freeze* psychological processes into more or less separate compartments. The end result is likely to be eventually discrete classification of hundreds of items as mechanisms which might include *"perceptual offense,"* as well as "perceptual defense" and many others. The rather negative labeling of consequential psychological processes as "defense mechanisms" reflects the gloomy conception of human nature built up chiefly on the basis of a selected sample of pathological cases. Recently Eysenck, a psychologist who has close access to pathological cases, called our attention to the fact that this pessimistic edifice of psychology built upon the study of pathological cases can scarcely be adequate for people on the whole. In actual practice there are quite a few individuals who do not just stay put and use their defenses in perceiving and acting as situations arise, but actively move out in their striving to single out certain objects, certain persons to make focal in their experience and strivings. It would not be any more fantastic to work on a psychology of *perceptual offense* than on the established groove of perceptual defense.

It does not seem necessary or parsimonious to use terms such as "projection," which crop up frequently in the discussion of intergroup relations, and more specifically in the explanation of the institution of prejudice. To be sure, perceptual variations, perceptual distortions under given conditions are facts too well established to be denied. Perceiving is not a cut-and-dried cognitive affair; its organization and the sequence of organization in time is, on occasion, determined largely by the preoccupations, fixations, attitudes of the individual. In some instances, in the face of harsh reality around him, the individual may shut himself in to build castles in his own confined psychological horizon. In this case, his motives, his passions reign supreme. That is why remembering, which in this case becomes imagining, as experiments have shown, is satisfying, frequently engaged in. The checks of reality are reduced to a minimum. It is even true that as a consequence of frustrations experienced in the face of unjust treatment, of discriminations suffered, the whole world may be constricted to only two narrow categories. The whole world may be experienced as consisting of just a few friends and a great mass of all the rest, lumped together as unfriendly, as hostile.

We cannot compile here the whole gamut of perceptual distortions with their direct implications for action. But there is no need for a clutter of separate mechanisms to handle the perceptual variations. They can be adequately handled in terms of the conception of perception and experience as jointly determined by external and internal (motivational) factors, and in terms of recurrences of particular events. As such, perceptual structuring is both motivational and cognitive in its determination. In short, the psychology of motives and attitudes is included in this conceptual approach to perception.

Perhaps these points can be illustrated by the cases of misinterpretations in intergroup relations so prevalent today. When one reads the accounts of various newspaper correspondents or diaries of "first-hand" observers representing different points of view or ideologies dealing with the same critical spots of the world today, one sometimes wonders if they are writing from the same place at all. The accounts differ radically not only as to their explicit evaluations but in the "facts" reported. This selectivity of items reported and the stress that different items receive are not entirely due to editorial policies laid down by home papers or the directives of sponsors who send observers to get on-the-spot reports, although these social influences are not infrequently operating. If on-the-spot observers were categorically instructed to report in a strictly objective way, if the observers themselves had the good will honestly to report only what they actually observed, their reports would still not be free of the selectivity determined by their own points of view, their ideologies on the issues.

Scientists are not immune to such influence, as the findings on the "psychology of testimony" and the more recent experiments on perceptual selectivity demonstrate. But this fact does not mean that the prospect of validity in the study of controversial human issues is a hopeless one. A vantage point can be achieved which provides a comprehensive view over and above restricting entanglements. Such a vantage point is not gained overnight or by good will alone, although good will is essential. It requires disciplined training in social science with special emphasis on cross-cultural and historical studies carried out with deliberate recognition of one's own ethnocentrism and its deflecting influence.

IMPLICATIONS FOR GROUP RELATIONS

The principles presented have direct implications for the study of group relations. They impose on us the necessity of studying reactions against the whole background of factors coming from within the individual himself and influences from his surroundings. The internal and external factors are parts of a functional system and are not discrete influences in isolation, each giving rise to its particular reaction. An approach which recognizes various influences and even works out a careful syllabus of each in an unrelated way will give us only discrete, out-of-context snapshots.

The functional interrelatedness of factors determining behavior means that we cannot take a single factor and make it supreme and sovereign as though that particular influence were holding the individual by the hand and directing him here and there. No matter how potent a single factor is, it too is an interdependent part of a functional system. Its influence has to be studied by its relation to other parts.

On the other hand, factors coming from the individual and from his socioeconomic and physical surroundings which form a functioning system have relative *weights* in determining the character of experience and behavior. The more potent or weighty factors may effectively transform the character of the whole structure and other parts.

In the next chapter an aspect of this point is elaborated in our discussion of the *reference group* concept and its application to the area of prejudice. The concept of reference group is derived from the more general frame of reference conceptualization as an application to social psychology. It is particularly useful in showing the effects of a main anchorage in the regulation of man's experience and behavior in his social relations. In Chapter 8 we shall see some of the effects of shifting a main anchorage on changes of related attitudes.

A word of caution seems in order concerning this useful concept of reference groups. It happens too frequently that potentially valuable concepts are detached from the general framework in which they stand. Then they become further instances of those magic terms used to explain everything. If the concept of reference groups is used in this detached way, it very quickly loses its relational character, which is its main characteristic and the principal justification of its usefulness as a concept. We shall have more to say on this point in the next chapter.

Reference groups signify the main relatedness of the individual to the social world around him. This concept helps us to understand the regulation of his reactions to various stimulus conditions in terms of his main relatedness. Reference group relatedness usually develops through actual participations in the group in question. Once this relatedness is established by the individual, it serves as the main regulating agent in relation to a host of situations and circumstances he faces subsequently.

These considerations force us to bring into our work and keep in our work at every step the *structural properties* of group situations which produce differential effects on the experience and behavior of individual members. An effective way of demonstrating the structural properties of group situations is through the *state of reciprocity* that arises in the course of the interaction process. Reciprocity renders the experience and reactions of members in a group situation interdependent on one another. It may conveniently be described as a structure with qualities of its own which cannot be explained directly in terms of personal qualities of this or that member in isolation, but which are the product of the *interaction process*. If the interaction process continues, the tendency is crystallization of a more stable state of reciprocity which defines the lasting *statuses* and *roles* of the individual members with all the *reciprocal expectations* they imply in the way of loyalty, coöperation, responsibility, and duty. These are polarized in relation to the status and role of the leaders. To be sure, the unique personality characteristics and special talents of the individual members are among the important determinants of the emerging reciprocity and its stabilization into a definite organization with a peculiar hierarchy. But these personal characteristics are effective in terms of the framework of the special demands, special properties of the situation and interaction process at hand. In Chapter 8 these points will be made more concrete by illustrations of properties and organization of small groups.

If simple discrete weights, presented to the individual in close temporal sequence, or simple forms are judged or perceived in a relational way, it is reasonable to raise the question of how much more crucial it becomes to study the individual in the framework of interaction in group settings. We know that addition of a heavier or lighter weight to a series or addition of a few lines to a form may produce reversal of the judgmental trend or transformations in the structure of perception.

We cannot legitimately extrapolate the effects of motivational urges of the individual (his hunger, his sex, his desire for recognition and prestige) to group situations as if the group situation were a void, as if the interaction process and the reciprocities that arise in it were but a play of shadows. *Likewise the compelling material conditions (technology, socioeconomic forces) influence human relations as affected by the existing organizational structure and by the system of beliefs or norms.*

We cannot extrapolate from the properties of individuals to the characteristics of group situations. Similarly, the extrapolation of the properties of in-group relations to the explanation of relations between groups, as though the *area of interaction* between these groups consisted of a vacuum or even the cozy atmosphere of a conference room, is equally erroneous. The character of intergroup relations is determined not only by the character of relations and norms that prevail within the in-groups but also by the process of interaction between groups—exemplified by the give-and-take process which may be full of tension or which may be in a state of flow. This area of tension, in cases of negative relations, or of flow, in cases of coöperation or alliance, may produce consequential reverberations within the in-group itself.

The nature of interaction between groups is determined in large part by the reciprocal interests involved and the degree of their significance to the groups in question. The interests at issue in intergroup relations must be interests of common concern to a group. A matter of common concern may relate to various values or goals shared by group members. It may be a real or imagined threat to the safety of the group as a whole, an economic interest, a political advantage, a military consideration, prestige, or a number of others. Unless it relates directly to issues of common concern for the in-group in question and is recognized by the group as being related, personal frustrations in the life history of the individuals or other personal motives of individual members will have relatively little effect in determining the nature and direction of intergroup relations. Once a particular issue comes to the foreground as the dominant influence in intergroup relations, it may become the limiting factor or the main anchorage in the frame of reference at the time. The main anchorage may relegate to the background other factors which served as main anchorages in more usual times. The influence of the main anchorage may be so potent that under these new conditions out-groups usually kept at a distance are sought after as allies, thus making for strange bedfellows.

Technological developments, the means of transportation and communication have brought groups within countries and nations of the world into such close contact with one another, created such a state of interdependence among them that the interaction areas have acquired crucial importance in their own right. The reality of intergroup influences has acquired such proportions that the properties of in-groups themselves are being seriously affected by them. The extrapolation from properties of in-groups in the explanation of intergroup relations in the form of outworn clichés of national character, or stereotypes, or formal social systems is becoming a serious obstacle in the way of understanding the interaction process in intergroup relations. The processes of intergroup relations have become so consequential today that certain practices within the in-groups become incomprehensible if not related to the area of interaction with other groups. These influences are so pervasive that even personal matters, such as one's budget, life plans, mode of life maintained, are vitally affected.

In short, attempts to predict the nature of intergroup relations from the properties of in-group relations alone give us a distorted picture of the reality of intergroup relations. Probably this is the reason why practical attempts to base the solution of intergroup relations on such methods as improving coöperative habits within in-groups have been so singularly fruitless. In-group democracy does not necessarily imply democracy toward out-groups and their members. Unless this point is fully realized, research and practical attempts in the way of resolution of intergroup problems will not take a realistic trend. In Chapters 9 and 10 some striking discrepancies between in-group properties and intergroup relations are reported in experiments dealing with the formation of in-groups, the interaction process between in-groups, the intergroup relations produced, and their effects on the in-groups.

A SUMMARY STATEMENT OF INTERGROUP RELATIONS

Let us start again with the main terms of our problem. A group is characterized as a social unit (1) which consists of a number of individuals who, at a given time, stand in more or less definite interdependent status and role relations toward one another and (2) which explicitly and implicitly possesses a set of values or norms of its own regulating the behavior of individual members, at least in matters of consequence to the group. From the point of view of the members, the social units thus characterized may be referred to as *in-groups*. Again from the point of view of the individual member, those social units of which he is not psychologically a part are *out-groups*. The term "intergroup relations" is used to refer to relations between two or more in-groups and their respective members.

Intergroup relations manifest themselves both in relations between two or more in-groups as social units and in the interpersonal relations between members of the in-groups in the course of daily living. There are no mutually exclusive sharp lines of demarcation between the two. For example, a personal friction may develop in the course of the personal dealings of two members of different groups. Because of low thresholds, it may degenerate into a starting point around which the partisans of the two groups rally and take opposing stands. On the other hand, even in individual relations between two members of different in-groups, the individuals usually act as representatives of their own groups, each maintaining the *viewpoint* of his group, upholding its norms, interests, etc.

One overall implication for the social psychological study of intergroup relations that emerges from the principles which have proved their validity is that intergroup relations can be handled adequately only by placing individuals in their appropriate group settings first. Direct extrapolations of ideas of frustration, aggression, dominance, coöperation, help, sympathy, and the like, obtained under unique personal conditions or in isolation to the level of intergroup relations have brought us pitifully short of our aim. To be sure, motives of men are basic in understanding why groups are friendly or hostile, why groups are at peace or at war with one another. To be sure, these positive or negative states of intergroup relations will be incomprehensible if the goals toward which they are striving are not brought into the picture. But the motives and goals in question in intergroup relations are not the motives and goals of individuals in an isolated state. They are motives and goals of men as deflected, organized, and transformed in group settings. And if the motives or goals of individual members are perceived by the membership as out of step with or contrary to the shared and sanctioned direction and goals of the group, such individuals are either brought in line or discarded as undesirables. Some of the directive ego-concerns of individuals related to such matters as being securely accepted, improving status and prestige stem directly from the particular nature of hierarchical organization and status norms of the particular groups of which they are members.

It is well-nigh impossible to trace in an exact way the genesis of the structural organization of large social units such as modern nations and the genesis of the prevailing norms in them that regulate the status, prestige, and intergroup attitudes of individual members. The studies dealing with the genesis of formation and functioning of small groups give us unmistakable leads which are verified in various geographic areas and at various times.

Individuals under the stress of common deprivation of their biological needs, individuals confronting an uncertain or insecure situation, individuals in the throes of climbing up the prestige and power ladder, individuals facing a common fate do gravitate toward one another and interact as prompted by their common strivings. In the process of interaction they say things, they do things they would not have said or done in isolation. In short, they act in a differential way in the process of group interaction.

As the process of common activities toward common goals continues, the hit-and-miss moves of the early stage give way to lines of action in more established grooves. Concurrently, the matters of taking *initiative*, taking *responsibility* for regulating the interaction process itself and for making further moves toward goals which also are redefined and crystallized in time, tend to become polarized around certain individuals who are perceived to have contributed more successfully than others under the particular circumstances in question. The polarization of activities around a certain member (leader) and his lieutenants signifies emergence of definite group organization with hierarchical positions in it. This brings about a corresponding hierarchy of *power relations*.

The power invested in the leader is not arbitrary; it has to be used within certain bounds. If these bounds are violated the leadership position is subject to various kinds of reactions from the rest of the organization. The leadership position itself is a position within the organization and not outside of it with complete freedom of direction.

The reciprocities thus established among the members of the group are regulated by a *set of norms* which is the inevitable product of the interaction process. This set of norms regulates the reciprocal obligations, loyalties, and duties as well as other matters of consequence in the group's scheme of things. The demands and pressures of the group for *conformity* will be directly proportional to the degree of importance attached to the norms in question by the group. Especially in the matter of a norm related to the identity of the group itself, the latitude of tolerance will be narrow and strict in cases of deviation. And the leader himself, in spite of his vastly superior power, is no exception to this rule.

In periods of stability and proportional to the compactness and solidarity of the group, conformity to the norms of the group is not experienced by the individual member as an external coercive force, for the very stuff of his personal identity is in large part derived from the values or norms of his groups, which, in the course of his development, have become his own very personal values or norms. Take away the social values or norms internalized by the individual in his development and see how much content and form are left to his unique self and his unique conscience.

Once a line of action, a policy of consequence starts rolling in the group, it compellingly becomes the personal line of action, the personal policy of individual members. There may be some nonconformists, some dissenters within the group. The terms "nonconformist" and "dissenter" are relative terms which have meaning only in relation to a group in which the majority upholds group norms. Sometimes nonconformists leave the group and become conformists in a new group setting.

The shaping of an in-group organization delimits the "in's," the members, with unmistakable demarcation lines. The members regulate their roles, their expectations toward one another in terms of the established practices, established norms within the in-group. But evidence cautions us not to explain the nature of intergroup relations from the practices and norms prevalent within the in-group (Chapter 8).

It does not follow necessarily that the general pattern of in-group relations (e.g., coöperative, sympathetic, or the reverse) and norms regulating in-group practices will be the same as the pattern and norms regulating relations with the out-groups and their members. The pattern of relations and norms in regard to out-groups is shaped primarily by the nature of functional relations between the in-groups in question. In some cases, the greater the degree of coöperative, active, and free participation within the in-group, the greater the harmony within the in-group, the greater and more effectively may prejudice and hostility be directed against the out-groups, if relations with the out-group in question are conflicting.

Thus, every in-group develops and standardizes in time a *point of view* in relation to out-groups in the course of functional contacts. These standardized points of view become part and parcel of its social-distance scale and, through the vehicle of language and tradition, even outlast the particular circumstances which gave rise to them. They make the in-groups the center of the universe in terms of which intergroup relations are judged, evaluated, and acted upon. As pointed out by Emery Reeves and as emphasized by T. H. Pear in *Psychological Factors of Peace and War*, even educated people, though they have "abandoned the idea that their planet is the center and the most important part of the universe" and have embraced the Copernican perspective in regard to the physical world, still cling to their self-centered "fixed points" in considering intergroup relations. The resolution of conflicts and achievement of understanding in intergroup relations is well-nigh impossible on the basis of "such a primitive method of judgment."

Psychological experiments have shown time and again that judgments and evaluations are made in terms of our own well-ingrained reference scales. As long as the groups in question cannot go beyond judgments based on their particular scales, no agreement is possible in their evaluations. Even what might be considered simple and objective events are seen and interpreted in egocentric frameworks. The consequence is a distorted picture of reality. One of the first tasks is to achieve a perspective in viewing things so that the student of intergroup relations can give a picture which comes closer to reality. In the words of Pear: *"The world and history cannot be as they appear to the different nations, unless we disavow objectivity, reason and scientific methods of research."* (Italics in original.)

It becomes clear then that intergroup behavior of individuals is intelligible only when it is considered in terms of appropriate group settings. The group setting is not just the setting of ingroups in question independent of their relation to other groups. This picture of intergroup relations is further complicated by the circumstances brought about by modern technology and upheavals of recent wars. No group is a closed system any more. The political and economic lines drawn in recent times have created new situations of flux and tension among in-groups—so much so that an individual living within the physical membership of a given group may be still regulating his intergroup behavior in terms of in-group demarcations which are no longer objectively there. The implications of this fact will be systematically developed in the next chapter, and further extended in Chapter 8.

In our opinion, one of the first advances in the study of intergroup relations will come from a full recognition of the historically irreversible fact of the state of interdependence and flux among groups in the present-day world. This state of interdependence and flux has made obsolete the conception of intergroup relations in terms of scales and values of this or that constituent group or combination of groups. It is forcing upon us a scale of values which transcends the traditional bounds of identification in a more comprehensive and integrated reality of "we-ness" that is real, that is not contradicted by the demands and values of the more circumscribed "we-ness" of the constituent parts. The resolution of tension between groups which are in a state of interdependence can be a reality and not a constantly frustrated hope if factors from the constituent in-groups will cease to contribute their pull in conflicting directions. And this requires tuning in those aspects of in-group goals and activities which have a bearing on intergroup relations in such a way that they will not be crassly insensitive to the positive moves of intergroup relations. As long as the in-group values and goals which have a bearing on intergroup relations are egocentric in nature, they cannot help contributing their bit to the heritage of confusion and tension that prevails today.

As stated in the first chapter, the psychologist is not in a position to solve the staggering problems of intergroup relations independently of men in social sciences and in practical affairs. However, he can contribute his bit by honestly pointing to the tragic consequences of existing social-distance scales as long as the identification and action of individuals are regulated accordingly. He can show that the group goals inimical to harmony among groups, the individual's participation in sadistic, grim happenings that follow do not stem from an inherent impulse of human nature. Going a step farther, he can set up group experiments which will show convincingly that a state of tension between groups can be effectively reduced and, in fact, turned to harmony by eliminating functional relations which are conducive to friction, by introducing constructive, creative group goals which require for attainment pulling together of the groups involved with their utmost energy.

C H A P T E R 7

лплплплплплплплплплплплплплплплплплплпл

Reference Groups in
Human Relations

In Chapter 1, the point was made that whenever the members of
an in-group, collectively or individually, react in relation to an
out-group or its members, we have an instance of intergroup
relations. This may be an instance of relations between gangs,
between clubs, between labor and employer groups, or between
nations. No matter in what special area of human relations they
take place (ethnic, industrial, political, and so forth) they are all
special instances of intergroup relations. As such they should
have some common features as well as unique properties peculiar
to each instance.

If our aim is a comprehensive approach, we have to attain
concepts which will enable us to deal with any instance of intergroup behavior in whatever area it may occur. Historically, authors working in special areas of intergroup relations (ethnic,
industrial, political, and so forth), on the whole, used concepts
which carried the special flavor of their areas. It seems to us that
the concept of *reference groups* is a generic one which can be
used in dealing with any kind of group and its relation with any
other group.

The concept of reference groups has begun to be used in recent
years in dealing with the behavior of man in various cases of intra-
and intergroup relations. It seems to us that we can conveniently
use this concept in dealing with the problems of social distance,
marginality, inconsistency of behavior in intergroup relations,

status equilibration, formation and change of intergroup attitudes. This is the task of the present and next chapters.

As the concept of reference group is a new and a broad one, it is necessary to clarify first the exact sense in which it is used and also state in some detail the psychological facts on which it is based. In doing this, it will be necessary to bring into the picture the high points of the psychological principles stated in the last chapter.

Social psychology, on the whole, has been approached historically in contrasting ways. One approach starts with one or a few sovereign principles, such as imitation, suggestion, instinct, libido, etc. On the other hand, there have been attempts to study empirically every social psychological topic, every specific case of attitude in its own right, as though the results concerning the topic at hand are insulated from other facts in that general area.

The approaches which utilize one or a few sovereign concepts tended to start and end with premature formalizations, resulting in rather "closed-system" schools of social psychology, in spite of claims of being systematic and comprehensive. In view of the diverse problems that have to be considered, it has become evident that, especially in social psychology, we cannot just sit down and write off all the major principles and concepts in one or a few stretches.

On the other hand, approaches which claim to have facts speak for themselves uncontaminated with theorizing end up, or rather scatter around, in almost endless discrete results, in lists, inventories, or unrelated social psychological syllabuses. The main trend of "public opinion" polling and attitude studies of diverse kinds has, on the whole, been of the latter sort until very recently.

Fortunately, we do not have to be bound by either of these alternatives. There has been growing concern with attaining concepts which stem from serious preoccupation with persistent problems in social psychology, which are organically related to actual research (experimental and otherwise), and which can be utilized for pulling together in a comprehensive way seemingly unrelated facts in a major problem area. The *concept of reference groups* seems to be such a concept.

Even though this concept has started to spread only during the last four or five years, it has already received somewhat varied interpretations and usages. There are incipient signs of its becoming a magic term to explain anything and everything concerning group relations. It may more than pay if we spend some time at this early stage to clarify our understanding of the concept in terms of the experimental work of which it is an extension, and in terms of its application to problems in group relations.

The general problem is obviously that of individual-group relationship. During the past decades the impact of vital events brought the problem of individual-group relationships into sharp focus and this trend continues to gain momentum. The major character of this trend, as contrasted with the individualistic emphasis, is the realization that group situations generate differential effects of significant consequence. Group interaction is seen as the major determinant in attitude formation and attitude change, and in other phenomena of vital consequence to the individual. During the last decades both sociologists and psychologists, with various approaches, contributed to a fuller realization of this trend. In several chapters of this book we have presented brief surveys of this general trend at relevant points.

Then what is the use of cluttering the already confusing inventory of concepts relative to the individual-group relation with another? The use of the concept of reference group as differentiated from the more general term, "group," needs justification. For concepts are not mere constructs which people, even scientists, can posit at will. Nor does consensus of opinion among professionals in an area make the use of a concept valid. As we look historically, consensus of opinion has been abandoned a good many times because, we suspect, it did not do justice to the understanding of events dealt with.

Two sets of considerations in particular have forced some such specified group concept as reference group to the foreground.

One is related to socioeconomic conditions; the other is on the psychological side.

In a stable, integrated, and relatively less differentiated society, there would probably be little necessity for the use of reference group as a separate concept. Modern man, especially in Western societies, is caught in the throes of vertical mobility, in the "dilemmas and contradictions of statuses" and the painful predicament of marginality created by the demands and goals originating in diverse groups. He finds himself betwixt and between situations as he carries on the business of living in different roles in relation to diverse groups which not infrequently demand contradictory adjustment of his experience and behavior. He is exposed through actual face-to-face contacts, through the mass mediums of communication, to pressures, demands, goals of diverse trends and ideologies. These are some of the many aspects of the setting in which he operates, through which he becomes indoctrinated, forms his identifications, faces a great variety of alternatives to choose from in line with his special needs. If his psychological level of functioning were restricted largely to the impact of immediate ups and downs of his biogenic motives and conditionings on that basis, he would probably not be troubled so much by the demands of overlapping and contradictory groups.

Thus we are led to the second consideration, which relates to man's conceptual level of functioning. As he passes from one group situation to another from time to time, he reacts to the demands, pressures, and appeals of new group situations in terms of the person he has come to consider himself to be and aspires to be. In other words, he reacts in terms of more or less consistent ties of belongingness in relation to his past and present identifications and his future goals for security of his identity, and also status and prestige concerns. In short, this conceptual level of functioning makes possible regulation of experience and behavior in relation to values and norms that lie at times far beyond immediate group situations.

The conceptual level of functioning is, on the whole, taken too much for granted. We may be gaining a great deal if this conceptual level of functioning is deliberately brought into the discussion of motives and goals in relation to group situations. Of course, this idea is tied up with the notion of *levels* so cogently stressed by Schneirla, Lindesmith and Strauss, and others (17, 21, 22).

It is apparent, then, that the groups to which the individual relates himself need not always be the groups in which he is actually moving. His identifications need not always be with groups in which he is registered, is seen to be or announced to be a member. The concept of reference groups forces itself through such facts. It becomes almost indispensable in dealing with the relation of individuals to groups in highly differentiated and poorly integrated societies, in societies in the process of acculturation and experiencing the high tempo of transition.

With the above considerations in mind, reference groups can be characterized simply as *those groups to which the individual relates himself as a part or to which he aspires to relate himself psychologically.* It is apparent that the characterization of reference groups just presented is a psychological one; that is, it is made from the standpoint of the individual in the individual-group relationship.

In many cases, of course, the individual's reference groups are at the same time his membership groups.[1] However, in cases where the individual's membership groups are not his reference groups, it does not follow that the groups in which he actually interacts will not have an effect on him. On the contrary, this circumstance creates important psychological problems for him to which we shall have occasion to refer later in this chapter when we deal with marginality as one instance of being caught between the positive attractions of one's reference group which is not one's membership group at the time, and demands and pressures of the membership group which is not his reference group.

---

[1] To make this point clear, we introduced our previous treatment of membership and reference groups under the title "Effects of Membership and Other Reference Groups." (M. Sherif, *An Outline of Social Psychology*, Harper, 1948, chap. 6.)

Numerous studies coming from both psychologists and sociologists have shown that the major source of the individual's weighty attitudes are the values or norms of the groups to which he relates himself, that is, of his reference groups. In fact, the values or norms of his reference groups constitute the major anchorages in relation to which his experience of self-identity is organized. This conception enables us to pull together a host of discrete data in various areas. The topics of social distances at which various out-groups are put by members of a given in-group, of marginality, of status regulation, and of inconsistencies in behavior revealed by individuals in intergroup relations acquire conceptual coherence when the implications of the reference group concept are applied to these topics.

Of course, the various facts and problems which are brought to focus through the reference group concept pressed for consideration whether or not the term "reference group" was explicitly used. A number of investigators, especially sociologists, as we shall see, provided interesting and valuable analyses of these specific problems.

Among psychological studies, Chapman and Volkmann's 1939 experiment merits attention (3). The conception of this experiment, which served as a model for numerous others, derived explicitly from the general fact that judgments, perceptions, etc., take place within referential frameworks. Specifically, level of aspiration was conceived as an instance of "the effect upon a judgment of the frame of reference within which it is executed." Goals set in relation to the task in question were lowered or raised as the case might be, as determined by the position of experimentally introduced groups with respect to the subject's own reference group. In short, the position of other groups relative to one's own reference group, which served as the major anchorage, determined the regulation of goals. The theoretical implications of this and related studies, especially Hyman's 1942 study on judgments of status, will be considered shortly.

More recently, the concept of reference groups has come to the foreground with varying emphasis in the works of Hyman (11),

Sherif and Cantril (24), Sherif (23), Newcomb (19), Lindesmith and Strauss (17), Merton and Kitt (18), Hartley (8), and Jahoda, Deutsch, and Cook (12), among others. In spite of the short history of its use, the concept is already being utilized in somewhat differing senses. Therefore, it is necessary to clarify its implications.

In studying the psychology of status, Hyman, who first used the concept of reference group, found shifts in judgments of status with changes of the group or individual in terms of which judgment was made. This was seen as a specific case of an anchoring point in the frame of reference determining judgment and was called "reference group" or "reference individual." Unfortunately, since the appearance of this important study in 1942, Hyman's contributions have not to date utilized the reference group concept.

In dealing with changing attitudes during adolescence, Sherif and Cantril (24) found the term most valuable. However, the characterization of the concept used in this book was presented first in 1948 (23).

Newcomb demonstrated the usefulness of the reference group concept by recasting the previously reported results of his important Bennington Study on attitude change in terms of the shifts or resistance to shifts in reference groups (in 23). Newcomb in his *Social Psychology* (1950) characterized membership and reference groups as they are characterized in this book. However, he introduces the notions of positive and negative reference groups. A positive reference group, in his terminology, "is one in which a person is motivated to be accepted and treated as a member (overtly or symbolically) whereas a negative reference group is one which the person is motivated to oppose or in which he does not want to be treated as a member" (p. 226).

In addition, Newcomb speaks of one group's being both a positive and a negative reference group for the same person, in the sense that he may willingly conform to some of its norms and not to others.

In line with their stress on conceptual factors in human social behavior, so well expressed especially in their chapter "Men Without Symbols," Lindesmith and Strauss (17) emphasize that the individual's relatedness and identifications with groups need not be in terms of actual face-to-face relations. They found the concept of reference groups useful in dealing with such relatedness in particular. It seems, however, that reference group refers specifically in their discussion to groups with which the individual identifies himself but of which he is not actually a member.

Merton and Kitt (18) gave numerous illustrations of how many of the attitude studies in the American Soldier Series can be conceptualized more parsimoniously in terms of reference groups. In this way, scattered data are pulled together in coherent fashion. Beyond the rich concrete illustrations, this account is somewhat confusing because, in extending the applicability of the concept, an attempt is made to establish a general reference group theory with rather intricate terminology. For example, the attitudes of enlisted men who conform to official army norms are spoken of "in the language of reference group theory" as "positive orientation to the norms of a non-membership group that is taken as a frame of reference" (p. 86). In terms of the concept of reference groups, one might say more simply that the army organization and its officers serve as a reference group for such enlisted men and not the informal groups that emerged among their fellow enlisted men.

We can proceed in the task of clarifying the concept, reference groups, by looking at indications of relevant facts in the psychological trend from which it stems. But this is not sufficient.

Psychological studies which demonstrated the effect of reference groups, whether or not the term was used, have stemmed from the more general concept of frame of reference. The theoretical approaches of the Chapman and Volkmann experiment and the Hyman study briefly summarized before are explicitly stated by these authors in terms of the frame of reference concept. In both of these studies, variations in judgment are shown to be determined by anchorages in the reference scales in question.

As can be seen in these examples, the concept, frame of reference, is a relational term. It does not in itself refer to any specific psychological item or function, such as judging, perceiving, remembering, etc. But perceiving, judging, remembering, etc., take place within a system of relationships, i.e., within their appropriate frame of reference. During the last decades it has become increasingly clear that a reaction can be adequately understood only in terms of the frame of reference within which it takes place.

Likewise, frame of reference is not equivalent or interchangeable with attitude, social norm, or reference group. But a social norm, an attitude, a reference group *may be* factors within a frame of reference at a given time.

It is necessary to make these distinctions because such terms have been used interchangeably at various times by different writers.

Briefly stated, the term "frame of reference" is used to denote the functional relatedness of all factors, external and internal, that are operative at a given time. All these external and internal factors enter jointly in determining psychological organization, perceptual or otherwise. Observed behavior is a consequence of organization thus produced. The *external factors* are the stimulus factors, some properties of which have been studied by Wertheimer and others. The fascinating problems of figure-ground relationship, properties of membership character of different parts, which come to the foreground in this connection, have their counterparts in social stimulus situations.

Internal factors include motives, both biogenic and sociogenic, attitudes, ego-attitudes, concepts, and other products of past experience acquired through learning. Internal factors are inferred from observed behavior.

Now, we can take up the point which links all this discussion with our problem. This point, which will now occupy the central position, is the consideration of *relative weights*, that is, the weights of external factors and internal factors in the joint determination of psychological organization and hence behavior. In more specific terms, this is the problem of relative weights, relative salience, relative importance (as you will) of external and internal anchorings.

Historically, the early studies of Gestalt psychologists and in more recent times the studies carried out by psychologists in the area of judgment have tended on the whole to show greater preoccupation with the unmistakably weighty effects of external anchorings in the determination of perceptual organization, or (in the case of judgment studies) the demonstrable effects of experimentally introduced anchoring stimuli. The main fact that emerges from such studies is that not all stimuli contribute equally to the determination of patterning. To illustrate the point with a recent study which has social implications: various adjectives used to form an impression of an individual contribute differentially to a total impression of the person (1). Change of certain adjectives will not change the general impression. But when certain others are changed, the character of the whole impression changes. (These adjectives which transform the whole impression may be designated as the *key* ones just to make our meaning clear.) Volkmann and associates have shown that the positional values of stimuli in a scale and, in fact, the whole scale are affected by the introduction of anchoring points within or without the stimulus scale (27).

Within a reference frame at a given time, anchorings which contribute heavily in determining the special character of perceptual structure need not be always and predominantly on the side of external factors. There are cases in which the main anchoring points are internal. As Volkmann stated, *"Anchoring can be achieved by appropriate verbal instructions, without the use of anchoring stimuli."* In more complex social situations, the individual's motives, his attitudes, do come as still more potent anchorages to determine his perceptions. These internal anchorings take a decidedly directive role, especially in cases of social situations that are unstructured, that are in the state of flux.

In this connection, we have to stress again the implications of the fact of perceptual selectivity. No matter how strong internal factors may be, no matter how strong social pressures or lures may be, nobody will see a rectangle as a circle, a dime as a fifty-cent piece. In short, my perception of external objects is not just what I want to make them out to be. There are compelling structural properties of stimulus objects which shape my perceptions. In this respect, the critique by the experimentalists in perception, like Gibson, leveled against "social perception enthusiasts" is a much needed corrective (6). On the other hand, in actual life situations, thousands of objects can potentially acquire figure character. Out of so many perceptual objects, probably those will be reacted to which are relevant to internal anchorages operative at the time. In the experimental situation, the subject is exposed to definite objects chosen by the experimenter with hardly any other alternatives, and his range of perceptual selectivity is necessarily limited.

In this brief discussion of anchoring points, the implications of one fact stand out with particular relevance to the concept of reference groups. And this fact is that anchoring points, external or internal, contribute heavily and, at times, decisively to the organization of experience and behavior. The properties of other parts in a reference frame become defined and regulated in terms of their relation to the anchoring points.

Reference groups, which are the groups to which the individual relates himself as a part or aspires to relate himself, serve functionally as major anchorings. In fact, reference groups might just as well be called *anchoring groups.* The individual's directive attitudes, viz., ego-attitudes, which define and regulate his behavior to other persons, other groups, and to an important extent even to himself, are formed in relation to the values and norms of his reference groups. They constitute an important basis of his self-identity, of his sense of belongingness, of the core of his social ties.

With this theoretical scheme in mind, the formation and functioning of many of the individual's directive attitudes can be pulled into a coherent picture. For example, as was shown in Horowitz' study on prejudice or social distance, the positive and negative attitudes of the single individual toward other groups are formed not on the basis of actual positive and negative contact with the groups in question but in terms of social proximity or social distance of these groups as defined by the prevailing norms of his reference group (10).

The individual is, of course, positively oriented toward his own reference group. We will be missing the main point, however, if we refer both to the group with which the individual identifies and to other groups toward which he has attitudes as reference groups. This view could conceivably lead to making lists of reference groups containing as many as there are groups in relation to which the individual has an attitude or anything to do. Nothing is to be gained by calling every group in relation to which the individual has formed an attitude a reference group, positive or negative. We can certainly speak of group high or low in the social-distance scale as positive or negative groups, but *not* as positive or negative *reference* groups. If "groups" and "reference groups" become interchangeable terms, there is no particular need to use "reference group" as a separate term. The concept of reference groups can be advantageously used to denote groups to which the individual relates or aspires to relate himself as a part.

This same conclusion is reached when the problem of positive and negative attitudes toward various groups is approached developmentally. As the child acquires his group membership, he also acquires established relatedness with other groups which is crucially mediated through verbal symbols of his own reference group. On the whole, the direction of this relatedness with various groups can be predicted from the social-distance norms of his own reference groups. These reference groups serve as the main anchorages in determining his perceived relations with his social world.

THE EGO OF THE INDIVIDUAL AND REFERENCE GROUPS

As everyone knows, the relatedness of the individual to his surroundings is not merely in terms of the positive or negative appeal of objects, persons, and groups as regulated *momentarily* by the ups and downs of his hunger, thirst, sex desires, and the like. As he develops beyond infancy and childhood, his relatedness to objects or situations displays an increasing degree of consistency, and a continuity of this consistency. At times these may be at variance with the ups and downs of his momentary needs.

The consistency of reactions regulated in terms of anchorages provided by reference groups is part of the more general problem of consistency of the individual from situation to situation.

The problem of personal consistency from situation to situation is being expressed more and more in terms of self or ego. We may, then, consider individual-group relationships in terms of the concept of self or ego. We shall be unifying and further specifying related problems if we deliberately bring ego into the picture in dealing with reference group behavior. For reference group standards or norms are internalized in the individual (through learning) as parts of his ego.

We may characterize ego or self as a developmental formation or a "subsystem" in the psychological make-up of the individual consisting of functionally interrelated attitudes which are acquired in relation to his own body, his family, and groups, objects, values, and institutions which define and regulate his relatedness to all these in so many concrete situations.

This conception of ego as consisting of many attitudes in relation to identifiable stimulus situations lends itself readily to the study of the individual's relatedness to his surroundings in many specific dimensions.

These ego-attitudes function as weighty anchorings in determining the individual's experience and behavior in relevant situations. Owing to man's conceptual level of functioning, his ego-attitudes are not subject ordinarily to abrupt variations from each situation to the next.

These ego-attitudes may be in relation to anchorings that lie far beyond his perceptual range in space and time. Otherwise, for example, great ideological identifications that cut across state boundaries, even national boundaries, so prevalent in our times, would not have been possible. (By this we do not mean that the causes of identifications are due to verbal factors. The causes are, of course, in the reality of motives of individuals and goals of groups under given conditions.) There is abundant evidence indicating a relationship between conceptual or language development from infancy on and development of ego-attitudes which increasingly expand the relatedness of man in space and time.[2] Here we can give only one or two items of this evidence. For one thing, there is a positive relationship between language development and ego development or expansion. Erection of consistent goals in relation to the future by the child has been found to appear by Gesell (5), Goodenough (7), and others only after about the age of five—that is, only after reference to the future is made possible with the learning of appropriate words or symbols (16).

At this point, the implications of the conception of ego or self presented above for various concrete problems related to reference groups may be stated in summary form. The constellation of interrelated ego-attitudes is situationally aroused in this or that capacity or role of the individual in the situation as superior, equal, inferior; accepted, rejected, etc., in relation to others in that particular situation. Whatever other goals we may be pursuing, whatever other tasks we may be engaged in, the ego-attitudes appropriate to the situation do also come in to determine the reactions—the way we strive toward the goal, the degree of effectiveness exerted in the performance of the task at hand, as experiments on ego-involvements indicate. For example, when we are hungry, we want to eat. But we want to eat in certain places and with certain people. We prefer to satisfy our sex desires with as "classy" a person as we can find under the circumstances.

In short, almost always this or that ego-attitude comes in as a factor, no matter what other goal we may be pursuing, what tasks we may be engaged in. If we, as respectable middle-class members of society, discover that we have landed in a disreputable hotel, we want to move to a reputable one, even if our bed is comfortable and the hotel is quiet and relatively inexpensive. We become

---

[2] The difficulty of even relatively simple discriminations by subhuman animals in the absence of spatial cues, when delays are not larger than ten seconds, is attributed by Yerkes and others (29) to the lack of symbols.

mindful of our status in relation to the attitudes of people important in our eyes, viz., our reference groups. We cannot relinquish these ego-attitudes at will from day to day with the ups and downs of other motives that may be operative at the time. Relevant ego-attitudes are situationally elicited whether or not we are conscious of them.

These various kinds of relatedness, which are formed or learned in the course of contact with the surroundings, may be studied as factors coming from this developmentally formed subsystem designated as ego system. We could readily supply experimental evidence to show that in many situations, whatever other immediate goals or tasks may be at hand, ego-attitudes do take part in determining the psychological organization, hence behavior. In the Chapman and Volkmann study mentioned, the instructions specified only the names of the out-groups (viz., literary critics and WPA workers) and their supposed level of performance on the task. No mention was made in the instructions to the subjects of the standing of their own groups. *The subjects raised or lowered the estimates of their performance by spontaneously using their own group as the main anchoring point and regulating the estimates of their performance according to the place of these groups (high or low) in relation to their own group in the same task.*

We will be moving in the direction of testable experimental possibilities along many directions if we make a special point of singling out the various factors coming from the individual in determining his experience and behavior. This consideration becomes especially relevant in the case of factors coming from ego or self, which, we repeat, almost always comes into the picture in human psychological functioning. For there are times when factors coming from within the individual himself may be in opposite directions. We may be very hungry in a room full of food, but may have to wait for the socially appropriate time to pay appreciable attention to the food. So in our present problem, when an individual who is strongly identified with an out-group is participating even as an announced member in actual interaction in a face-to-face group, his appraisals and conformity in the momen-

tary situation will be deflected in terms of anchorages provided
by the group of which he considers himself a part, that is, his reference group.

SOME SPECIAL PROBLEMS RELATED TO
INTERGROUP RELATIONS

The usefulness of the concept of reference groups, as we have
seen, stems from the fact that it is attained on the basis of a host
of facts which reveal the regulation of experience and behavior
by their appropriate anchorages. Whenever problems of conflict
of anchorages arise, or whenever status anchorages are dispropor-
tionately high or low in relation to one another, we face significant psychological problems. Reduced to its bare essentials, *marginality* is the condition of being caught between two conflicting
reference groups; or being caught between one's own reference
group and a group which is capable of exerting pressures, putting
demands on him and requiring conformity of him. Again, in bare
outline, at least some cases on inconsistency revealed by the individual in intergroup relations are due to the fact that, as the
individual goes through various situations, they activate situationally roles prescribed by contradictory norms of his multiple reference group affiliations. Likewise, having attained a high status
in some dimension of human relations, one finds that being still
in low status in some other respect becomes insufferable; hence
some of the comedies and tragedies that accompany the efforts
for *status equilibration*.

Marginality in Human Relations

Personal conflict, uncertainty, or insecurity follows lack of stability of anchorings in reference groups. These situations have
been extensively studied by sociologists—notably Park and Stonequist—as *marginality* (25).

The state of marginality gives us a good opportunity to emphasize certain points which we could touch upon only briefly in
the course of this discussion. Since our task in this chapter is the
clarification of the reference group concept, the emphasis has

been on instances in which the groups are not face to face, or which are not within the perceptual range of the individual. However, such emphasis should not imply that immediate face-to-face group situations in which the membership group is *not* a reference group do not have some effect on the individual. On the contrary, even in cases in which a sharp cleavage exists between the group in which he is registered or taken for granted and his reference group, he is bound to feel the immediate pressures and demands for conformity of the group situation he moves in. In such cases, he will be pushed in one direction by his actual membership group, pulled in the opposite direction by his reference group.

In cases of marginality, however, the situation is ordinarily one of lack of stability in reference group ties. The individual cannot relate himself in a consistent way to either group. Both groups, at times, are reference groups for him, however unstable his ties with one group. The degrees to which he is ego-involved with the value scales of one or the other may vary.

The most common example of marginality is that of individuals belonging to an ethnic group, religious group, or color group in a minority position who, because of their inability to be accepted in the larger society and their tendency to reject standards or position of their own group, feel insecure in their reference group affiliations in a major way.

Among psychologists, Kurt Lewin has written on these problems (15), and Hartley has done interesting studies with children on the conflicting values of groups to which they relate themselves (9).

Marginality is not confined to members of minority groups. The *foreman* in industrial life is often in a similar position. Ordinarily, of course, the foreman rises out of the rank and file of workers. But as a foreman he is betwixt and between management and the workers. He cannot consistently relate himself to management, partly because of his origins and his economic situation, and because he does not actually take part in making policy decisions, but just carries out the directives of management. Roethlisberger (**20**) pointed out that management calls the foreman the "grass roots level of management" or "front-line personnel man." But the foreman calls himself a "go-betweener." He has to uphold management's standards and regulations and at the same time try to get workers to conform to them spontaneously. "Again and again he is put in a position of either getting the worker's cooperation and being 'disloyal' to management or of incurring the resentment and overt opposition of his subordinates" (p. 290).

The workers, in turn, think of the foreman as "the boss." In an interview from a study by Whyte and Gardner (**28**), one worker said: "You can't talk about this sort of thing with the boss. After all, he's part of management and you couldn't expect him to see things as we do. He's a good guy, as far as that goes, but he's a management man" (p. 19).

The foreman thus is unable to take either management or the workers as his reference group in a consistent way. The result may be, in the words of one foreman: "You don't know where you stand. It's a hell of a situation because I get on edge and blow my top and say things that I really didn't mean to say" (p. 20).

In the American Soldier Studies of World War II, Stouffer and associates apply a similar analysis to the conflicting situation of the noncommissioned officer (**26**). Here the "noncom finds himself in a conflict situation involving official responsibility to his officers on one hand and unofficial obligations to the other enlisted men on the other hand" (p. 410).

Inconsistency in Intergroup Relations

We have mentioned the relative consistency and continuity of the individual's identity. However, especially in modern complex societies, his behavior may appear highly contradictory and inconsistent in various situations. As an example, Jahoda takes the case of some union members who actively participated in the Detroit race riots of 1943 even though in their union they were taught and practiced nonsegregation. Now if these union members had been *nothing but* good and stanch union members, they would not have participated in the riots. But they were also members of families, neighborhood groups, churches, ethnic groups, and, as they have been reminded in so many ways from childhood on, a "white" group, which, they have learned, stands at definite distances to other groups. These groups were major reference groups long before these individuals became members of a union with an anti-discrimination policy. It is not surprising that, in a situation in which they could either act as a "regular person" in terms of their major reference groups of neighborhood, color, etc., or as good union members, many of them—probably with no thought of doing otherwise—acted contrary to their union's practices.

To be sure, behavior of individuals may be inconsistent for a number of reasons, perhaps idiosyncratic ones related to continual thwarting of basic biogenic motives or persistent conflict situations of a personal nature. However, a large proportion of instances of inconsistencies in *social* behavior can be understood in relation to conflicting norms of various reference groups which have been internalized and may be situationally aroused. Charters and Newcomb (19) showed that when Catholic subjects are situationally ego-involved as Catholics, their reactions to general statements are substantially different from their reactions to the same items when Catholic group reference is not activated.

When an individual has multiple reference groups, the norms of which conflict in various areas, he will sooner or later find himself in a situation where the norms of different reference groups point in different, even opposite, directions. Consider the situation of modern professional woman. In her work, of course, her professional group is the major reference group; in social life, perhaps the ladies of the community; in her home, her family. It is not unusual for her to find herself in a situation where the norms of two or more of these reference groups are in conflict. Of course, she will probably react in terms of one or the other. She may even be aware of the source of her dilemma, feeling resentment toward one or the other or her reference groups responsible for the conflict in this area. It is doubtful, however, that this situation is clarified by speaking of that reference group as a negative reference group in that respect and positive in another respect, as Newcomb and others do. Probably at some time or other almost every group member is negatively inclined toward at least some norms of his group. If these terms were used, every group to which the individual relates himself could be both a positive and a negative reference group.

Killian (14) has made an interesting analysis of "the conflict of civilian and army norms in a military railway service." Although the men studied were all in the army and subject to all rules and customs of "military courtesy," the usual behavior between them, whether officers or enlisted men, was in terms of status in civilian railroad groups. In spite of "constant pressure from the general headquarters for compliance with traditional military practice," the railroad group and its norms persisted as the major anchorages, and resulted in behavior quite inconsistent with the army situation.

In an analysis of the significance of multiple group membership in a disaster situation in four southwestern communities, Killian (13) studied the reactions of individuals to a situation where by necessity a choice in reference groups had to be made. For example, frequent conflict was found between loyalty to family or friends and loyalty to occupational groups. An example of apparently inconsistent behavior in the eyes of those who watched was that of the state trooper who decided after a tornado struck that as a patrolman his job was to drive to the next town for help. But to the friends and acquaintances who called for his help as he drove out of town his action must have seemed inconsistent, even heartless. He stated that this was "one of the hardest things I ever had to do." The behavior of telephone workers in two disaster communities who were on strike at the time reveals the conflict between reference groups within the community and those outside of the community. "In both communities the striking workers were allowed to return to duty by union leaders, but were ordered to walk out again a few days later. In both cases the union officials considered the emergency to be over sooner than did the townspeople of the stricken communities. In one town the workers obeyed the union's orders only to find themselves subjected to harsh criticism by their fellow-townsmen. In the other community the workers resigned from the union rather than forsake their loyalty to their other membership group" (p. 313).

Status Equilibration

To the degree that the individual has interiorized the norms of his various reference groups, conflict or contradictions of these norms will be experienced as personal conflict or insecurity. This relationship becomes more precise when individuals' statuses in their various reference groups are specified. Groups are necessarily hierarchical along some dimension. Status denotes the relative position of each member in these respects. Of course, to have a relative position, the individual must in some degree relate himself or belong to the group. This relatedness implies experience of the hierarchy of the group and ego-involvement with it. Once a member, his aspirations for status and standards of attainment are determined in terms of this scale.

Now what happens when the individual's status in various reference groups differs? In delineating the concept of *status equilibration,* the sociologist Benoit-Smullyan suggests that "there is a real tendency for the different types of status to reach a common level" (2, p. 160). For example, a millionaire who finds himself admired only for his money teams up with a college professor or public relations expert, or endows a research foundation, in the effort to attain prestige socially commensurate with his financial status. Or a lady newly arrived in a financial sense may indulge in literature or the arts, or psychology, in order to bring her social status in the community to the level of her financial status. In the process of striving, she may be a little ashamed of her associates on the wrong side of the tracks and try to minimize or even break off her relationship with them. As Hartley suggests, another way the individual may seek to adjust his statuses is by trying to raise the prestige of one of his reference groups to the level of the higher group. Hartley's study with Fenchel and Monderer on college students' status and status strivings in five significant reference groups found the tendency to be expected from the notion of status equilibration (4). Striving for status was significantly greater in reference groups in which status was lower. "The results indicate a definite tendency for the status ratings to approach a common high anchorage level within the individual's status structure, as defined by his different reference groups" (p. 477). The explanation for this, we should think, lies in the ego-involvement in these anchorages defined by reference groups, and in the personal uneasiness at being exposed to situations of conflict and contradiction.

The personal problems that are produced by concern over equilibration at the highest attained status have their serious counterparts in intergroup adjustments of individuals, especially those who are members of minority groups in a country with heterogeneous ethnic composition.

Minority group members, at the same time, are citizens of the larger society. The tendency for the general run of minority group members is to internalize the social-distance scale that exists in the country as a whole, putting various groups at various positions on the hierarchy of social distance standardized from the point of view of the group on top of the scale (Chapter 4). Having accepted the social-distance scale with its relative positions for various groups, they tend subjectively to place their own group close to the highest position and to keep the rest of the social-distance scale intact. In the last analysis this tendency reflects an attitude which means that the minority group members in question reject discrimination against their own particular group but at the same time accept discrimination applied to other minority groups.

Probably this subjective placement would not have been made if the upward move had been perceived as impossible, as it is considered by members of the low caste in a country where lines between hierarchical positions are more sharply drawn and more or less frozen, e.g., until a few decades ago, in India. But in a society in which there is a greater degree of fluidity, a greater degree of give-and-take in a greater number of social functions (business, education, social intercourse, and so forth) between groups high and low on the social-distance scale, special complications arise. Here we shall cite only two important cases.

1. Some members of the minority groups not high on the social-distance scale do actually arrive at topmost status in business, education, art, or some other area of social life through their personal achievements. There are some among these individuals who have attained topmost status in some respect who strive to equilibrate their statuses in other areas to this highest one. The consequence of such strivings is reflected in pulling away from the norms of their original group even to the point of depreciation of the group from which they stem. This phenomenon is described as "self-hatred" of one's own group by Lewin and others. Whether a person in this situation will turn against his own group or instead stand with his own group involves intricate personality problems which we cannot consider here. The important point in this connection is to note the occurrence of such cases due to the intergroup relations mentioned above.

2. The depreciation of the group from which one stems may be due to the unsatisfactory nature of one's belongingness and status in his own group. The anchorages in one's own group having become precarious through the lack of motivational support, the aspiration to belong to a higher group determines his subjective acceptance of the anchorages related to the higher group. Usually in such cases there is a wide gap between actualities of real belongingness and statuses and subjectively desired belongingness and statuses. This gap between actual belongingness and status on the one hand and fantasied identification and status on the other becomes the source of personal conflicts, insecurities, and painful experiences in social adjustments.

REFERENCES

1. Asch, S. E. Forming impressions of personality, *J. abn. & soc. Psychol.*, 1946, *41, 258–290.*
2. Benoit-Smullyan, E. Status, status types and status interrelations, *Amer. Sociol. Rev.*, 1944, *9,* 151–161.

3. Chapman, D. W., and Volkmann, J.   A social determinant of the level of aspiration, *J. Abn. & soc. Psychol.*, 1939, *34*, 225–238.

4. Fenchel, G. H., Monderer, J. H., and Hartley, E. L.   Subjective status and the equilibration hypothesis, *J. abn. & soc. Psychol.*, 1951, *46*, 476–479.

5. Gesell, A., and Ilg, F. L.   *Infant and Child in the Culture of Today.* New York: Harper, 1948.

6. Gibson, J. J.   *The Perception of the Visual World.*   Cambridge: Riverside Press, 1950.

7. Goodenough, F. L.   *Developmental Psychology: An Introduction to the Study of Human Behavior.*   New York: Appleton-Century-Crofts, 1945.

8. Hartley, E. L.   Psychological problems of multiple group membership, in J. Rohrer and M. Sherif (eds.), *Social Psychology at the Crossroads.*   New York: Harper, 1951.

9. Hartley, E. L., Rosenbaum, M., and Schwartz, S.   Children's use of ethnic frames of reference: an exploratory study of children's conceptualizations of multiple ethnic group membership, *J. Psychol.*, 1948, *26*, 367–386; Children's perception of their ethnic group membership, *ibid.*, 387–398; Note on children's role perception, *ibid.*, 399–405.

10. Horowitz, E. Development of attitudes toward the Negro, *Arch. Psychol.*, 1936, No. 194.

11. Hyman, H. H.   The psychology of status, *Arch. Psychol.*, 1942, No. 269.

12. Jahoda, M., Deutsch, M., and Cook, S. W.   *Research Methods in Social Relations.*   New York: Dryden, 1951.

13. Killian, L.   The significance of multiple group membership in disaster, *Amer. J. Sociol.*, 1952, *57*, 309–314.

14. Killian, L.   The conflict of civilian and military norms in a military railway service.   Manuscript made available by the author.

15. Lewin, K.   *Resolving Social Conflicts.*   New York: Harper, 1948.

16. Lewis, M. M.   The beginnings of reference to past and future in a child's speech, *British J. educ. Psychol.*, 1937, *7*, 39–56.

17. Lindesmith, A. R., and Strauss, A. L.   *Social Psychology.*   New York: Dryden, 1949.

18. Merton, R. K., and Kitt, A. S.   Contributions to the theory of reference group behavior, in Merton, R. K., and Lazarsfeld, P. F.

(eds.), *Continuities in Social Research: Studies in the Scope and Method of the American Soldier.* Glencoe: Free Press, 1950.

19. Newcomb, T. M. *Social Psychology.* New York: Dryden, 1950.

20. Roethlisberger, F. J. The foreman: master and victim of double talk, *Harvard Bus. Rev.,* 1945, *23,* 283–298.

21. Schneirla, T. C. Problems in the biopsychology of social organization, *J. abn. & soc. Psychol.,* 1946, *41,* 385–402.

22. Schneirla, T. C. Chapter 3, this volume.

23. Sherif, M. *An Outline of Social Psychology.* New York: Harper, 1948.

24. Sherif, M., and Cantril, H. *The Psychology of Ego-Involvements.* New York: Wiley, 1947.

25. Stonequist, E. V. *The Marginal Man.* New York: Scribner, 1937.

26. Stouffer, S. A., *et al. Studies in Social Psychology in World War II, The American Soldier, Combat and Its Aftermath.* Princeton: Princeton University Press, 1949.

27. Volkmann, J. Scales of judgment and their implication for social psychology, in J. Rohrer and M. Sherif (eds.), *Social Psychology at the Crossroads.* New York: Harper, 1951.

28. Whyte, W. F., and Gardner, B. Problems of the foreman, *J. appl. Anthrop.,* Special Issue, Spring, 1945.

29. Yerkes, R. M., and Nissen, H. W. Pre-linguistic sign behavior in chimpanzee, *Science,* 1939, *89,* 585–587.

C H A P T E R   8

Intergroup Behavior as Determined by Various Group Settings

In this chapter we shall discuss more concretely various factors determining specific cases of intergroup behavior in terms of empirical findings of sociologists and psychologists. Intergroup behavior (as defined in Chapters 1 and 6) is that behavior which the members of an in-group reveal, collectively or individually, toward out-groups and their members as a consequence of influences stemming from their group membership.

As in any kind of behavior, there are immediate psychological factors impelling the individual to behave this or that way in intergroup relations. These psychological factors, e.g., frustration, rivalry, desire to dominate, to be mightier and wealthier than others, or coöperation, sympathy, and altruism, have bearing on intergroup relations as they are patterned, deflected, channelized, or altogether transformed in their appropriate group settings. This statement is based on generalizations presented in Chapter 6.

No matter how strongly this or that psychological tendency may be operative at the time intergroup behavior is exhibited, positing such impulses as the main explanatory principle of intergroup behavior is inadequate. For these impulses are products of antecedent conditions in a social setting. If our aim is prediction and control of intergroup behavior we have to bring these antecedent factors into the picture. As Gordon Allport, one of the leading exponents of the "psychological" approach to human relations, cogently stated: "Therefore, the psychological and psychiatric emphasis is correct and proper so far as 'immediate' causation is concerned. Now, it is equally true that the warlike expectations, hates, and anxieties that give a hostile bent to personality may be the result of hunger, exploitation, tradition, and social structure. Hence for 'long run' causation, social, historical, and economic influences are often decisive" (2, p. 136).

Under ordinary circumstances, intergroup relations are regulated in terms of social-distance scales of the group of which the individual is a member (Chapters 4 and 7). Ladylike or gentlemanly behavior, or a kindly act appropriate in relation to ingroup members may be out of place, even weird, when bestowed upon a member of an out-group placed at considerable social distance. On the other hand, an act of cruelty may not be perceived by the person engaged in it or by members of his in-group as unladylike or ungentlemanly when meted to that out-group member. It may be viewed as simply putting the impertinent person in his appropriate "place."

Very deliberately we prefaced the generalization in the above paragraph with the phrase, "under ordinary circumstances." The state of flux and interdependence that characterizes relations among groups in the present-day world has gone beyond the state of regulation of intergroup relations only in terms of surviving social-distance scales of the groups in question.

1. The changed nature of functional relations between groups from negative to positive or vice versa,

2. The discrepancies in the directions taken by the subordinate groups belonging to the same general social system,

3. The situational factors operative at the time which demand the type of behavior that runs counter to the mode of reaction prescribed by the surviving social-distance scale,

4. The introduction of new technological practices which transform the existing pattern of human relations within and between groups,

5. The individual crossing of group lines under the influence of strong personal motives made possible in a world of increased contacts so intricate and enmeshed

—all these have made obsolete the accounting for intergroup behavior in terms of social distance *alone*. All these influences, which are becoming so powerful in a shrinking world, tend to reduce the relative weight of the heritage of social-distance scales at many places today. It is not a rare case today to observe the new emerging influences mentioned above wielding the greater weight in the patterning of intergroup behavior.

INTERGROUP BEHAVIOR IMPLIES PARTICI-PATION IN THE TREND OF GROUP ACTIVITY

The intergroup behavior of individuals which is of sufficient consequence to make its study crucial in the scheme of human relations today is *not* composed of discrete, unrelated acts of love or hate exhibited by this or that individual toward out-groups. If an act of love exhibited by an individual member toward an out-group and its members is not in line with the directional trend (formal or informal) of the in-group, it will be considered wasted, out of place, queer, or a personal idiosyncracy. Consequently it will have practically no effect in the course of intergroup relations. If such an out-of-line exhibition of love or friendship is viewed to be a serious deviation from the trends that prevail in the in-group, measures will be taken to bring the offender into the fold or to reject him. Likewise, if individual members exhibit manifestations of prejudice or hatred not in line with the trends within the in-group, they will be considered as going beyond the bounds of propriety and reason. If such out-of-line manifestations of prejudice or hatred go to extremes, the members who commit them will be treated as offenders or criminals.

Such manifestations of prejudice or hatred might very well be, in some cases, the products of the unfortunate frustrations suffered by the individuals in question. But still the central question remains. Such displaced acts of aggression are directed, on the whole, against out-groups low on the social-distance scale. In

short, if not in line with the trends of the in-group, manifestations of prejudice and aggression are handled as matters of justice
and restitution. It can be concluded, then, that friendly or hostile
acts directed toward an out-group which are not in line with the
ongoing trends within the in-group constitute a problem in the
area of *deviate behavior*. And the central problem of intergroup
relations is not the problem of the deviate behavior.

The fact that renders the problem of intergroup relations so
central today both as a topic of study and as a matter of grave
practical importance is that intergroup behavior is not primarily
the problem of deviates. It is the problem of participation of the
great body of individual members in the intergroup trends that
take shape within their respective in-groups. The individual members are not outside of the shaping and direction of these positive
or negative trends in relation to out-groups. They do participate
as initiators of a trend toward a particular out-group with all the
means of mass communication and other appeals at their disposal.
They do participate, at times, as eager recipients of these appeals.
They do participate as personally involved followers. Whether
they contribute in the capacity of leaders, or as aroused followers,
or as rank and file caught in the drift of the rolling band wagon,
they are all participants in the intergroup trend. As such they
come to consider it only proper and decent to contribute their
bit in line with the trend in question. And this is essentially the
same as the basic problem of social psychology—viz., the problem
of *conformity* to the trends and standards of the group of which
the individual is a member.

As has been noted by so many writers, there are strong demands
and pressures for conformity to the norms and trends of the
group. These demands for conformity come both (1) from the
group and (2) from the individual himself. In the literature on
conformity to group norms the usual emphasis has been on pressures coming from the group. The psychological factors within
the individual impelling him to conformity are not sufficiently
stressed.

The pressures for conformity to group norms and goals are

exerted through both positive and negative measures. Conformity is approved, encouraged, and rewarded in many ways. Nonconformity is viewed with disfavor, disapproval. Depending on the importance of the norm to the group and the degree of deviation, nonconformity is reacted to with various corrective and even coercive measures: ridicule, scorn, silent treatment, ostracism, actual punishment, or death.

Pressures to conformity are not exercised only by formally organized groups. They are exerted by any kind of group that has some structure. One of the best-documented illustrations of informal group pressures is the concerted set of correctives applied by employees against the rate busters among them. In this connection, the production norm that emerged among the workers' group in the Roethlisberger and Dickson study, and the correctives applied to those who broke the norm give us a typical case. "Beliefs regarding a day's work and the dangers involved in exceeding it were not confined to a few persons but were held quite generally, both by the men in the observation room and in the regular department. It was apparent that there existed a group norm in terms of which the behavior of different individuals was in some sense being regulated" (64, p. 423).

The deviates who busted the production norm standardized in the group were viewed with disfavor. Various forms of correctives were applied to these deviates to pull them into the fold—disfavor, ridicule, scorn, warnings, and even physical punishment, for which the group used their standardized term, "binging." ". . . Binging was used to regulate the output of some of the faster workers." This was one of its most significant applications and is well illustrated in the following entry:

W_8: (To W_9) "Why don't you quit work? Let's see, this is your thirty-fifth row today. What are you going to do with them all?
W_9: "What do you care? It's to your advantage if I work, isn't it?"
W_8: "Yeah, but the way you're working you'll get stuck with them."
W_9: "Don't worry about that. I'll take care of it. You're getting paid by the sets I turn out. That's all you should worry about."

W$_8$: "If you don't quit work I'll bing you." W$_8$ struck W$_6$ and finally chased him around the room.

Obs: (A few minutes later) "What's the matter, W$_6$, won't he let you work?

W$_6$: "No. I'm all through though. I've got enough done." He then went over and helped another wireman. [64, pp. 422–423]

In the more systematic studies by Festinger and his associates we find clear-cut substantiation of the consequences of deviation in line with the above observations (21, 22).

The group correctives to pull the deviate back to the norm and to hold the vacillating in line need not be coercive. They can be in the form of highly gratifying experiences.

Critical periods of the strike occur most frequently in connection with Sundays and other holidays. At these times the strikers are especially inclined to desert because of the absence of picketing or other mass activities and because of the sight of privations at home. Reflection upon private needs is likely to cause a return of individualism. Means for combating these crises are Sunday picnics, celebrations, entertainments, special meetings—anything which will help the participants to forget themselves and keep them within the stream of group influences. [30, p. 93]

Conformity to group norms is not only or even primarily a consequence of demands, pressures, correctives, and coercion exerted on individuals. Conformity to group norms primarily through the impact of forces coming from outside the individual may be the typical case of members who deviate or show symptoms of deviation. The representative fact of conformity is the conformity of members whose very sense of self-identity, sense of pride, sense of security, sense of achievement are derived, in no small degree, from the fact of belongingness in a group with a definite status and role within it. This being the case, in their eyes conformity to the group norms is not perceived as an act of coercion imposed from outside. It is their group, their norm. As good members, as proud members, the desirable, the proper mode of behavior is to conform, to uphold, to cherish, and actively to defend their group norms. When the autonomous, willing observance of group norms weakens or disappears, the group itself is weakened or disorganized. And not all groups are in a state of disorganization.

The willing, the autonomous, the sought-for conformity to group norms on the part of individuals is not due to an inherent instinct or need for conformity, as has been posited by some recent writers. Conformity to one's group norms is the inevitable functional consequence of belongingness in a group. Being a part of the group, identifying oneself with a group and having a definite status in it is not an inconsequential matter. It necessarily means making the values and norms of the group one's own values and norms—in short, constituent parts of one's ego.

A group is not only a repressive, coercive agent in the lives of individual members. Besides direct gratifications and experiences of success as well as direct frustrations and experiences of failure resulting from the ups and downs in one's status and prestige relations, the vital matters of economic gain, sexual gratification, occupational satisfaction take place within the group setting. In the words of Festinger and his associates, "Friendships, companionship, and the warmth and pleasures of close emotional ties are, of course, available only as a result of our relationships with other people. Prestige, social status, and approval of others are in themselves group-oriented goals. They exist only as a particular kind of relationship with other persons. Membership in groups also tends to make accessible to people goals which otherwise would be far out of reach" (22, p. 3). No wonder then that the recent line of development which is handling the problem of attitude formation and change in terms of interaction in group situations is proving to be effective.

The evidence concerning regulation of one's own directive attitudes in terms of the values and norms of reference groups may be called to the attention in this connection (Chapter 7). As we have seen, the regulation of one's attitudes in terms of one's reference groups is not confined only to cases in which there are immediate group demands and pressures. The reference group

regulation of attitudes occurs even when immediate social demands and pressures are not present or, at times, when they are
in the opposite direction.

The approach presented in the above paragraphs becomes even
more plausible when the consequences of disruption of stable ties
with one's group are considered. The stability of one's sense of security and personal identity consists, to a large extent, of the
stability of his anchorages in relation to the physical and social
world around him. In this system of anchorages, relatedness and
identification with one's reference groups occupy no small part.
When these anchorages are disrupted through being let down,
losing faith, rejection, or other circumstance, the consequence is
floundering around in a fluid, undependable, unchartered atmosphere in which instability is ubiquitous. The striving is to hold
on to something that is stable, dependable (69, 70). In critical
times, when these strivings are general in the population, the
slogans, the solutions offered by the demagogue in clear-cut pro-
phetic dicta are highly effective in their appeal value. Such facts
make perfectly understandable the reasons why the new convert is
more zealous, more uncompromising in his devotion to the norms
of his newly embraced faith, group, or whatever his brand of new
haven may be.

Now we can summarize the main point of this discussion. Intergroup behavior, for good or for evil, that is consequential in
human relations today is not typified by this or that kind of
deviate behavior. The representative type of intergroup behavior
consists of participation in conformity with the developing trend
or existing social-distance scale in one's own group in relation to
the out-groups in question. Conformity in intergroup relations,
as well as in other areas, is brought about both (1) by group demands and pressures exerted on the individual members and (2)
through the very fact of group belongingness, being identified,
loyal, and dutiful members of the group. It is more realistic,
therefore, to approach the understanding and solution of intergroup relations through (1) the implications of belongingness,
status and role relations of members within a group, and (2) con-

sequences of the nature of functional relations between delineated in-groups, such as social-distance scales, and new developing trends in intergroup relations produced by new conditions. The following two sections will deal with these topics.

SMALL GROUPS STUDIED AS PROTOTYPES

Man in modern societies functions in many in-group and intergroup settings. Some groups are so large and intertwined that it may seem next to impossible to handle them without losing track of the central problem or deviating from scientific methods at some step. Largely for this reason, the study of man in informally organized small groups, which has occupied sociologists for some time, has become a major concern for social psychologists.

This is not the only methodological advantage in studying small, informally organized groups. *We may observe such units in the process of formation.* The rise of group structure and the stabilization of tradition and their effects on individual behavior —in short, the formation of reference groups—can be traced here and now in longitudinal fashion. This process would appear to bring our problem to a greatly simplified level. But observing man in the setting of small in-groups as though these possessed the structural properties of all group settings is not the panacea it was once thought. Even when brought to the quiet confines of a laboratory, informally organized groups are *parts* of larger group settings and are related to other groups, small and large. Attempts to derive broadly applicable principles for man's behavior in group settings cannot merely *allow for* the operation of the interrelationships of various group settings. Rather the relations among various group settings must be basic in these attempts.

It is true that large formal organizations differ in some ways from informally organized groups. An obvious example is that formal organizations are frequently much larger. As Whyte (79) has pointed out, "bigness" in itself brings new problems. For example, face-to-face communication tends to be replaced by indirect, even mass, communication. Flexibility in meeting group problems may be drastically reduced. The compellingness of structural properties in large-scale, formal organizations cannot be minimized. Later in this chapter we will consider briefly the well-nigh inescapable impact of modern mass mediums in almost immediately involving individuals in group values and goals. It seems unlikely, however, that formal organizations and informally organized groups need be sharply dichotomized in understanding man's behavior in group settings. The differences from this point of view are largely in their origin and not, on the whole, in their functioning.

Many formal organizations start as informally organized groups. Several religious sects, for example the Mennonites, Quakers, and Mormons, began as relatively small groups with informal organization. The contemporary society on the isolated isle of Tristan da Cunha began with a small informally organized group of three individuals (55). One of the early labor movements in the United States, the Order of the Knights of Labor, grew from an informal basis and functioned for twelve years in secrecy (46). The first coöperative store in England, which marked the beginnings of the coöperative movement during the last century, developed from the informal meetings of twelve unemployed weavers who "met together to discover what they could do to better their industrial condition" (33).

Especially since the work of Cooley, sociologists have been aware of the prevalence of informal human groupings and their importance in socialization and in individual behavior in general. As Faris (19) points out, the well-nigh universal tendency for individuals sharing common circumstances of life to form spontaneously into small cliques has been so impressively documented in recent years that their prevalence and significance can scarcely be subjects of doubt. Even preschool children tend to cluster in small groups with some stability and status structure (49, 53). Informal cliques and groupings become especially frequent and central to individuals in modern societies during adolescence, when formal status as adults is not yet secured and reformulations of the relation of self to others are in shaky, tentative form (32, 69).

So widespread and potent are informal groups within formal industrial organizations that Gardner speaks of them as "one of the characteristics of human organization; a characteristic that may be understood and modified but never done away with" (25, p. 7). Certainly studies of that most formal of all organizations, the military, substantiate such a conclusion (5, 72).

Some Essential Features of Small Groups

The activities of informally organized groups run the gamut from respectability to criminality, from peaceful pursuits to antisocial acts and violence. Extensive study of such in-groups reveals that all informally organized groups have at least the following features:

1. Common motive or motives conducive to interaction among individuals.
2. Differential effects of the interaction process on individuals.
3. Rise of a group structure with hierarchical statuses within it and clear-cut in-group demarcations.
4. Standardization of values or norms and other group products in terms of which activities within the group are regulated.

We shall discuss each of these features briefly in the above order. Further discussion of these minimum common features may be found in M. Sherif, *An Outline of Social Psychology*.

1. Informal organization of groups occurs spontaneously through the interaction of individuals with *common goals or motives*. The potential variety of these is as wide as the range of human wants, desires, and interests which may be shared by individuals. Perhaps there are a few cases of group formation in which only one motive figured. But two or more are usually central in the process, and these weigh heavily in determining the type of activities engaged in, the sort of status structure which develops, and the goals and traditions which form in the interaction process. The individual who does not share these motives with others in the developing in-group soon finds himself out of place, a misfit. While all individuals need not interact with predominantly the same motives, motives central to the group forma-

tion must be experienced in common by all to some degree. These may be basic, biogenic needs for food, shelter, and the like. A common threat or danger to life itself or to means of livelihood may bring people together for mutual protection and aid. Note the statement of the Knights of Labor: "When bad men combine, the good must associate, else they will fall, one by one, an unpitied sacrifice in a contemptible struggle" (46, p. 4).

Individuals facing uncertainty or insecurity in their social ties may gravitate toward one another to establish some social anchorage of their own in terms of which they may achieve clarified and stable personal identities. This is a common basis for interaction in a modern world of rapid change where old loyalties overlap and conflict with the new, where thousands are "alone" in cities teeming with people, where youth struggles through a longer transition to adulthood amid the clashing of old and new in themselves and in the social world. A desire for some place in life, any status at all, or better status, prestige, power—all these have brought people together to interact as a group.

Individuals sharing a common fate, say, as married college students of similar background in a housing project or as prisoners of war with diverse backgrounds, may interact and form in interaction all the characteristics of little in-groups in terms of their proximity to one another. But proximity itself is not adequate basis for in-group formation, as thousands of city apartment dwellers who greet neighbors with no more than a passing nod could tell us. Informal groups of more than momentary duration form on the basis of matters of some consequence to the individuals in question. In such a serious situation as a prisoner-of-war camp, early groupings within living units quickly give way to more enduring in-group formations centered around modes of meeting the situations shared in common. Thus in a German prison camp, in-groups arose based on defiance to the Germans (refusal to work), desires to escape, the wish to have it as easy as possible or to gain the favor of the captors (3).

No matter what the original motives which brought individuals into interaction, once in-group formation begins new motives and goals will arise and may perhaps acquire greater importance than those which were central in bringing the individuals together in the first place. Very often, just being with the in-group becomes a goal in itself. Group association holds many pleasures and opportunities which are impossible in isolation. Since in-groups never function in a vacuum, since they constantly meet new situations and problems, since they operate in relation to other groups and within larger social settings, it is hardly surprising that new desires and new goals emerge during in-group functioning which in time may become as vital to individual members as those which drew them together.

2. When individuals interact with one another, the *structural properties* of the group situation produce *differential effects* upon their experience and behavior. Group situations are not the only situations in which qualitative changes in behavior occur. Whenever compelling new factors are introduced in the frame of reference determining behavior at a given time, we may expect shifts or even reversals and transformations in experience and behavior, depending on the weight of the new factors in the reference frame. But group situations, especially those of sufficient duration so that a status hierarchy and role structure take shape, produce alterations in behavior which are, at times, dramatic.

This feature of group situations has been found in experimental social psychology from its beginnings, irrespective of the theoretical interpretations put upon the findings. The early studies by Moede (51), F. H. Allport (1), and Dashiell (15), for example, produced alterations in such functions as judgment, thinking, attention, work performance, and the like, as a result of group situations. Sherif (68) demonstrated experimentally the differential effects of group situations in the perception of unstructured stimulus situations. Using in-groups of children, Lewin, Lippitt, and White (45) produced shifts in behavior by varying a potent aspect of structure in children's interest groups —the kind of adult leadership. As noted previously, dramatic examples of differential behavior in group interaction were reported by early writers, such as Le Bon.

The differential effects of group situations do not result from

mysterious forces which tear all inhibitions from the individual
or strip pieces from a presumed "social veneer." They are the result of *structural properties* which every group situation possesses
in some measure, whether they are temporary or lasting to the
point of relative stabilization. Structural properties of group situations may be contrasted to bit-by-bit or piecemeal additions of this
factor or that. In group situations, the individual becomes a *part*
of a functioning system.

When the group in question is an organized in-group, the
structural properties are easily specified and their effects measured concretely in sociological study (point 3, below). But even in
temporary groupings, such as those in the street clustered around
a celebrity or an accident, or aggregations suddenly faced with
disaster and panic, the structural properties are not mysterious.
Killian's studies reveal that within four or five minutes after
disaster strikes, while panic reigns, small groups of survivors who
find themselves together interact as informal groupings to find
some solution for their personal plight or some remedy for the
situation of others. The result in many cases was heroic efforts
at rescue and relief before any organized agency was on the
scene (41).

The structural properties of such temporary groupings and of
any group in the process of formation can be specified. When
individuals with common motives, goals, or even temporary interests interact, reciprocities among the individuals begin. Even
in its beginnings, this state of reciprocity produces expectations
toward others in relation to oneself. The studies of "leaderless"
groups in which individuals are placed in a situation, perhaps
with a task or problem to solve in common without an appointed
leader or instructions, reveal concretely how the state of reciprocity develops and expectations, even though temporary, are
formed. If interaction continues, the reciprocities and expectations become stabilized, eventually standardized, into a group
structure with definite roles and statuses including leader-follower
relations. The sociological studies of clique formations trace the
stabilization of group structure in detail.

3. Whenever individuals with motives or goals in common

interact for any length of time, a *group structure* consisting of hierarchical statuses (relative positions) and roles takes shape. The reciprocities arising in any interaction of individuals with motives and goals in common are stabilized over a time span in terms of the respective contribution of individual members to the process of interacting toward the group's goals. Since individuals are not identical, the expectations engendered in this state of reciprocity fall into a hierarchical scale, which has considerable stability, though it is by no means immutable or static. The expectations in relation to each position are stabilized as *social norms* which define the functions of the various positions in the group structure. These standardized expectations define the roles of the group members. Henceforth, the individual member tends to act within the role prescribed by these standardized expectations (norms).

The aspirations of individual members tend to be set in terms of their defined roles. The individual occupying a particular status who attempts to substitute his own definitions and aspirations at variance with those prescribed by his role must be prepared to face obstacles and personal conflict, unless he is in the fortunate circumstance of a group structure in flux whose members may be tolerant of the new definitions as beneficial to their progress.

The rise of a group structure necessarily implies distinguishing those who are in the group from those who are not in the group. Thus the beginnings of "we feelings" as contrasted to "they"— the division of in-group from out-group—are products of the formation of a definite group structure. However, the fact of in-group structure does not necessarily imply the nature of attitudes toward out-groups, as we shall see when discussing the next feature (under 4).

It is certainly not inevitable that dominance, suppression, and ruthless competition should rule supreme in determining group structure. Anthropologists have taught us that the most coöperative person may be he with highest status in a group. But groups everywhere are hierarchical along some dimensions. Even when

men in groups explicitly set out to abolish all distinctions whatso
ever, a group structure develops. Thus the three men who originally banded together on the isolated Atlantic island of Tristan
da Cunha signed an agreement that "No member shall assume
any superiority whatever, but all to be considered equal in every
respect, each performing his proportion of labour, if not prevented by sickness . . ." (55, p. 19). But within the space of five
years, as new members found themselves on the island, a new con-
tract was drawn specifying by name the top status hierarchy which
had developed in the meantime. Today, status on Tristan da
Cunha is based chiefly on proficiency and diligence in work. Self-
assertion or attempts to dominate are not considered proper.
Rather distinction is achieved by quiet and diligent pursuit of
the work to be done.

In his studies plotting informal groups from kindergarten
through the eighth grade, Moreno found progressive capacity on
the part of individuals for reciprocal expectations as stabilized in
differentiated group structures (54). "Cooperative group action"
and "increased differentiation" of children's groups went hand
in hand with increasing awareness and practice of adult status
patterns, such as those based on sex distinctions, nationality, and
color differentiations.

Since the expectations of individuals which are standardized
as norms defining various roles in the group are *reciprocal,* the
positions within the group structure imply not only ways of acting, patterns of respect and deference toward others but definite
expectations of the ways oneself will be treated by other group
members. One of the early experimental studies of informal
groups, begun in 1926, found higher relationships between status
in the group and kind of treatment *received* by the person occupying that position than between status and various personality
"traits" of the individual (60). Just how traumatic an experience
it may be to have these standardized expectations of treatment
by others violated can be illustrated from the "front office" group
of a large modern business (where group structure may be almost
as rigid as in an isolated community or sect). In a shifting of

office space, a certain vice-president inadvertently was given a metal desk instead of the mahogany variety common to others in his group. "Why? He pondered and fretted, and began reading hurts, omens, and hidden meanings in every casual conversation. Eventually the matter came out in the open, for the V.P. could go on no longer; he was on the brink of a complete nervous breakdown" (6).

Group structure is polarized around the leader. As evidence in the final section of Chapter 2 indicates, the leader is clearly the most important single *part* of the group structure from the point of view of influencing group activity and maintaining stability of the structure. Toki's experiments substantiate the well-known tendency for groups to be disrupted or to disintegrate temporarily if the leader is removed (74). But the resumption of group activities and stabilization of structure is not necessarily dependent upon a particular person as leader. If the group is in early stages of formation, as in Toki's experiments, or is faced with a persistently unstable (unstructured) situation, as in periods of economic, military, or political crises when old leaders lose their magic, a new structure takes shape polarized around different individuals as leaders.

The standardized expectations (norms) defining the role of leadership are more exacting, require greater obligations, greater responsibility than those for other positions in the group (78). The group has higher aspirations for the leader, and the leader, in turn, sets higher levels of attainment for himself (29). Thus the leader operates within more or less definite limits defined in the interaction process. While the leader has the greatest opportunity for shifting or changing group activity, group aspirations, group values, his behavior is subject to a narrow latitude of tolerance or acceptability which does not apply to other group members. The leader may seek to widen this *range of tolerable behavior* at times; and he may be successful in doing so, particularly if the group faces situations fraught with serious problems and widespread uncertainty (unstructured situations). However, ordinarily if he steps too far beyond the limits of this range of tolerable behavior for his leadership role in matters of consequence to the group, he may look forward to a struggle to maintain his position, or he may wake up to find himself lower in the group's status hierarchy. An extreme possibility may be illustrated by the fate of one O'Brien, who was leader of the elite ore-trimmers' union on a Lake Michigan port. As president of the union, he was sent to Cleveland to negotiate a pay scale for the coming season. Instead, O'Brien became involved in a deal to transfer his men to a new union—one which would trim ore for less than he was delegated to demand. When he began to carry out the scheme, a furor arose. When the men caught up with him, "O'Brien was ready for ten months in a hospital and nobody on the street seemed to know who had prepared him" (31).

The focus of power in the group resides in the leader position. In informally organized groups, the leader emerges as a result of his relatively greater contribution to the interaction process in areas of consequence to the group. In terms of the primary choices by members for friendly association, the leader is not necessarily the most "popular" individual. But if the group achieves any sort of stability, the leader will be central in the choices of other "popular" members (36). Thus his channels of personal influence extend to all parts of the group. At the same time the leader may secure tangible means or weapons of power. As we shall see presently, few, if any, characteristics of in-groups are immune to influences of other groups. In power relationships, this is particularly the case where the means of exerting or expressing power within the in-group or outside the group are a matter of particular consequence to the group in achieving its goals. Then he who secures the means of power, whether from within his own group or with the interested aid of other groups, may be recognized as the leader without any coercion on his own part. The power structure of the group in this case is dependent upon other power structures outside of the group.

When reciprocities and expectations become stabilized into a definite group structure and each group member lives up to the standardized expectations defining his relative role, group *soli-*

darity is at its maximum. The state of affairs referred to as "morale" is a consequence of the relative degree of stabilization of reciprocal expectations of group members in various positions and the degree to which these expectations are consistently fulfilled. Being the polar zone of high expectations with a narrower latitude or range of tolerable behavior, the upper status hierarchies are more crucial in creating and maintaining the experience of group solidarity (high morale) (37).

To illustrate some of the above points concerning group structure, we will consider briefly some of the results of deliberate encouragement of informal groupings within a formal organization—the Marine Corps—and attempts to utilize this informal organization to achieve the ends of the Marine Corps in wartime. We refer to the famous "Carlson Raiders" of World War II (7). Carlson set out to foster the formation of an in-group of men with firm convictions about the war which would include both officers and men. (Informal groups among military rank and file customarily do not include officers.) Traditional distinctions between officers and men which Carlson felt were not essential to carrying out the tasks to be done were minimized or eliminated (e.g., separate mess for officers). At every step in the rigorous and varied training, the men were informed of the plans and the purpose of the plans. Thus reciprocal expectations were stabilized among the men and the function of each was seen in terms of the goals of the group. Necessarily the officers had to prove their worth as leaders. As the most important, Carlson demonstrated his "absolute fearlessness." "He was always cool as lettuce. . . . When the man who leads you has no fear, you feel safe" (p. 298).

"The Old Man showed that he admired and respected us, and we saw that there wasn't anybody who loved our country more than he did—and that's why we loved him" (p. 36).

These procedures resulted in an in-group formation capable of performing heroic deeds under terrible combat conditions. It was virtually unnecessary for Carlson to exert formal disciplinary measures. Group solidarity stemming from the stable and fulfilled expectations of the men made self-discipline a reality (i.e., norms were internalized).

A consequence of the group solidarity was personal security for individual members. During the terrible days of Guadalcanal, only one case of war neurosis occurred in the Raiders. *Fortune* quotes Lieutenant Commander E. Rogers Smith, naval psychiatrist, as saying that, with the exception of the Raiders, the strain and stress of Guadalcanal produced "a group neurosis which has not been seen before and may never be seen again" among "healthy, toughened, well-trained men" (7, p. 332).

The crucial feature for the sake of illustration is that a sequence of events occurred demonstrating the way in which group solidarity and high morale achieved in the Carlson Raiders were dependent upon the fulfillment of stabilized, reciprocal expectations defining the role structure. The leader in a military group necessarily has relatively greater obligations and responsibilities, if only because of the seriousness of the situations the group faces. In this case, the leader, Carlson, had deliberately fostered an in-group structure in which high expectations were standardized and had made himself the model in meeting them. After a year of difficult combat, there came a time when Carlson could not fulfill these high expectations. The Raiders counted on a rest period such as other groups had been given. Instead they were ordered to combat again. Carlson requested materials to make living conditions more bearable for the men. None were forthcoming. Evidently this was beyond Carlson's control; but being a loyal Marine officer, he refused to put the blame on higher Marine echelons. When his men asked questions, he answered in a general way which seemed evasive. It seemed that he had "let them down."

In contrast to the earlier period of solidarity, morale was low. Some of the men began to use the group's slogan (which signified their working together) in a derisive fashion. There was "hell in the ranks." Some men "began to accuse Carlson of being no different from other brass hats. There were words about Carlson spoken in the tents during this period which had never been spoken by his men before. Many of the men were convinced that all his talk had been a trick to get them to give more, work harder, sacrifice more. They held him responsible for their disappointments" (7, p. 313).

It was not until Carlson was removed from the Raiders for another duty that the men realized the truth. When he left, a correspondent reported seeing the men "cry like babies." When a more orthodox Marine officer took Carlson's place, "all complaint against Carlson vanished" (p. 317). They were aware that the in-group structure and its norms were "dead." One "amateur balladist" put it in a song: "Give up your Raider schemes, Give up your Raider dreams, In the memory of men, there were those who were brave. . . ."

The formation of group structure generates a variety of by-products, among them the standardized reciprocities and expectations referred to in the above paragraphs. We shall deal with these by-products of group interaction under the generic term *social norms*.

4. When interaction of individuals with common motives or goals endures for a sufficient time, *by-products* of the interaction process, such as catchwords, jargon, nicknames, slogans, customs, values, and the like, are standardized. Many of the most significant by-products of group interaction may be grouped under the generic term *social norms*. Norms, or group standards, may arise and be standardized in relation to any matters of consequence (or, to use Festinger and Schachter's term, "relevance") to the group. These norms relate to such areas as ways of doing things, expectations for various role positions, shared aspirations, notions of value, and the like. They crystallize in short-cut forms how the individual members should behave within the group and what things are important to the group. Social norms are values to be abided by, upheld, and cherished by group members. Noting the regulating function of group norms in social life, Sherif (68) demonstrated experimentally that social norms are formed in group situations and subsequently serve as standards for the in-

dividual's perception and judgment when he is not in the group situation. The individual's major social attitudes are formed in relation to group norms. Henceforth, hís behavior in related situations is governed by attitudes whose content and directions are derived from these norms.

In any group, separation of the in-group from out-groups which occurs as group structure takes definite shape implies some sort of norms in relation to the in-group and its members and in relation to out-groups and their members. The nature of norms standardized toward out-groups will, of course, be heavily dependent upon the goals, aspirations, and type of status hierarchy in the in-group, as these relate to the position, aspirations, and goals of the out-group. When those who comprise the "they" (in contrast to the in-group) are seen as obstacles in the way of achieving group goals, or as objects of manipulation to serve in-group ends, norms relating to out-groups will be negative in character. On the other hand, should the goals and norms of the out-group and its members be supplementary to those of the in-group, so that relations between the two groups are characterized by mutual dependence, or should achievement of the goals of the out-group be necessary for fulfillment of in-group aspirations, norms in relation to the out-group will tend to be positive in character. The positive or negative picture of relations between groups which is so crucial in determining the nature of norms toward the particular out-group may be determined by actual compatibility or conflict in the goals or aspirations of the groups or may result from the efforts of interested parties within the group, or even outside of the group in question, to spread a certain kind of picture to the rank and file. Experimental verification of these points is presented in Chapter 10.

Norms arise in group interaction even in cases where the group has organized around rebellion or deviation from the "rules" of organized society. The Labadist Colony in Maryland, an offshoot of the Reformed Church of Netherlands, centered around a belief in freedom from all law other than Divine Law. In the course of time, a hierarchical structure developed and "freedom from law," though applied to laws external to the group, was not applicable for norms which inevitably were standardized within the in-group (38).

In summarizing some of the characteristics of sects which isolate themselves (either socially or geographically) through nonconformity to the norms of the larger society, Gillin noted: "In the beginning, their tenets are negative in their origin. They do *not* swear, do *not* take arms, do *not* wear gaudy clothing or ornaments, do *not* baptize infants, and do *not* have church sacraments. Then gradually they build up a body of positive doctrines and practices which easily can be seen to have been brought into the circle of social consciousness by their opposition to the social class holding the other doctrine" (27, p. 429).

Even such fluctuating and variable groups as migrant workers ("hobos") have definite norms which developed as they came together in work situations and in camps ("jungles"). For example, definite norms are standardized concerning the proper ways to act when using a camp (which may be nothing more than a place where cooking and sleeping can take place without detection of authorities). Anderson lists seven norms in relation to hobo jungles the violation of which constitute "jungle crimes" (4).

If he is to be considered a member with any standing at all and not an object of pity, derision, or ridicule, the individual must act in terms of the norms of his group (reference group). This fact comes out clearly in the clique and gang studies of Thrasher, Shaw, and Whyte (67, 75, 78). In order to take any place in the group structure, the individual must show that he is a worthy group member by abiding by its major norms. Merei's studies of children's groups referred to in Chapter 2 demonstrate this strikingly in the case of individuals who strive toward the upper levels of the structure. Children who were older than the group and had been leaders in other situations were introduced into the group after a clear-cut tradition (set of group norms) had taken shape. In order to achieve a place in the group structure, these individuals had first of all to conform to the group's norms. Leadership was attained by some within the framework of these established norms. A few exceptional individuals succeeded in altering tradition (norms), after becoming a good member, through introducing minor variations and then bringing new elements into the weakened norm system. Merei finds the "plus" that appears in group situations a consequence of the set of norms standardized in the group: "Thus the group 'plus' is not some substance hovering above the group: it is the hold their customs and habits have on the members; it is tradition, the carrier of which is the individual, who, in turn, is strengthened by it. Conceivably, the feeling of heightened intensity always evoked by group experience is the experiencing of just this 'plus' " (49, p. 35).

Studying children's play groups from kindergarten through middle childhood, Piaget (62) demonstrated that the capacity to internalize group norms or "rules of the game" develops hand in hand with the increasing ability to see that others have a point of view and to deal with others on a reciprocal, give-and-take basis. These findings imply that internalization of group norms is not possible until the individual's self is delimited from other persons and elaborated in the course of social interaction. The significant conclusion is that norms are internalized when they become a part of the individual's self-system—a constituent part of his ego. When group norms are internalized by the individual, he behaves as a group member even though he is not with the group because the internalized group norms are a part of his personal identity (69).

When individual members participate in the formation of group norms, they assent to them internally. This is the significance of the studies by Lewin and his associates on "group decision" (43). When group members take part in the formation of a group norm, it is internalized. If they are good members of the group, violating the norm will arouse pangs of "conscience" even though no one may know of the violation.

The degree to which norms are internalized is highly related to the *solidarity* of the group. Thus in time of defeat, crisis, or disorganization, deviations from norms may become rampant. When group ties are weakened or cut, internalized norms tend to lose their potency. On the other hand, group solidarity implies that more or less definite reciprocal expectations among group members are fulfilled, consequently that self-discipline with little or no external coercion is the rule.

Earlier in this chapter we noted some of the external means by which production norms are maintained in informal groups in industry. Gardner reports that in one such group, where rates were established for work finished by the group but the foreman checked on individual output, "fast workers would let the others have part of their output. If too high, they would either 'give it away' or just not report part of the work actually done" (26, p. 157). Thus even when external coercion is not applied, group members may spontaneously regulate their behavior in terms of group norms though other personal benefits are reduced.

In the group which formed the first coöperative store in England, it became apparent that members must trade with the store if it was to survive competition from merchants. In one instance, a woman who had been sending her child to a nearby store insisted that the child walk to the coöperative, more than a mile away, in spite of the effort and inconvenience involved (33).

When the individual internalizes group norms which run counter to individual capacities and trends, he is in for a difficult time, even if the group understands his conflict and exerts only mild correctives. In a German prisoner-of-war camp, a tall Basque prisoner "who was extraordinarily powerful and adept," being a good member of the prisoner group, tried to slow his work performance in accordance with the group norm of equalizing work production for each member so that none would be punished by the Germans. ". . . Try as he might to control his movements, little by little his energy would get the better of him and he would resume his normal rhythm. 'I don't know how to slow down' he would say with sincere embarrassment. So when the foreman's back was turned he would throw shovelfuls into his neighbor's wagon in order to satisfy both his need to expend himself and his spirit of solidarity" (3, p. 37).

It should be noted that the form of external coercions exerted to secure conformity to group norms is itself standardized in the interaction process. We have noted the practice of "binging" (hitting) in work groups. In a community which has been more or less isolated over a long period, both positive norms, or imperatives, and group sanctions are clear cut, well known, and—so long as life goes on in the familiar pattern—relatively rigid. Brummitt surveyed such a community in Casey County, Kentucky. People who came into the community with new ideas from the outside saw them "laughed out of use." "People who do not live as it is generally felt would be best for themselves and everyone else concerned are almost forced to move away. There is certainly order in what will follow as a result of all action. No individual lacks social security in whatever level of society he chooses, yet every social sin has a punishment well known to any member" (10, p. 126).

Of course, the same degree of conformity is not required in relation to every norm of the group. Deviation of minor norms may be overlooked or merely frowned upon. The demands for conformity will be proportional to the importance of the norm in question to the smooth functioning of the group toward its goals. Therefore, in cases of norms regulating matters concerning the identity and existence of the group, its maintenance and well-being, the demands for conformity are stricter and deviation is less tolerated. It is probably possible to make a scale of the *range of tolerable behavior* for various norms of a group. The more consequential the norms, the narrower the limits of this range.

Sussman (73) tells of IBM operators in an office who had formed a tight little in-group. Outside of working together, their chief function seems to have been lunching together in the company cafeteria, where they occupied the same table every day. Because they had special training in their work and received more pay, they considered themselves superior to other groups. They dressed for the superior position and were unfriendly to others. The company, thinking this an undesirable situation, publicly urged all employees not to engage in "snobbery." One group member took this to heart and started eating occasionally with other girls. Now since eating lunch together constituted the major social activity of the group, this girl was at first censured mildly, then subjected to a silent treatment, and finally ostracized by her own group. No one would speak to her in the office; her only communication was with her superior. This seems harsh treatment indeed for such an apparently harmless act as eating lunch outside the group. But the range of tolerable behavior for this norm was very narrow because it was central in importance to this little group. Perhaps if the girl had merely smiled and acted in a friendly fashion to others she would not have crossed the limits of the range of tolerable behavior and incurred ostracism by the group.

Another implication of this illustration is that every group has norms defining a *range of tolerable behavior* toward various out-groups. This range will, of course, vary, being broadest in the case of out-groups with whom friendly or coöperative relations are maintained and narrowest for those groups kept at greatest social distance. If the behavior of the individual member goes beyond the limits of this range standardized in relation to the particular out-group in question, he will be the object of correctives from the group just as he would be if he exceeded the range of tolerable or permissible behavior in relation to any other group norm. For example, if lynching were considered beyond the limits of tolerable behavior in relation to members of an out-group, external force outside the group would not be required to stop lynching. In-group members would consider it an intolerable act and would take measures to prevent it as criminal.

SOME RECURRENCES OF INTERGROUP BEHAVIOR IN CONTEMPORARY HUMAN RELATIONS

The material presented in this book permits us to draw certain conclusions concerning intergroup behavior. At this point we shall concentrate on three conclusions which appear to us particularly important, both from the point of view of practical relevance and for the fruitful research possibilities they embody.

1. The typical case of intergroup behavior, as we have seen,

does not pertain to the area of deviate behavior. The typical case of intergroup behavior is that which is represented by the great body of group members when they comply, in word and in action, with the in-group trends and social-distance scale in relation to out-groups and their members. Every group, whether formally or informally organized initially, has a definite structure of its own and a set of norms defining the attitudes, the expected modes of behavior, and hence the roles of individual members in relation to (a) other members in the group occupying various statuses within it and (b) out-groups and their members as prescribed by their respective places on the social-distance scale.

This major conclusion is reached on the basis of our survey of prejudice studies in Chapters 4 and 5 and of the principles presented in Chapter 6. It became necessary to discuss at some length the behavior of individuals as in-group members with

a. an account of the formation and functioning of in-groups consisting of individuals who gravitate toward one another impelled by some common motivation, and

b. an account of the conformity to group norms achieved both through inner necessity and desire felt by the members and through correctives exerted by the group.

2. In-group demarcation is coincidental with the rise of norms and stereotypes regulating the behavior of members in relation to out-groups and their members (Chapters 5, 7, 8). These norms toward out-groups constitute the social-distance scale of the group with standardized attributions (stereotypes) attached to the out-groups in question. The norms toward out-groups are primarily determined by the nature of relations between groups. As such, norms toward out-groups need not correspond to the positive or negative nature of relations practiced within the in-group. Norms followed within the in-group may be democratic and coöperative in nature. It does not follow that norms developed toward out-groups in general will be democratic and coöperative. Depending on the nature of intergroup relations, at times the greater degree of solidarity and coöperativeness within the in-group may mean more effective friction with out-groups. In ethnological literature,

we find cultures which are neither quarrelsome nor bloodthirsty among themselves but most ferocious to outsiders. This is not a fact peculiar to "primitive" cultures alone. The case of colonial powers during recent centuries who had one code for their in-group members and a quite different code in relation to "natives" is too well known to need documentation. Full realization of the fact that developing harmonious in-group practices need not necessarily resolve intergroup friction has significant theoretical and practical implications. For one thing, this realization will lead us to put greater emphasis on conceptions of "we-ness" and "they-ness," and on functional relations between groups as such.

3. In-groups today are no longer closed systems. They are no more the independent and autonomous systems that they might have been once. Their functioning is considerably—at times, decisively—affected by their relations to other groups in the present-day state of increased technological, economic, and cultural interdependence. The regulation of intergroup behavior primarily by the prescriptions of the existing social-distance (prejudice) scale is, therefore, no more the preponderant general rule. Under more stable, more settled conditions, intergroup behavior exhibited by in-group members was largely a function of the prescriptions of the prejudice scale. It still is to an impressive degree. But in numerous instances today, the impact of other influences proves to be weightier in determining the structuring of the trend and practice of intergroup relations. In such cases the weight of the social-distance scale as a factor is no longer great enough to serve as the main anchorage in the frame of reference of intergroup behavior. Some other influence stemming from the rising conditions of modern life becomes the weightier, and on occasion the decisive, factor. This influence may be the changed nature of vital interests between groups. It may be the changes brought about in intra- and intergroup relations through the transforming effect of a technological advance. It may be a situationally determined factor which weighs more heavily when two or more opposing factors are operative. It may be due to discrepancies in the conflicting influences coming from the unintegrated nature of superordinate

and subordinate values fighting for supremacy at the time. Or it may be due to the individual's change of reference groups in a setting of flux of contacts which are conducive to such crossings. The above generalizations are based on typical recurrences we noted in our survey of a good many empirical observations reported in the literature dealing with intergroup behavior. We shall illustrate each major type with what appears to us a representative example.

When the area of relations between two groups is of vital concern for the groups in question, intergroup relations affect not only norms toward the out-group but in-group norms as well. In some cases, the influence of relations between groups is sufficiently strong to make in-group norms seem incomprehensible without reference to intergroup relations. Earlier in the chapter we noted that informal work groups set rates for their own production. As Roethlisberger and Dickson found, this rate setting constitutes a group norm. The reasons why the in-group norms are set at a particular level are not adequately explained by relations within the in-group. Take the case of a new radial drill operator in a machine shop. He understood that the piecework rates would permit him to average $1.25 an hour. But this notion was quickly corrected by a fellow worker with high seniority:

"Well, what do you suppose would happen if I turned in $1.25 an hour on these pump bodies?". . .

"They'd have to pay you, wouldn't they? Isn't that the agreement?"

"Yes! They'd pay me—once! Don't you know that if I turned in $1.25 an hour on these pump bodies tonight, the whole God-damned Methods Department would be down here tomorrow? And they'd retime this job so quick it would make your head swim! And when they retimed it, they'd cut the price in half! And I'd be working for 85 cents an hour instead of $1.25!"
. . . .

According to Jack, a couple of operators . . . got to competing with each other to see how much they could turn in. They got up to $1.65 an hour, and the price was cut in half. And from then on they had to run that job themselves, as none of the other operators would accept the job. [65, p. 430]

Whyte reports a case in which hostile relations between the workers and management resulted in the workers' setting low rates for themselves, at times to the point of actual "slowdowns," with considerable financial loss to themselves. However, after the two groups passed a critical period and arrived at some stability in their relations with each other, production went up. "For the first time, stepping up production became a good thing to do—from any point of view. . . . They went after money—to be sure —but only when it fitted into the proper social setting" (79, p. 194). Intergroup conflict may, as Whyte found, exert an even more pervasive influence on in-group expectations and behavior by creating a prolonged unstructured situation with accompanying personal insecurity for group members (p. 210).

Compelling features of intergroup relations may also affect the structure of the in-group. As the most frequent representative of the group in intergroup relations, the leader is particularly vulnerable to such influence. If, perhaps through no fault of his own, he is unable to fend for his group, protect it, support its goals when he ventures into the area of vital relations with other groups, the result may be increased frustration of the group expectations and consequent loss of influence by the leader (61).

In the area of behavior toward out-groups, shifts in the nature of functional relations between groups are conducive to changes in behavior toward the out-group, even though these may run counter to the regulation of the existing social-distance scales. Killian's investigation of southern white migrants in Chicago provides an instructive illustration of this point (40). The migrants came from specific local areas in the South to definite local communities in Chicago. Other white groups on Chicago's West Side looked down on them as culturally inferior "hillbillies." Coming from an area where their native, white, Protestant stock assured them a position in the dominant southern group, the migrants regarded themselves as "real Americans" who were being unjustly disliked and mistreated, whose superiorities were not recognized. In many ways these transplanted southerners took on characteristics of a minority group.

In contrast to intergroup relations in the South, where their position, though lowly, was definitely superior to that of Negroes and was supported by law and tradition, their new situation in the poor section of Chicago was characterized both in work and in the city by nonsegregation of Negroes. Did they cling to the southern position in their behavior toward Negroes?

Briefly, Killian found that some members tried to do so initially, but most came to realize the impracticality of such attempts in the new situation.

. . . The predominant reactions of the southern whites to non-segregation of Negroes were *acceptance* of the situation or *avoidance* by self-drawal; overt aggression or attempts to force withdrawal of Negroes were exceptional rather than normal. Acceptance was accompanied by certain standard explanations, including: (1) "When in Rome, do as the Romans do," (2) "you can't go against the law," and (3) "the Negroes are more powerful than the whites and you can't fight them". . . their behavior in the new situation did not conform to the old group norms of "asserting white supremacy"; in spite of lip-service paid to the old norms, behavior now conformed to the new norms of accommodation evolved in an novel situation. [40]

This is a striking case of new behavior patterns running counter to the existing social-distance scale in response to different functional relations between groups.

Advances in technology which make the use of certain devices, methods, or employment obsolete are conducive to bringing about change in the scheme of human relations sanctioned by the older devices. New technological developments may also result in the formation of new in-group structures.

Technological innovations may result in breakdown of the existing in-group structure or its cleavage into smaller in-groups. Sayles reports the case of a group of metal polishers whose precision work had given them considerable prestige in the plant and who had been a solid core for union organization (66). Then the company introduced a new extrusion machine eliminating the need for as many polishers. At the same time, the falling off of orders after the war resulted in production cutbacks. The in-group of polishers split into cliques chiefly on the basis of seniority. The union leader had little enthusiastic backing. "Absent is the unified spirit that motivated the 'reckless' attitude of the war years. The changes management induced in the department and the conflicts that resulted have sapped these energies" (p. 10).

When technological change is more extensive in scope and produces breakdowns of old in-group alignments, new in-group structures of broad scope may take shape. Warner and Low trace the rise of industrial unions in "Yankee City" due to the technological developments which leveled off the groupings based on skill and made the majority of workers "interchangeable cogs in a machine" (77). At the same time, the factories had become but units in impersonal and distant organizations. The gap between owners and workers was widened from both sides, and the situation was conducive to common group membership of all workers in the factories.

Relatively sudden technological changes may result in abrupt shifts in the direction of intergroup relations, depending on the common or antagonistic interests of groups facing the change. Such shifts in alignments were the striking finding in Cottrell's study of a town which actually faced "Death by Dieselization." The town had been built in the middle of a desert by a railroad to service steam locomotives. The people had been encouraged by the company to live and settle down there, and relations between company and workers were friendly. Then the company shifted to Diesel engines, a change which ordinarily might have been gradual but was hastened by the heavy demands of the war years on old steam engines. This change made the town obsolete, for Diesel engines do not require such frequent servicing. The railroad workers reacted with hostility toward the railroad, putting the friendly relations into the past. On the other hand, groups of townspeople who had been regarded with suspicion or hostility by the workers, e.g., merchants, now became strong allies in the workers' efforts to keep the town alive (14). Similar close coöperation and mutual support occurred between workers and supervisory personnel when a steel company decided to move a plant to another city for reasons of increased efficiency and economy (76). Such a relationship is not wholly in accordance with usual norms of either group relating to the other. But this was a small consideration when both groups faced so serious a threat to their welfare.

Since individuals in modern societies are usually members of more than one in-group (reference group), interpersonal relations within an in-group may be changed as a result of relations between two different groups having overlapping memberships with the in-group in question. If this intergroup relationship is one of intense conflict, much depends on which side in-group members take. For example, striking workers have refused to participate in the services of their church when a non-striker was present, and when in a majority have made the church group so uncomfortable for members who did not support the strike that the latter withdrew (30).

Conflicting group norms and trends on the same issue tend to produce contradictions between verbally expressed opinion and actual behavior. This stems from the fact that individuals today in highly complex Western societies are members, at the same time, of different groups which are all interrelated parts of one society. Therefore, they are caught now in a *situation* which favors behavior in line with the norm or rule from one source and then in a *situation* which favors behavior required by the opposite norm stemming from another source.

In public entertainment places, restaurants, and taverns in states in which liberal trends and old norms exist simultaneously, one finds striking cases of contradictory intergroup behavior. The following observation in Elmira, New York is a typical illustration of the point: "Five Negroes (two of them fieldworkers) stopped in at another tavern to have a drink. The bartender was extremely friendly. A few hours later, white fieldworkers asked him if Negroes ever came to his place. He denied that they did. Another fieldworker put the same question to his wife a few days later. She also denied it" (16).

The most serious cases of discrepancy in intergroup relations creating conflict situations for people caught in them are due to conflicts among the norms and regulations of local groups and the superordinate of which local groups are parts. Various authors on intergroup relations have called attention to the fact and consequences of discrepancy between norms of subordinates and superordinates (58, 80, 81).

The analysis of the intergroup behavior of individuals who belong to different subordinate groups of a larger society in terms of the points developed in connection with our discussion of reference groups has significant practical implications (Chapter 7).

The relative positions on the social-distance scale of various groups within a country are functionally related to one another. In this scheme of things, the group at the upper end of the scale, being the more powerful in all areas of living, exerts greater weight than others. There is a strong tendency for the group at the upper end of the scale to serve as the main anchor. Status, occupation, prestige strivings are in the direction of equilibration with the main anchor. When members of groups low on the social-distance scale find themselves barred from their moves in the upward direction in so many respects (social, occupational, etc.) because of vertically standardized segregation demarcations, the psychological consequence is continual thwarting of aspirations, frustrations, and conflicts.

These psychological consequences become intensified in periods of change. During such periods, members of a subordinate group come to realize more and more their potentialities on a par with any other group. As they prove their competence in the arts, in science, in professions, and in industrial life, the conception of self limited to a "place" subordinate to the dominant group tends to be rejected. And in times of emergency, such as war, the larger society may require of them the same service demanded of any other citizen. Such times serve as a compelling reminder of the democratic ideals announced today as applying to all individuals. The demarcation lines prescribed by the social-distance scale stand in marked contrast and conflict to such values.

Situations and opportunities in periods of change tend to encourage, or even demand, of the member of a minority group that he conceive of himself also as a full-fledged citizen of the larger society like anyone else. Inevitably the equilibration of status and role relations in terms of common standards for all groups (majority and minority) becomes more compelling. These standards serve now as a common anchorage for all groups, including the minority groups. But at the same time, the established demarcation lines require that the member of a minority group conceive of himself not just as different but as inferior. Thus he is placed simultaneously in two psychologically incompatible positions.

For the subordinate group, low on the social-distance scale, problems of obtaining the vital necessities, means of livelihood, adequate housing, and medical, educational, and recreational facilities, are of course matters of central and basic importance, as they are to any group. But if these things were actually provided on the "equal but separate" basis, serious experiences of frustration and conflict would still be generated for individual members as long as demarcation lines were drawn demanding that they regulate their status and role relations in many areas of life (economic, social, political, etc.) at a lower level than that of common standards for the society as a whole. The "equal but separate" formula requires the impossible psychological feat of conceiving of oneself and of regulating one's strivings, aspirations, goals simultaneously in terms of two conflicting sets of standards —the common standard for all citizens in a society and the lower standards of a subordinate group. This feat is psychologically impossible in the sense that it will always result in varying degrees of personal conflict, frustration, insecurity with all their by-products and results.

PROBLEMS OF CHANGE OF INTERGROUP ATTITUDES

As noted in Chapter 1, many groups and agencies, impelled by practical considerations and sincere desires for more harmonious intergroup relations, are engaged in attempts to reduce tension among groups. It is difficult to assess the results of such efforts. Probably, while some have contributed to reduction of intergroup hostility in specific instances, others have had little or no effect on the people to whom the efforts are directed, and some may have resulted in reaffirmation by group members of their stand toward out-groups held at considerable social distance (23, 80).

However impressive the quantity of such efforts, it is well to keep in mind that they are but "drops in the bucket" when compared to forces directed toward perpetuating existing demarcations. Numerous studies are available showing that the practices and emphasis in the bulk of popular literature, newspapers, presentations by mass mediums of communication, educational texts, and opportunities are much more favorable to maintenance of existing social-distance demarcations than to their change (12, 13, 71, 83).

The reduction of group prejudice, as Horowitz' studies of children's prejudices demonstrated, implies change of attitudes derived from social-distance scales established for a group. When the implications of the problem so stated are seriously considered, it is really not surprising that piecemeal attempts at changing intergroup attitudes through exposure to brief contacts or information bring conflicting and generally inadequate results (80).

The implications of the outline of in-group formation and functioning presented in this chapter offer leads for the problem of changing intergroup attitudes based on empirical evidence and established principles. Ordinarily the factors leading individuals to form attitudes of prejudice are not piecemeal. Rather their formation is functionally related to becoming a group member— to adopting the group and its values (norms) as the main anchorage in regulating experience and behavior. When individuals cease to conform to group situations merely in response to external pressures from the group and internalize group standards or norms, the group becomes a *reference group* for the individual (Chapter 7). After the early childhood period, the self becomes a classificatory system based on demarcation lines prevalent in one's reference groups (56). Other groups are evaluated by one in terms of their relation (social proximity or distance) to his reference group. His goals and aspirations in matters relating to these out-groups are, on the whole, regulated by standardized expectations of his group (reference group) in relation to other groups and are shifted up and down accordingly (11, 20, 47).

Lasting and consistent changes in attitudes toward out-groups, therefore, can be expected (1) when individuals become psychologically related to a new reference group with differing norms in relation to out-groups or (2) when the norms established in the individual's present reference group are changed. In the words of Lewin and Grabbe: "Re-education influences conduct only when the new system of values and beliefs dominates the individual's perception. The acceptance of the new system is linked with the acceptance of a specific group, a particular role, a definite source of authority as points of reference" (44, p. 68).

Thus, the girls of conservative background who adopted the Bennington College group with more liberal out-group norms as their *reference group* changed their attitudes in the liberal direction, while those whose main anchorage remained the home, old friends, or small conservative groups in the Bennington setting continued to be more conservative (59). Change in intergroup attitudes with changed reference groups is no doubt the representative case for individuals who are "nonconformists" or "dissenters" from the larger social setting in these respects (34, 57).

Social-distance scales retain remarkably similar characteristics over a period of time; however, as mentioned in Chapter 4, they are by no means unchanging. Having developed historically as a product of specific types of relationships among groups, established scales are altered by striking changes in intergroup relations over a period of time. Thus the events of World War II resulted in the falling of the Germans and Japanese down the scale, and the moving upward of some other groups, the Chinese for example (8, 48).

The use of communication from outside to effect shifts in in-group norms is subject to all the handicaps of piecemeal attempts mentioned above. It is true that radio, movies, television, and other mass mediums of communication are dramatically effective in involving individuals in group values and influencing their choices of goals. But as Flowerman has pointed out, it is one thing to make a certain kind of soap irresistible by involving the individual through his group's norms of cleanliness and attractiveness, and quite another to use mass mediums in attempting to involve the individual in norms which run counter to the norms of his group (24). A very common reaction of individuals to such attempts seem to be to ignore, avoid, or forget them, or to perceive the communication as so foreign to oneself that it can only be attributed to sources alien and hostile to one's own groups (23, 42, 80). In some cases, communication contrary to the norms of one's own group boomerangs, producing effects opposite to those intended (24, 80).

From a theoretical point of view, such reactions to propaganda differing from the norms of the individual's reference group seem closely akin to the contrast and assimilation effects observed in simple perceptual and judgmental situations. Since every in-group has a set of norms toward out-groups, we can predict that communications which fall within the *range of tolerable viewpoints* within a group may be assimilated to its scale of values under favorable conditions. On the other hand, communication representing a stand far beyond the in-group's scale of values may result in a shrinking or restriction of the group's range of tolerable views and a reaffirmation of them. When communication represents a viewpoint so distant from the in-group's that it is alien to values either within the in-group or within the large unit of which the in-group is a part, it may have no effect whatsoever on the in-group's value scale. Coming from an entirely different value system, it may easily be ignored or forgotten.

Persons of good will often express the belief that *contact* breeds friendly association between members of different groups. The difficulty here is that contact may also very well breed increased hostility and sharpening demarcations between in-groups, as certain reports of intergroup contacts in industrial situations indicate (35). A study in the Near East shows that in-groups may be most hostile to those groups with which they come in closest contact (18). Ram and Murphy's analysis of intergroup relations in India substantiates the point that contact between members of bitterly hostile in-groups exerts surprisingly little influence on the attitudes of in-group members (63). Members of antagonistic groups may be almost completely unaware of the other's problems or hardships because their perspective in intergroup contacts is the standardized viewpoint of their own group. Even personal suffering in intergroup relations may contribute little to the individual's view of the out-group. Hindu refugees who had suffered at Muslim hands and those who had escaped without personal tragedy seemed equally hostile toward Muslims.

Obviously, "contact" is a blanket term. Therefore, in any discussion of the effects of contact on intergroup attitudes, we must specify: What *kind* of contact? Contact in *what capacity?* Summarizing very briefly a considerable body of evidence accumulated in recent years, the overall picture seems to be as follows: While friendly associations with an individual member of an out-group held at considerable distance may *become* important in changed attitudes toward the out-group, it is more likely that the out-group member in question will be considered simply as an *exceptional* member of the out-group, therefore not possessing the stereotyped traits attached to the out-group. In situations in which in-group members meet with members of an out-group held at considerable distance on a very limited scale, such as a tea party, there is little likelihood of change in attitudes of in-group members. When members of socially distant out-groups work in the same place of employment (e.g., a department store) with approximately equal status, and this condition is set forth in unequivocal terms as necessary for the employment, individuals are likely to develop more favorable attitudes toward out-group members as these relate to employment situations (28). This development does not necessarily imply transfer of favorable attitudes to other situations. When individuals of socially distant in-groups live in adjacent or the same dwelling units, changes in attitudes toward the out-group may occur in either positive or negative direction, depending in part upon the opportunities presented for neighborly association by being physically relatively close or distant to out-group members (**17, 82**). Positive changes tend to occur among individuals *"who have relatively intimate contacts with Negroes and perceive these contacts as socially approved, and, as a result change in their attitudes"* (**82,** p. 69, italics in original). However, there is some indication that individuals who do, under these circumstances, change to a more favorable attitude toward Negroes do not change in the same degree their attitudes toward members of other out-groups (**17,** pp. 104 f.).

At the opposite pole from discrete or isolated contact of individuals as members of different in-groups are situations in which members of traditionally hostile out-groups work, live, and spend leisure time together over a period of time in an in-group with norms favoring the reduction or elimination of prejudice. The indications are, in this case, that individuals may change their attitudes as they become in-group members and share experiences within the group with individuals belonging to traditionally delineated out-groups (**9**).

This highly generalized picture substantiates the main theme of the present discussion: When contact between members of socially distant out-groups involves joint participation as members in an in-group whose norms favor such participations, the individual's attitudes toward members of the out-group are likely to be altered.

However, so long as individuals belong to different in-groups with conflicting norms in relation to out-groups, such changes may be relatively specific to the area of contact or may be subject to fluctuations as the individual moves from one group setting to another, resulting in apparently inconsistent behavior. Conflicting norms of various functionally related in-groups result inevitably in inconsistencies, not only for members of minority groups, but for majority group members as well. In the latter case, personal conflict is sometimes minimized by socially established demarcation lines marking the point where one shifts from one set of norms to another. Thus miners who work daily with

Negroes as fellow workers leave the darkness underground, go to their segregated washroom, and live the rest of the day in a world having norms of superiority with comparative ease (50).

In the previous section of this chapter, we mentioned again problems of multiple reference groups and the influence of superordinate groupings upon subordinates. In this connection, there is a commonly held belief to the effect that prejudice cannot be legislated out of existence. The effects of superordinates on the intergroup relations of subordinates can perhaps be clarified by conceiving of subordinate groups as parts of the superordinate structure. Now the superordinate, either by legislation, court rulings, pronouncements, or action in specific instances, sets limits for the behavior permissible in intergroup relations of subordinate parts. If the range of permissible behavior set by the superordinate is very wide, or has no clearly defined limits, open conflict between subordinates may be encouraged or at least possible. On the other hand, when the superordinate sets limits to the *range of tolerable behavior* subordinates must keep their intergroup behavior within these limits or suffer correctives of the superordinate. It is possible, of course, that elaborate means for evading or secretly overstepping these limits may be devised by subordinate groups. But so long as subordinate in-groups remain a functional part of the system, they will have to abide by the limits set by the superordinate on the whole, unless they have sufficient weight in the system of functional relationships to change them. Recent evidence indicates that at least in certain areas the setting of definite limits to the range of tolerable behavior for subordinate in-groups may result in the formation of new norms in these areas (39, 52).

REFERENCES

1. Allport, F. H. *Social Psychology*. Boston: Houghton Mifflin, 1924.
2. Allport, G. W. In H. Cantril (ed.), *Tensions That Cause Wars*. Urbana: University of Illinois Press, 1950.
3. Ambriere, Francis. *The Long Holiday*. Chicago: Ziff-Davis, 1948.

4. Anderson, Nels. *The Hobo: The Sociology of the Homeless Man.* Chicago: University of Chicago Press, 1923.

5. Anonymous. The making of the infantryman, *Amer. J. Sociol.,* 1946, *51,* 376–379.

6. Anonymous. Problem for the front office, *Fortune,* 1951, *43,* May, 78 f.

7. Blankfort, M. *The Big Yankee.* Boston: Little, Brown, 1947.

8. Bogardus, E. S. Changes in racial distances, *Internat. J. Opin. & Attit. Res.,* 1947, *1,* 55–62.

9. Brophy, I. N. The luxury of anti-Negro prejudice, *Public Opinion Quart.,* 1946, *9,* 456–466.

10. Brummitt, Jessie A. A survey of an isolated community, Casey County, Kentucky. M.A. thesis, Sociology Department, University of Chicago, 1942.

11. Chapman, D. W., and Volkmann, J. A social determinant of the level of aspiration, *J. abn. & soc. Psychol.,* 1939, *34,* 225–238.

12. Committee on Discrimination in College Admissions. *On Getting into College.* Washington: American Council on Education, 1949.

13. Committee on Study of Teaching Materials. *Intergroup Relations in Teaching Materials.* Washington: American Council on Education, 1949.

14. Cottrell, W. F. Death by dieselization: A case study in the reaction to technological change, *Amer. Sociol. Rev.,* 1951, *10,* 356–365.

15. Dashiell, F. Experimental studies of the influence of social situations on the behavior of individual human adults, in C. Murchison (ed.), *Handbook of Social Psychology.* Worchester: Clark University Press, 1935.

16. Dean, J., and Kohn, M. L. Situational diagnosis and intergroup relations. Unpublished manuscript personally communicated by Professor John Dean of Cornell University.

17. Deutsch, M., and Collins, M. E. *Interracial Housing.* Minneapolis: University of Minnesota Press, 1951.

18. Dodd, S. C. A social distance test in the Near East, *Amer. J. Sociol.,* 1935, *41,* 194–204.

19. Faris, R. E. L. *Social Psychology.* New York: Ronald, 1952.

20. Festinger, L. Wish, expectation, and group standards as factors influencing level of aspiration, *J. abn. & soc. Psychol.,* 1942, *37,* 184–200.

21. Festinger, L., Back, K., Schacter, S., Kelly, H., and Thibaut, J. *Theory and Experiment in Social Communication.* Ann Arbor: Research Center for Group Dynamics, 1952.

22. Festinger, L., Schacter, S., and Back, K. *Social Pressures in Informal Groups.* New York: Harper, 1950.

23. Flowerman, S. H. Mass propaganda in the war against bigotry, *J. abn. & soc. Psychol.,* 1947, *42,* 429–439.

24. Flowerman, S. H. The use of propaganda to reduce prejudice: a refutation, *Internat. J. Opin. & Attit. Res.,* 1949, *3,* 99–108.

25. Gardner, B. B. The factory as a social system, in W. F. Whyte (ed.), *Industry and Society.* New York: McGraw-Hill, 1946.

26. Gardner, B. B. *Human Relations in Industry.* Chicago: Irwin, 1947.

27. Gillin, J. L. A contribution to the sociology of sects, *Amer. J. Sociol.,* 1910, *16,* 236–252.

28. Harding, J., and Hogrefe, R. Attitudes of white department store employees toward Negro co-workers, *J. soc. Issues,* 1952, *8,* 18–28.

29. Harvey, O. J. An experimental approach to the study of status relations in informal groups, to appear in *Amer. Sociol. Rev.,* 1953.

30. Hiller, E. T. *The Strike.* Chicago: University of Chicago Press, 1928.

31. Holbrook, S. H. *Iron Brew, A Century of American Ore and Steel.* New York: Macmillan, 1946.

32. Hollingshead, A. B. *Elmtown's Youth.* New York: Wiley, 1949.

33. Holyoke, G. J. *The History of the Rochdale Pioneers.* New York: Scribner, 1893.

34. Horowitz, E. L. "Race" attitudes, in O. Klineberg (ed.), *Characteristics of the American Negro.* New York: Harper, 1944, Part IV.

35. Hughes, E. C. Race relations in industry, in W. F. Whyte (ed.), *Industry and Society.* New York: McGraw-Hill, 1946.

36. Hunt, J. McV., and Solomon, R. L. The stability and some correlates of group-status in a summer-camp for young boys, *Amer. J. Psychol.,* 1942, *55,* 33–45.

37. Jacobson, E., Charters, W. W., Jr., and Lieberman, S. The use of the role concept in the study of complex organizations, *J. soc. Issues,* 1951, *7,* 18–27.

38. James, B. B. The Labadist Colony in Maryland, *Johns Hopkins Studies in Historical and Political Science,* 1899, *17,* 7–45.

39. Jones, B. A.   The influence of new legal requirements upon patterns of race relations in the South.   Mimeographed paper read before American Sociological Society, Chicago, September, 1951.

40. Killian, L. M.   Southern white laborers in Chicago's West Side. Ph.D. dissertation, University of Chicago, 1949.   Quotations from summaries kindly made available by the author.

41. Killian, L. M.   Disaster and social organization.   Manuscript kindly made available by the author.

42. Lazarsfeld, P. F.   Some remarks on the role of the mass media in so-called tolerance propaganda, *J. soc. Issues*, 1947, *3*, 17–25.

43. Lewin, K.   Group decision and social change, in T. M. Newcomb and E. L. Hartley (eds.), *Readings in Social Psychology*.   New York: Holt, 1947.

44. Lewin, K.   *Resolving Social Conflicts*.   New York: Harper, 1948.

45. Lewin, K., Lippitt, R., and White, R. K.   Patterns of aggressive behavior in experimentally created "social climates," *J. soc. Psychol.*, 1939, *10*, 271–300.

46. Lindsey, Almont.   *The Pullman Strike*.   Chicago: University of Chicago Press, 1942.

47. MacIntosh, A.   Differential effect of the status of the competing group upon the level of aspiration, *Amer. J. Psychol.*, 1942, *55*, 546–554.

48. Meenes, M.   A comparison of racial stereotypes of 1935 and 1942, *J. soc. Psychol.*, 1943, *17*, 327–336.

49. Merei, Ferenc.   Group leadership and institutionalization, *Human Relations*, 1949, *2*, 23–39.

50. Minard, R. D.   Race relationships in the Pocahontas coal field, *J. soc. Issues*, 1952, *8*, 29–44.

51. Moede, W.   *Experimentelle Massenpsychologie*.   Leipzig: Hirzel, 1920.

52. Moore, L. H., and Clark, V.   Attitudes toward Negro education. Mimeographed manuscript kindly made available by the authors.

53. Moreno, F. B.   Sociometric status of children in a nursery school group, *Sociometry*, 1942, *5*, 395–411.

54. Moreno, J. L.   Who shall survive?, *Nervous and Mental Disease Monogr. Series*, No. 58, Washington, 1934.

55. Munch, P. A.   *Sociology of Tristan da Cunha*, Oslo, Norway, 1945.

56. Murphy, G.   *Personality*.   New York: Harper, 1947.

57. Murphy, G., and Likert, R. *Public Opinion and the Individual*. New York: Harper, 1938.

58. Myrdal, G. *An American Dilemma*. New York: Harper, 1944.

59. Newcomb, T. M. Attitude development as a function of reference groups: The Bennington Study, in M. Sherif, *An Outline of Social Psychology*. New York: Harper, 1948.

60. Newstetter, W. I., Feldstein, M. J., and Newcomb, T. M. *Group Adjustment: A Study in Experimental Sociology*. Cleveland: School of Applied Social Sciences, Western Reserve University, 1938.

61. Pelz, D. C. Leadership within a hierarchical organization, *J. soc. Issues*, 1951, *7*, 49–55.

62. Piaget, J. *The Moral Judgment of the Child*. London: Kegan Paul, Trench and Trubner, 1932.

63. Ram, P., and Murphy, G. Recent investigations of Hindu-Muslim relations in India, *Human Organization*, 1952, *11*, 13–16.

64. Roethlisberger, F. J., and Dickson, W. J. *Management and the Worker*, Harvard University Business Research Studies, *21*, No. 9, 1939.

65. Roy, Donald. Quota restriction and goldbricking in a machine shop, *Amer. J. Sociol.*, 1952, *57*, 427–442.

66. Sayles, L. R. A case study of union participation and technological change, *Human Organization*, 1952, *11*, 5–15.

67. Shaw, C. R. *The Jack-Roller*. Chicago: University of Chicago Press, 1930.

68. Sherif, M. A study of some social factors in perception, *Arch. Psychol.*, 1935, No. 187.

69. Sherif, M., and Cantril, H. *The Psychology of Ego-Involvements*. New York: Wiley, 1947.

70. Sherif, M., and Harvey, O. J. A study in ego functioning: Elimination of stable anchorages in individual and group situations, *Sociometry*, 1952, *15*, 272–305.

71. Southern Regional Council, *Race in the News*, Atlanta, Ga.

72. Stouffer, S. A., *et al*. *The American Soldier: Combat and Its Aftermath*. Princeton: Princeton University Press, 1949.

73. Sussman, M. B. Case from personal files kindly communicated to the authors.

74. Toki, K. The leader-follower structure in the school-class, *Japanese J. Psychol.*, 1935, *10*, 27–56; English summary in E. L. Hartley and

R. E. Hartley, *Fundamentals of Social Psychology*. New York: Knopf, 1952.

75. Thrasher, F. M. *The Gang*. Chicago: University of Chicago Press, 1927.

76. Walker, C. R. *Steeltown, An Industrial Case History of the Conflict Between Progress and Security*. New York: Harper, 1950.

77. Warner, W. L., and Low, J. O. The Factory in the Community, in W. F. Whyte (ed.), *Industry and Society*. New York: McGraw-Hill, 1946.

78. Whyte, W. F. *Street Corner Society*. Chicago: University of Chicago Press, 1943.

79. Whyte, W. F. *Pattern for Industrial Peace*. New York: Harper, 1951.

80. Williams, R. M. *The Reduction of Intergroup Tensions*. New York: Social Science Research Council, Bull. 57, 1947.

81. Williams, R. M. *American Society*. New York: Knopf, 1951.

82. Wilner, D. M., Walkley, R. P., and Cook, S. W. Residential proximity and intergroup relations in public housing projects, *J. soc. Issues*, 1952, *8*, 45–69.

83. Writers' War Board. *How Writers Perpetuate Stereotypes*. 1945.

CHAPTER 9

꒒꒒꒒꒒꒒꒒꒒꒒꒒꒒꒒꒒꒒꒒꒒꒒꒒

The Rise of Attitudes Toward
In-Group and Out-Group:
Experimental Verification

Attitudes are factors which enter into the determination of behavior from within the individual; that is, they are internal
factors (Chapter 6). But the understanding of attitude formation
and the content of attitudes toward groups, like other social attitudes, cannot be gained merely by studying single individuals
independent of their setting, no matter how intensive such study
may be. In the last chapter, the findings on group formation
stress that the content of the individual member's major attitudes
toward the group is derived from the social norms of the group.
These norms are internalized by individual members. The resulting attitudes of members in the group may vary in terms of
status position and role attained and in terms of individual, perhaps unique, characteristics of members. But if any degree of
solidarity exists within the group, their attitudes toward the
group are shared, held in common by all group members.

In Chapter 4, studies of children's attitudes toward out-groups
showed us that, as the child becomes a member of groups in the
course of his development, he also forms attitudes toward out-
groups. These attitudes are derived from the prevailing norms
of his groups toward the out-groups in question.

In order to understand the origins of attitudes toward in-group
and out-group, we must study the rise of social norms as a part of

the interaction process, within the in-group and in relations between in-groups. In the sociological study of small groups and in the studies of "group decision," we have learned much of the essential conditions for the formation of norms within the group. In Chapter 5, the historical examples of norms of social distance and prejudice toward out-groups indicated that such norms relative to out-groups are to an important extent a function of incompatible goals, interests, or directions of the groups in question.

In this and the following chapter, two experiments are presented which verify some major conclusions reached on the basis of such findings concerning in-group and intergroup relations.

The first experiment was undertaken with the conviction that real understanding of attitudes toward in-group and out-group lies in longitudinal study in which the major influences can be specified. It starts, therefore, with the experimental production of in-group formation. It constitutes a deliberate attempt to create a *reference group* for the individual members. The in-groups thus formed were then brought into functional contact in specified situations of competition and of frustration of one group by the other. Thus in-group formation, the formation of group structure consisting of status and role relations of the members, a set of norms peculiar to the in-group with its distinct character of "we-ness," the rise of norms relating to the out-group, and the attitudes of individual members can be traced as determined by the character of interaction within and between the in-groups.

The period of this experiment that deals with intergroup relations is summarized in the next chapter. It is followed by a second study dealing more specifically with the development of stereotypes as a result of interaction between groups. This experiment shows that stereotypes which one group develops and maintains about another are products of functional relations existing (in the present or the past) between the two groups. The relations between groups, as experienced by the rank and file of the group, may reflect the state of affairs that exists objectively or may be induced perceptually through manipulation of beliefs and selective use of mediums of communication by a powerful faction pursuing certain interests. The experiment indicates that the traits embodied in the stereotype are selected because they reinforce the stand of the in-group in the perceived state of affairs between the groups.

In short, stereotypes are standardized short-cut evaluations which reflect present or past relations between groups, or a picture of these relations presented to the group. Whatever objective truth may be reflected in them concerning the qualities of the members of the group in question does not constitute the main core of the rise of stereotypes. The main core is an evaluative one —the nature of the evaluation being determined by the nature of actual or perceived relationships between groups. Our review of social-distance scales of various groups and of stereotypes in Chapters 4 and 5 brought out these facts impressively.

Once stereotypes reflecting particular relations between groups are standardized, they become a part of the culture of the group through the vehicle of language and tend to survive, at times long after the disappearance of actual conditions or deliberate manipulations which were operative at the time of their origin.

The hypotheses tested in these studies are advanced on the basis of recurrent observations of reactions manifested in in-group and intergroup relations. The area of group relations is highly complicated and vital, yet it is still academically erratic. It would not seem to advance the development of a sound and unified approach to engage in feverish experimental activity testing hypotheses advanced in a hit-and-miss way or hypotheses stemming from theories not firmly established even on the relatively simpler level of individual behavior. As a matter of fact, even hypotheses formulated on the basis of recurrent observations of individual reactions have not proved very fruitful to the area of group relations. In the complicated area of human relations, fruitful hypotheses can be attained only after absorbed attention to the more concrete world of observations. After acquiring intimacy with the more concrete findings of sociologists and noting recurrent features or trends in their findings, we can reasonably hope that the hypotheses we formulate will serve as starting points of studies that have something important to do with the actualities of group relations. With this sort of background, we shall probably be less vexed with the troublesome problem of validity as our results start coming in.

As elaborated in the last chapter, spontaneously formed small groups studied in various places over a period of time have certain features which seem common to them all. Since these common features served as guide lines in formulating the hypotheses and in planning the study reported in this and the next chapter, we shall mention them again briefly.

1. When individuals come together to interact in a more or less lasting way, we note a major common *motive*. This common motive (or motives) may be common deprivation of means of livelihood, sex, or the like; it may be lack or instability of social anchorages, common strivings for recognition, social climbing, prestige, or many others. The common motivating factor weighs heavily in determining the direction of activities. As W. F. Whyte and others have noted, if individual members expect different objectives from the group, there will be poor organization and little productivity in whatever they may do.

2. The structural properties of group situations produce *differential effects in the experience and behavior of interacting individuals* (Chapters 6 and 8). This feature becomes particularly compelling if a well-defined status and role structure has emerged in the course of interaction. It necessarily leads to studying the social behavior of individuals by *first* placing them in their appropriate group settings and proceeding to investigate individual motives, capacities, talents, etc., as affected by this setting as well as contributing to this setting.

3. If the interaction process is not transitory but continues for some time, a *group structure* with hierarchical statuses and reciprocal roles emerges. Every individual who is part of the group is necessarily a part of this structure, including the leader. In this process, the group structure is distinguished from others as an

in-group. As such, it becomes a *reference group* for individual members.

4. In the process of the formation of group structure, norms concerning matters of consequence to the group will arise. The standardization of norms is a natural process in group interaction and need not be conscious or deliberate. As in-group delineation takes place, appropriate norms concerning the in-group will be standardized. Unless carried over and introduced by group members as the in-group forms, out-group norms will be standardized as the in-group comes into functional contact with other groups. The attitudes governing in-group relations and out-group relations of individual members as well as those governing other matters of consequence to the group will henceforth be derived consciously or unconsciously from these norms standardized in the process of interaction.

The norms, and hence attitudes, regulating relations of group members with out-groups and their members need not be of the same nature as norms regulating in-group relations (Chapter 8). Norms regulating in-group relations may be democratic in nature; but this does not necessarily imply democratic norms in relation to out-groups. Norms concerning relations with out-groups cannot be extrapolated from the nature of norms concerning in-group relations.

Since the considerations implied in the foregoing remarks are crucial in the formulation of our hypotheses, it may be helpful to make them more explicit. As noted above, one of the products of group formation is a delineation of "we" and "they"—the "we" including members of the in-group or reference group. The "we" thus delineated comes to embody a host of qualities and values to be upheld, defended, and cherished. Offenses from without or deviations from within are reacted to with appropriate corrective, defensive, and, at times, offensive measures. A set of values, "traits," or stereotypes are attributed to all those groups and individuals who comprise the "they" groups from the point of view of the "we" group. Now these characteristics attributed to the out-groups are neither a direct outgrowth of in-group practices or norms nor entirely independent of them. Such attributed traits may be favorable, unfavorable, or both, depending upon the nature of actual or perceived relations between the groups in question. (In some instances, interested parties within or without the in-group may exert influence so that a certain type of relationship appears to exist to in-group members, even though this may not be the case objectively at the time.) If the interests, directions, or goals of the groups involved in functional contact with one another are integrated or harmonious (or are made to appear so), the "they" group is pictured in a positive or favorable light. However, if the activities and functional views of the interacting groups clash, then the characteristics attributed to the out-group are negative and derogatory. If one group takes the position that another group is in its way, that for some reason the other group interferes with the goals or interests of the "we" group, or that it should be working in the interest of the "we" group, all sorts of stereotypes develop to justify this position. As we saw in Chapter 2, race superiority doctrines are deliberate or unconscious justifications for this kind of relationship.

These facts are amply supported by the evidence from the sociological studies of small groups, from "race relations," and even from experiments which were *not* primarily designed to study in-group and out-group delineations. For example, in Sears, Hovland, and Miller's study of the effects of frustration caused primarily by sleep deprivation, with numerous other frustrations provided for the subjects as well, an in-group formation was observed in the making. Jokes and unflattering adjectives were bestowed not only on the experimenters involved but on psychologists in general (2). Likewise, in the Minnesota study of semistarvation during World War II, the men sharing semistarvation "built up a tremendous in-group feeling that tended to exclude both their non-starving friends and administrative and technical staff" (1, p. 31). In short, the world was delineated into "haves" and "have-nots," with appropriate attitudes.

More recently, Thibaut's study of group "cohesiveness" or

solidarity yielded some relevant results for intergroup relations
(3). The procedures in this study were somewhat parallel to the
well-known Lewin, Lippitt, and White leadership study in that
the principal variable was differential treatment of groups of boys
by the adult experimenter. In this case, previously organized
athletic teams and camp groups were each divided into two experimental groups which participated together in a session of
games. One group received the preferred activities and positive
treatment from the experimenter; the other group was assigned
subordinate and less favored activities in the games and was
otherwise discriminated against by the experimenter. After a
time, the "underprivileged" groups were encouraged by another
adult to appeal for better treatment. In some cases their pleas
were granted; in others they were rebuffed by the experimenter.
Here we cannot go into the rather complicated experimental design which seemed necessary for Thibaut's particular problem.
Our interest is in the effects of such differential treatment on
relations between the experimental groups. As would be expected, these relations were complicated especially by the fact
that in each case members of the subgroups receiving differential
treatment were at the same time all members of an organized
group which included both temporary subgroups, and by the fact
that the primary source of frustration and recipient of hostility
was the experimenter. While clear-cut results for our problem
were not obtained because of these and other complications,
hostile actions between members of the two subgroups did occur.
The effect of rejecting the pleas of the less-favored groups for
better treatment seemed to be to reduce direct intergroup aggression. On the other hand, this treatment did result in more rejection of members of the more-favored group as friends. Thibaut
concluded: "The evidence from the present experiment suggests
that if two groups interact with differential status and the hostility
deriving from discriminatory treatment remains unexpressed, the
original cohesiveness of the group increased. If the hostility is
expressed through acts of aggression against the favored group,
the cohesiveness of the group returns to approximately its original

value" (p. 278). If the experimental procedures had succeeded in producing clear-cut in-group formations rather than temporary divisions in an established in-group, somewhat different results might have been expected.

A PRELIMINARY STUDY OF INTERGROUP RELATIONS

The plans for this study were formulated and predictions made on the basis of the repeated findings in the study of small groups and intergroup relations. The experiment was conducted in a camp in northern Connecticut during the summer of 1949 by M. Sherif. This study was carried out as the first part of a series of related research all of which will be integrated with the aim of giving a more rounded picture of the vast topic of relations within and between groups. In the research to be reported here, we have started with the negative aspect—the experimental production of friction and negative stereotypes between groups. Our main interest is to proceed to a realistic understanding of conditions and means of bringing about harmony and integration between groups. But in view of so many efforts toward reducing tensions between groups which have not proved to be so rewarding in spite of the good will of people engaged in them, this study is based on our conviction that only by understanding adequately the conditions that bring about tensions can we hope to cope with them effectively. With this conviction, we started with the experimental production of in-groups themselves and proceeded to create conditions which resulted in friction and attribution of derogatory stereotypes between these in-groups, which had no friction between them at the outset. Our next step is the reduction of such tensions, equipped with the knowledge of conditions producing tension. This procedure stems from the idea that a realistic understanding of underlying factors or diagnosis precedes effective measures in the way of improvement.

On the basis of lessons learned from the study of small in-groups and functional relationships between in-groups, the following hypotheses were formulated:

1. When individuals having no established relationships are

brought together in a group situation to interact in group activities with common goals, they produce a group structure with hierarchical positions and roles within it. This group structure implies positive in-group identifications and common attitudes, and tends in time to generate by-products or *norms* peculiar to the group, such as nicknames, catchwords, ways of doing things, etc.

2. If two in-groups thus formed are brought into functional relationship under conditions of competition and group frustration, attitudes and appropriate hostile actions in relation to the out-group and its members will arise. These will be standardized and shared in varying degree by group members.

As earlier chapters indicate, the testing of this prediction involves, in prototype, the formation of group stereotypes. Various more specific predictions which can be made on the basis of previous studies will be noted as we proceed.

Subjects

In order to test these hypotheses, it was necessary to eliminate as much as possible the formation of groups and the development of positive or negative relations between them on the basis of factors other than those to be introduced experimentally in the situation. Chief among these were background factors, such as ethnic differences and differences in class, religion, education, age, sex, etc. In short, the subjects had to be homogeneous in as many background and individual respects as possible.

Interviews were held with parents of prospective subjects in their homes and with the ministers of their church groups. Information sheets were filled in for each subject, including relevant background material as well as the subject's interests, play-group activities, school experiences, etc.

The possibility that groups would form on the basis of previous acquaintance or hostility was minimized by selecting subjects from different neighborhoods and towns in the New Haven area. Thus there were no definitely established bonds of friendship or hostility among the subjects.

Before the experiment, several tests were administered to the subjects by psychologists, who did not appear to the subjects again after the experiment began. These tests were deliberately given before the subjects went to the experimental situation to prevent suspicion on their part that the tests were directly related to their behavior in the experimental situation. The tests given were an intelligence test, the Rosenzweig Picture-Frustration test, and selected pictures of the TAT.

In attempting to satisfy the requirement that subjects be of homogeneous background, twenty-four boys were selected. All were close to twelve years of age, all came from settled American families of the lower-middle-class income group in the New Haven area. All of the boys were Protestants; nineteen came from the same denomination and the other five from highly similar denominations. The educational opportunities and backgrounds of the boys were similar. The group had a mean I.Q. of 104.8. All of the boys might be called more or less "normal"; none had been labeled "behavior problems."

With these factors equated as much as possible, the kind of groupings, statuses within groups, and attitudes produced between groups could not be attributed to differences in cultural and social background factors, such as ethnic, religious, or class differences, or to existing bonds of close friendship. As we shall see, further precautions were taken to equate individual and personality variations in the groups formed in the experiment on the basis of the test results, physical characteristics, skills, etc.

The possibility remained that the formation of a particular in-group might be determined chiefly by personal preferences or attractions among the boys, or by their common personal interests. For this reason, the experiment was planned so that the weights of personal preferences and interests, as well as personality factors, between the experimental groups could be neutralized.

General Plan of the Experiment

This study of in-group formation and intergroup relations was conducted at an isolated camp site near the Massachusetts state line and lasted for eighteen days. The nearest town was eight miles away, and there was no bus service in the neighborhood; consequently there were no immediate distractions from neighborhood soda fountains, movies, townspeople, etc. Neither boys nor staff members were permitted to have any visitors during the course of the study. As far as the boys were concerned, they were attending a summer camp sponsored by the Yale Psychology Department.

The camp site consisted of about 125 acres of land, largely hills and timber, with a stream having suitable places for swimming and fishing running through it. (See Plates I and II, following page 272.) There were two bunkhouses, an open mess hall, kitchen, infirmary, administration building, latrines, and equipment tents. There were broad level areas for athletic events. There were no electric lights.

The experiment was planned in three stages or periods:

Stage I was planned as the period of informal groupings on the basis of personal inclinations and interests. All activities were camp-wide, offering maximum freedom for choice and "mixing up" of boys in various games and camp duties. Thus it became possible to single out budding friendship groups and, more or less, to equate the weights of such personal factors in the two experimental groups of Stage II.

Stage II was planned as the stage of formation of in-groups as similar as possible in number and composition of members. Each experimental group would participate separately in activities involving all the members of the group. Activities were chosen on the basis of their appeal value to the boys and their involvement of the whole group. Different activities afforded varied situations in which all members of a group could find opportunities to participate and "shine." All rewards given in this period were made on a group-unit basis, not to particular individuals.

Stage III was planned to study *intergroup relations* between the two experimental in-groups thus produced when these groups were brought into contact (1) in a series of competitive activities and situations and (2) in mildly frustrating situations so arranged that the actions of one group were frustrating to the other. In line with the findings of frustration studies mentioned in Chapter 5, special frustrations of *individuals* were not experimentally introduced; rather, on the whole all individual members of a group saw the frustrations as their own precisely because they interfered with *their group*. Great care was taken that these frustrating situations not be blamed on the adults in the situation, but on the other group of boys. This effort was successful to a major degree.

The particular activities chosen in the three periods or stages were selected from those for which the boys themselves expressed preference. They were timed in terms of the demands of the three stages of the study. Thus the activities and situations in which the boys participated had the motivational or appeal value of life situations and were not simply situations and tasks prescribed by adults or chosen from a very limited number of alternatives. Specific activities and procedures will be described with the findings of each stage.

Before giving more detailed description, however, it is necessary to emphasize a few points relating to the ways observations were made and the role of adults in the camp. It is very well known that individuals behave differently when they know they are being watched or studied, especially by psychologists. This consideration cannot be "allowed for" in evaluating results or explained away. For this reason, all those associated with the study were strongly urged to prevent the boys' suspecting that their behavior was being observed or that various periods of camp activities were planned following an experimental design. (Some of the techniques for avoiding such conclusions are noted below.) The parents and boys were simply told that new methods in camping were being tried out. Parents were, of course, assured that the health and safety of their children would be safeguarded by every means.

The bulk of the observations was obtained by two participant observers who were graduate students. They appeared in the role of senior counselors to the two experimental groups. Each participant observer had the assistance of a junior counselor who was under his direct control and was instructed to follow his lead. Since the junior counselors were experienced in camping activities, the participant observers were comparatively free to observe their groups and to stay with them throughout the camp period.

However, the participant observers were instructed not to make notes in the boys' presence unless the situation clearly called for writing something, such as a cabin discussion in which "minutes" could be taken down. Otherwise, the participant observers withdrew or surreptitiously jotted down short notes which were expanded each evening after the boys were asleep.

The other staff members, including an official camp director, activities director, and nurse, were instructed to perform their duties in the camp in strict accordance with the planned activities and stages. The specific demands of the experiment for the next day were discussed in detail each night after the main observations for the day were obtained from the participant observers.

As far as the boys were concerned, therefore, the situation was as natural and attractive as the usual summer-camp situation. In order that the principal investigator might also be free to observe and that the criterion of homogeneity among subjects and staff members be satisfied, he appeared on the premises as a caretaker with the name of "Mr. Mussee." This role gave him freedom to be at crucial places at crucial times doing odd jobs without attracting the boys' attention. In addition, it was sometimes possible to make naïve statements and ask naïve questions of the boys about matters which every other staff member was expected to know as a matter of course. For example, he usually pretended not to know what group a particular boy belonged to, and was sometimes able to elicit information that might not have been available otherwise.

According to the participant observers and other staff members, who were instructed to watch carefully for any sign to the contrary, this role of caretaker was not suspected. The boys customarily came to Mr. Mussee for repairs of their personal belongings or camp property and for help in moving supplies, equipment, etc. Some typical examples of the boys' reactions to

Mr. Mussee will illustrate the role. The rather patronizing attitude accorded a caretaker is seen in one boy's reaction when Mr. Mussee was following his group to a cook-out. The boy yelled: "Hey, Mr. Mussee, hurry up. We can't wait for you!"

On the last day when the whole camp was breaking up and the premises were being cleaned, the "caretaker" was busy putting data in order and did not appear. Several boys, not seeing him at his job, complained, one of them remarking, "Where the hell is Mr. Mussee? This is his job."

In addition to the observational data collected, the friendship choices of each boy were obtained informally at two crucial points in the experiment. Charts of seating arrangements at meals, of bunk choices, of athletic teams chosen, of partners or buddies in various activities and situations were made for each day throughout camp. A record was kept of outgoing and incoming mail.

A fundamental point to be kept in mind in understanding the results that follow is that the participant observers, who appeared in the role of counselors, were in the camp primarily to observe. Both they and other staff members were repeatedly urged not to be leaders in the usual sense of adult leadership at boys' camps. They were instructed, rather, to make provisions for the activities, to look after the safety and health of the boys, and to set things right if behavior went too far out of bounds. Neither the counselors nor the boy leaders who emerged during the course of the experiment were asked to exercise any particular kind of leadership technique, democratic or authoritarian. Nor was authority to be delegated or suggested to the boys by the staff members. If any staff member showed a tendency to depart from observance of these instructions, it was forcefully called to his attention so that it might be corrected. Another pitfall about which staff members were cautioned by the principal investigator was a tendency to identify with one or the other group of boys. The necessity for this caution became particularly important during the period of intergroup relations (Stage III). The boy leaders and their lieutenants emerged from the ranks of the two experimental groups in the course of group interaction, especially during the period of in-group formation (Stage II).

The daily camp program was made up of activities for which the boys themselves expressed preference. Especially during the first few days of camp (Stage I) and the period of intergroup relations (Stage III), these activities were formally scheduled. However, their appearance on the schedule was made as if answering the boys' requests. The adult staff members had at hand the essential equipment for most of these activities. For example, if a hike was scheduled, tents, canteens, food, equipment, etc., were available as they asked for them. But a special point was made of leaving the boys to their own devices in organizing the activity. Until the experiment was concluded, at the end of Stage III, the boys were not preached to or organized from above to discuss among themselves the manner in which they would execute their activities. The attitude of the adults was to be that these were their affairs, their discussions, and their action. This attitude runs counter to that of the usual adult camp leader. It was encouraged among the staff by daily thrashing out together the relation of the purposes of the experiment to each specific procedure and plan.

On the whole, the demands of the situations, not adult leadership, led the groups to discuss their affairs collectively. For example, the participant observer at one time gave his group a whole watermelon, leaving the division strictly to them. On another occasion, four large chocolate bars were given to each group of 12 boys as a reward in their collective Treasure Hunts. The ways in which the watermelon and chocolate were distributed were up to the boys. Of course, these boys were used to camp situations in which such decisions were made by adults. But it was comparatively simple to turn the situation over to them, and this was successfully done.

RESULTS OF THE EXPERIMENT

The data obtained related to in-group formation, the rise of group structure with relative positions and leader-follower relations, the development of in-group products, and the development of intergroup tensions with appropriate attitudes and stereotypes to be presented in the next chapter. Information concerning individual variations in personality and skills will help us in understanding how particular roles and statuses in the groups were achieved and maintained, including the leadership positions. Observation of those boys who participated least in group activities and were inconsistent in their identifications may give leads for the study of marginality and social isolates.

Stage I

The first three days of camp were planned as the stage of "natural" or "spontaneous" groupings based on personal likes, dislikes, common interests of the boys. The main purpose of Stage I was to rule out, or at least to minimize, the possibility of interpreting results of the in-groups formed later and relations between these in-groups on the basis of personal inclinations of individual members for one another.

The boys were brought to camp in a bus, and all twenty-four were housed in one large bunkhouse during this period. They were free to select their own bunks, seats at meals, buddies for play activities, athletic teams, etc. All activities were camp-wide, i.e., potentially including all boys. They were selected to get each boy in contact with all the others and to give each an opportunity to contribute in his own way. For example, swimming, softball, mass soccer, a two-hour hike as well as a talent show, stunt night and small-group activities, such as ping-pong, horseshoes, fishing, tossback, and card playing were scheduled.

During these three days, budding friendship clusters and leader-follower relations were observed. The leaders tended to emerge in specific activities, and their role was maintained only temporarily, usually for the duration of the activity. These boys were not necessarily those who rose to leadership or high ranks later in the study. (For example, Billings, who emerged as a leader in softball, was later in the lower-status ranks of his group in Stage II.)

One particularly striking instance of a developing friendship cluster will be noted so that the relations between the boys in question can be followed at a later period of the experiment. The following is an excerpt from a summary of a two-hour hike. (Only the first letters of the names used throughout are the same as those in the boys' actual names.)

"The hikers did not proceed according to plan up the river toward New Boston. Along the highway, the boys saw a dirt trail veering off to the left and, with the assent of the lead counselor, they took it. The trail ended abruptly and the hikers decided to climb the mountain. About half way up it was decided to have a race to the top. The three boys who won the race were Hall, Miller and Crane. Hall told [staff member] that they all walked to the top abreast by mutual agreement, so that no one of them would arrive before the other two."

After this incident the three boys called themselves "The Three Musketeers." The next morning they went out to catch salamanders while the other boys were playing softball. Upon their return, they talked to Mr. Mussee and a participant observer telling them of plans to build a wire basin to hold salamanders. When asked why they had not been swimming with the others, Crane replied, "When one of us doesn't do something, then none of us do it."

At the end of Stage I, boys were taken aside informally at a "free activity" period for informal interviews held on the pretext of getting suggestions for favored activities and improving the camp. During these interviews, friendship choices were obtained casually and were written down by another staff member hidden from the boy's view behind a curtain. The main results of the poll of favored activities were:

Softball and hiking—20 choices each
Football—14 choices
Swimming—13 choices
Soccer—12 choices
Fishing—9 choices
Ping-pong—7 choices
Horseshoes and volleyball—5 choices each
Several other activities—4 choices or less each

The friendship choices obtained informally were used to make popularity ratings (sociograms). As other studies have found, the sociograms showed, as had observations, that the boys were beginning to cluster in budding friendship groups of two, three, or four boys. These sociograms served as the most important criterion in assigning the boys to the two experimental groups for the period of in-group formation which followed (Stage II). The division of the subjects into the two experimental groups was deliberately done to split the budding friendship groups which developed. For example, if two boys showed preference for one another, one was put in one group and the other boy in the second group. If more than one friendship choice was made, we attempted to put the boy in that group holding the *fewest* of his friendship choices. In the case of larger clusters, the other criteria mentioned below formed the basis of the particular division made.

At the start of Stage II—the stage of experimental in-group formation—the number of friendship choices given to members of the experimental in-group was fewer than the number of friendship choices given to members of the experimental out-group. One of these experimental groups came to be known as the Red Devils, the other as the Bull Dogs. Therefore, it will be helpful to refer to them by these names, although at this point in the experiment the groups had existence only on paper. As Table 2 shows, of the total friendship choices made by boys who

TABLE 2.   Total Choices of Friends, End of Stage I

| | Choices Received By: | |
| | Eventual Red Devils | Eventual Bull Dogs |
Choices Made By:		
Eventual Red Devils	35.1%	64.9%
Eventual Bull Dogs	65.0%	35.0%

were to become Red Devils, only 35.1 percent were choices of other boys assigned to their group. The remainder, almost two-thirds, of the friendship choices made by future Red Devils were directed to boys who were placed in the Bull Dog group, that is, the out-group.

Similarly only 35 percent of the total friendship preferences of boys who were to become Bull Dogs were for other future Bull Dogs. Sixty-five percent of their friendship choices were for boys who were placed in the Red Devil group.

In addition, the two experimental groups for Stage II were equated in other respects as much as possible without violating the requirements of the sociogram results. Chief among these characteristics were physical size and strength, ability in games, and intelligence and personality ratings made previously on the basis of tests by psychologists.

Stage II

Stage II was the period of experimental in-group formation, which lasted five days. After breakfast, the boys were told that the camp would be divided into two groups to make it easier to carry out their preferred activities. The lists of names in each group were read, and for identification purposes one group was assigned the color red and the other blue. The groups were then told that they could decide which of the two bunkhouses they would take. As it happened, the *red* group (which came to be known as the Red Devils) voted to remain in the old bunkhouse while the *blue* group voted to move to the new bunkhouse.

It had been anticipated that this split into two groups might not be taken easily by some of the boys. For this reason, immediately after the bunkhouse change was made, cars took each group separately from the camp for a hike and cook-out, activities which had first preference with most of the boys. The cook-out supplies were particularly sumptuous, including steak for broiling over open fires. This rather quick separation to highly appealing activities dispelled the unpleasantness felt by some boys at being separated from their new friends. One boy, Thomas, had cried for ten minutes after the announcement of the split, which meant his separation from another camper with whom he had struck up a friendship in camp.

During Stage II, the two experimental groups were separated physically as much as possible chiefly by scheduling their activities on the camp grounds and away from the immediate vicinity of the buildings and play area at alternating times. They lived in separate bunkhouses, ate at separate tables, served on K.P. on alternate days, and engaged separately in frequent hikes, overnight camping trips, etc. Swimming was engaged in separately by the two groups. The groups very soon found their own special swimming places some distance apart. One of these, the Bull Dogs', was secret from the other group.

The activities of Stage II required that members of each group coöperate collectively in achieving their ends. In addition to hiking, overnight camping trips, and swimming, other group activities were carried out. For example, each group had a "Treasure Hunt" which had to be solved as a group and engaged in such games as bean toss, in which each member had to collect beans so that the whole group found the required number of beans to win a group reward. A sum of money ($10.00) was given to each group to spend as they chose. These activities were, of course, scheduled by staff members and were enthusiastically participated in by the boys. However, each group was left free to participate in the activities in its own way. In addition, the size of the camp and of the groups allowed opportunity for the boys to choose other activities as well. Considerable group effort went to improving their cabins, stenciling insignia on T-shirts, making standards, signs, game equipment for the group, etc. Both groups had private hide-outs which they worked collectively to improve. (The Red Devils built a lean-to; the Bull Dogs worked hard to improve their swimming place by removing stones.) In addition, the groups sometimes engaged in craftwork, collecting wildlife, and the like. The activities were varied and afforded *ample opportunity for each boy to show his worth in some line of pursuit.*

Developing In-Group Structures. The major outcome of these participations in both groups during Stage II was the formation of well-defined in-group organizations or structures. By in-group structure is meant simply the development of relative hierarchical positions and roles within the group unit ranging from highest to lowest position. At the end of Stage II, friendship choices were again obtained in an informal way. In addition, the hierarchical roles within each group were manifested in terms of attempts to initiate group activities and the acceptance or rejection of such attempts by other group members, the degree of responsibility taken in the planning and execution of group activities, the initiation and effectiveness of group praise and punishment, and the like.

The sociograms made from the friendship choices of the boys in each group reveal the hierarchical positions in terms of *popularity* (see accompanying figures). They can be considered as one index of group structure, and are useful in this regard. The sociograms do not, however, adequately reflect the *power relationships* within the group. We will consider important examples of these in each group. In the Red Devil group, Lee (L) is shown as receiving one more friendship choice than Shaw (S) at the top of the group. However, Shaw was the acknowledged leader of the group. During Stage II he acquired and maintained power over Lee as well as Miller (M) and Bray (B), who also had high status in the group. Through these boys, and by exerting physical dominance over the others, Shaw was the leader and the focus of power in the Red Devil group during this period.

An example of a discrepancy between popularity rating and power position in the Bull Dog group is the case of Hall (H, at 5, left). Two other boys received as many popular choices as Hall, and one boy below Crane, the leader, received more. But Hall exerted greater direction over the group than the popularity rating indicates by itself, because of his acknowledged ability and leadership in athletic events. This leadership in athletic events (which were very important to these boys) was approved by Crane, the Bull Dog leader, who was not so proficient in sports. Hall, in turn, acknowledged the overall leadership of Crane. Our analysis of the two in-group structures will be based on both popularity ratings and behavioral manifestations of the role and status relationships within the groups.

A general finding concerning the structures of the two groups

POPULARITY   BULL DOGS

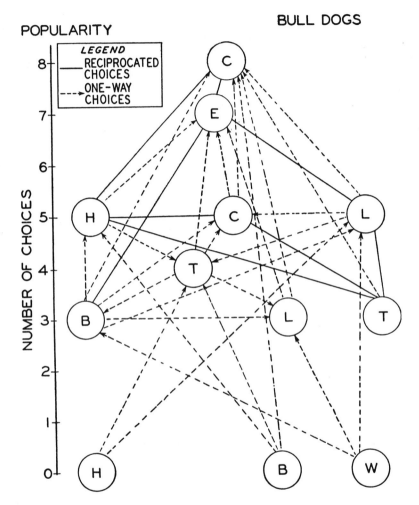

End of Stage II, in-group formation.

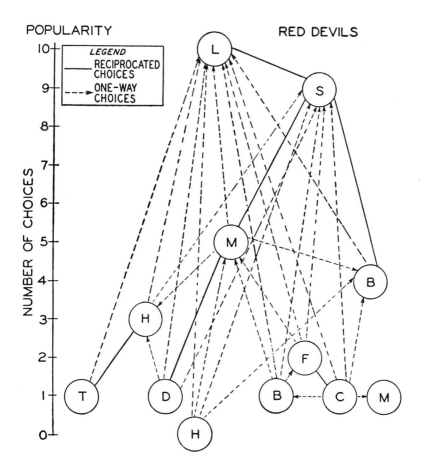

POPULARITY   RED DEVILS

NUMBER OF CHOICES

LEGEND
——— RECIPROCATED CHOICES
- - -→ ONE-WAY CHOICES

End of Stage II, in-group formation.

was corroborated both by the sociograms and by the behavior of the boys. By the end of Stage II, the Bull Dog group was a more closely knit, well-organized, and functioning unit than the Red Devil group, as is reflected in the sociograms. It is easily seen that the gap between the leaders and the majority of group members in the Red Devil group is much greater than that in the Bull Dog group.

Since group structure is focalized around the leadership role or roles, we will consider the leaders who emerged in the two groups first.

Status Relations in the Bull Dog Group.   In the Bull Dog group, Crane rose to the leadership position by his greater contribution in the planning and execution of common activities and by regulating and integrating the tasks and roles of the group members. Crane was one of the taller boys, though not one of the best athletes. Like the other boys, he came from a lower-middle-class family. He was the youngest of three children, being seven years younger than his sister. The psychologist noted prior to the experiment that his I.Q. was 100. At the outset, Crane successfully swung the vote to move to the new bunkhouse. When they arrived at the bunkhouse, a general discussion ensued concerning what could be done to fix it up. One boy, noticing a small picture of a dachshund on a bedpost, said, "Why don't we get some pictures of some animals?" Crane: "Yes, we have the blue and white colors. Let's get a big picture of a bulldog and call ourselves the Bull Dogs." There were shouts of "Yes!" followed by the singing of the Bull Dog song made famous at Yale. (The influence of the larger setting is apparent here, in addition to the immediate situation. One of the staff members had on a Yale T-shirt; blue and white are Yale colors; the boys were from the New Haven area.)

Crane's suggestions for improving the bunkhouse, by putting the letter *B* on the door and by building a chinning bar, for example, were from the first almost always adopted as good ones. He proved to be very effective in leading the group on its first hike and cook-out. He took charge of the first-aid kit, and on the second day of a toolbox which Mr. Mussee brought to the cabin.

Of course, Crane did not make all the suggestions for his group, but his approval was usually necessary for a suggestion to carry. The way in which his influence was exerted can be seen in a summary of the group's reaction to receiving ten dollars to spend as they pleased. Carlson (C, center of Bull Dog sociogram) first suggested improving the latrine. He was shouted down. Crane suggested wood for shelves. This suggestion received polite but unenthusiastic approval. Another boy suggested that orange boxes would do for this purpose. Two boys suggested better lights for the cabin and three others agreed. Crane then suggested wax for the floors. The boys agreed that the camp would furnish this anyway. Bromley, one of the lowest-status members, then suggested a basket of fresh fruit. Crane endorsed this suggestion and then the others enthusiastically agreed. Lowe, of lower status, suggested blue hats. "Yeah," Crane said, "and let's get some letters—B—to put on them." This proposal was adopted.

In another instance, the group turned decisions over to Crane to make. When a whole watermelon was given to the group, the boys thought the counselor should cut it. He replied that it was their melon. After about three minutes, Thomson (T, middle of Bull Dog sociogram) offered to do it. The group shouted "No!" Evans, one of Crane's lieutenants, offered to cut it but did not move to do so. Then Wood, at the bottom of the hierarchy, stepped up and took the knife. At this, Hall, another lieutenant, grabbed the knife and handed it to Crane. Crane cut the melon, saying "You guys who yell the loudest will get yours last."

Crane helped, assisted, or showed concern about other group members more than any other boy. For example, he administered first aid. Lowe asked the counselor how to fix the belt on his canteen. Crane said: "Here, I'll show you." When Thomas hurt his leg, Crane counseled him: "Take a rest." As Carlson carried rocks out of their pool, he was advised, "Carlson, don't strain yourself." Such concern was not confined to special buddies or lieutenants in the group. One boy in the group, Harvey, was low in status and was the only boy having waves of homesickness. He was particularly interested in nature study, and Crane showed concern about the welfare of Harvey's collection of pets and specimens on several occasions, at times helping him hunt. He frequently praised other group members and instigated group praise. After the group had worked long and hard on a project to improve its secret swimming pool, Crane said, "We did a good job, boys. We should be proud of ourselves." This was followed by cheers for the group effort and the suggestion that they give the pool a name (Bull Dog Pond). (See Plate III, in group of pictures following page 272.)

Crane was successfully able to organize the group for fairly complicated activities in such a way that the boys were usually pleased. On the third day of Stage II, he organized a detail to build a latrine at their hide-out, led by Evans. This detail worked hard while the rest of the group was swimming, but there was no evidence at all of dissatisfaction among the boys digging the latrine.

Here is a verbatim account of some of Crane's directives during a group Treasure Hunt: "Stop right now—walk—no, go ahead—all together—If you guys don't stick together we'll lose the prize." A short time later, Crane got a splinter in his foot. While he tried to remove it, Hall and Evans, his lieutenants, took the lead, but the group became temporarily disorganized. With the splinter out, Crane quickly got the group together for a successful finish.

On the second day, Mr. Mussee asked one of the boys, "Who is your leader?" The reply was, "Crane." "What Crane says goes."

As he became more and more absorbed in his leadership activities in Stage II, Crane neglected to write his family. After writing five letters which went unanswered, his mother telephoned the camp director to see if he was all right.

The Bull Dog group was, then, polarized around Crane. He did not lead in every situation. For example, he was not as good in athletic events or those requiring muscular skill as Hall. Hall took the lead in such situations with Crane's approval. However, Crane would occasionally overrule a decision of Hall's in athletics, telling him, for example, not to put in a substitute player. In no instance did Hall dispute such decisions. A third boy, Evans, was delegated authority by Crane in other tasks, such as camping or hiking. On one occasion, the Bull Dogs wanted to leave camp without revealing their direction to the Red Devils and staff. Crane devised a circuitous route, half of the boys going one way in diversionary action and half slipping out another. He led one group and Evans the other. Thus during specific occasions, during which the group was engaging in athletic games, for example, Hall would actually take more initiative and assume more responsibility than Crane. But we gain a very discursive picture of the group structure if it is not realized that all such initiatives and responsibility were taken with the sanction of Crane, who was the acknowledged leader and focus of power relations within the group.

The personal abilities and skills of various boys contributed to their achieving and maintaining status. For example, Thomas, who had cried when the two experimental groups were separated, might well have remained unhappy had he not achieved recognition on the cook-out and hike on the first day of Stage II. When the group tried to decide who should be cook, Thomas volunteered. The results were highly successful, and Thomas became the cook for the group. Although he was not in the top level of the hierarchy (see T at right of sociogram), he achieved a fairly stable status, especially because he also had ability in athletics. For example, he was one of the boys Hall depended on in games, and Crane sometimes called for his assistance in tent building and similar activities. On the second day of Stage II, he was observed to come from mail call with a letter. His former friend, Taylor of the Red Devils, was right by him. However, he deliberately moved to his own group, clustered some distance away, and sat down among them to read his letter.

The case of Lambert reveals a struggle for status, chiefly because he set his goals high. He was resentful of Hall's higher position in the power structure (he received as many friendship choices as Hall) and did not hesitate to express the fact. "Why should Hall get to do that?" At the same time, he made some approaches to Hall, who naturally smarted under his verbal attacks and criticism. (When the group was collecting polliwogs on the first day, he gave some he had collected to Hall.) By the second day, Lambert was getting the "silent treatment" from Hall, with the coöperation of Crane. Lambert cried and told a staff member that he wished that he could move to the other cabin or better that Hall would move out of their cabin. Later the same day, he made a poster glorifying his group with the slogan "The Red Devils are a bunch of jerks." On day three, the group came upon Lambert, who was tugging and pulling at some horseshoe stakes deeply embedded in the ground to take them near the Bull Dog cabin. Hall helped in this endeavor. When Lambert finished, he fell to the ground exhausted amidst the cheers of the group. Lambert said, "It was me and Hall. We did it!" By the third stage of the study, his status seemed to be much more stable, in terms of his relations to Hall and other top Bull Dogs, and indirectly from his close adherence to the group activities and decisions. In the next chapter we shall note the effects of some breakdown in the group structure on Lambert, after the experiment was formally concluded.

Two members lowest in status in the Bull Dog group, Bromley and Wood, were as much a part of the group as any others. (Harvey, who was also low in status, will be considered later in more detail.) Their low status did not mean that they were subjected to derision or that they were isolated from the group. Rather, they contributed relatively less to the particular activities important in the group, and their initiative was not usually acted upon unless a high-status member backed it. (We have noted that Bromley suggested buying a basket of fruit for the cabin, a suggestion which was adopted only *after* Crane, the leader, backed it.) Otherwise, their initiative was likely to be blocked, as when Wood started to cut the watermelon and Hall took the knife away. (All three of these boys were average or above in the intelligence tests, and did not seem atypical according to the clinical examiner.)

Status Relations in the Red Devil Group. In the Red Devil group, the focus of power relations during Stage II was Shaw, as noted above. In contrast to Crane of the Bull Dogs, who gained leadership principally through his planning and coördinating functions, Shaw was recognized primarily for his daring, his athletic skill, and his "toughness." Shaw was an attractive blond boy, among the more athletic in the camp. He was an only child and average in intelligence, according to the test results. On the first day of Stage II, there was little evidence of Shaw's emerging as leader. He stuck close to Lee during the cook-out and hike. On day two, the group was given ten dollars to use as they pleased. There was considerable discussion and a number of suggestions concerning disposal of the money. One boy suggested a tether ball game outside the cabin. This suggestion was received rather favorably; but Huston (a boy who was at this point somewhat dissatisfied with being in this group) asked, "What about the other boys? Wouldn't they use it?" Another boy, even lower in status, suggested that they build a fence around it. This suggestion led to the notion of setting up boundaries around their cabin and marking them out by stakes. When the limits of "their" area were being discussed, Shaw said: "We're the Red Devils, and all these things are ours." (This was the first time that the name "Red Devils" had been used by the group. This name was, unfortunately, influenced by one of the junior counselors. The boys all knew that the other group had adopted the name "Bull Dogs." They were already interested in making their cabin and group a good one. The junior counselor in this instance overstepped the role assigned him by suggesting the name "Red Devils." This lapse was called to his attention that evening. The boys did not make any response at the time. Shaw's use of the name in this context achieved its adoption.) After thus crystallizing the situation, Shaw seized a red and white standard (made from a broomstick) and led the boys out to set up their boundaries around the cabin, an action which led to some skirmishing with some members of the Bull Dog group. (This incident will be referred to later.)

That afternoon, upon returning from a swim, the boys found that in their absence the Bull Dogs had been in their cabin. Shaw had not yet arrived. The group postponed decision on what to do about this uninvited intrusion. Fenwick (F in sociogram) said "Let's wait for our captain" (meaning Shaw). Shaw was sent for and arrived on the run. He was all for making reprisals on the Bull Dogs for this invasion of their territory. Since this conflict between the two groups was occasioned by their being in proximity to one another, it was necessary to reduce further opportunities for contact between them during this stage. At the moment, the staff members had to change the direction momentarily by influencing Shaw. When he changed his mind, several members of the group remarked that "We all have friends in the other group" and that "We're just playing."

These were the situations which brought Shaw to the focal position in the group. That night on the way to their own campfire meeting in the woods, Shaw led the way and the boys agreed (verbally, but not by vote) that Shaw was their "captain." Shaw led the group effectively in games and in daring expeditions into the woods, etc. But he was not so effective in organizing and coordinating other in-group activities. Since Lee, the other boy who might have achieved the leadership position, did not make moves to do so, the group attacked common plans and problems which they made or met in relatively unorganized manner. On the third day, the Red Devils decided to build a lean-to in the woods. No clear-cut group plans for building it emerged. The boys tended to go at the job individually. But Shaw's influence was revealed by the following incident: When Shaw scratched his hand and withdrew temporarily, the others became listless and the work came almost to a standstill.

On day five of Stage II, when the Red Devil group had achieved some stability, Shaw tried to direct the breaking up of an overnight camp. The counselors estimated that the job would have taken two adults about ten minutes. The Red Devils did the work in half an hour. Unlike Crane of the Bull Dogs, Shaw did not organize work details. Rather he ordered the boys individually, "Do this," "Don't **do** that," etc., or worked hard at the job himself.

Group decisions could not be made, however, without Shaw's

sanction and help. For example, on the fourth day of Stage II there was extra ice cream at lunch. Canfield, who was low in group status, called to Shaw to come settle its disposal. It had already been suggested that the extra ice cream be given to the counselors, and there had been no objections. However, this was not done until Shaw put the question up for a vote in an approving tone of voice.

Shaw tended to be "cliquish," confining his favors and his attention on the whole to a few other boys high in status (Lee, Miller, and Bray) and preferring to be with them. He sometimes enforced his decisions by threats or actual physical encounters. On the third day of Stage II he actually led the group in throwing green apples at two members low in status (Harding and Marshall). These members cried at the time but did not react with rebellion. On the contrary, after recovering from the incident, they made approaches to Shaw, tried to help him and sit by him at campfire. Had Shaw given members thus attacked the satisfaction of being accepted in a consistent way, it seems likely that his position would have been more secure. As it was, he was really more interested in his lieutenants. ("My first successor is Lee, then Bray is third.") As a consequence, Shaw's leadership position was sometimes shaky. In fact, as we have seen, Lee received more friendship choices at the end of Stage II than Shaw. It was the consensus of the staff that Lee could have taken over the leadership of the group if he had wished to. But at no time did he assert leadership over Shaw. By remaining subordinate to Shaw on personal grounds, Lee insured Shaw's leadership in the group. On the last day of Stage II Shaw called for nominations of a softball captain. He was nominated, then Lee. At this Shaw said, "Hey, all the guys aren't here," and delayed the election until after lunch. Even with this delay, Lee was elected captain. But he continued to defer to Shaw in making decisions.

In spite of the ambivalence of some boys who had suffered under Shaw's attacks or neglect of them, he remained their acknowledged leader and had great prestige in the group. This fact is revealed, for example, when he spoke of his birthday, which was a week away. When the boys found that he would be only twelve years old, they all expressed surprise with such remarks as, "I thought you were at least fifteen."

In the analysis of statuses within the groups and the ways they were achieved, the role of individual variations in personal characteristics is certainly crucial. This role is not, however, as simple or direct as might be thought. The individual characteristics seem to have importance in these group situations in relation both to the demands of the situation and to other individual variations in the group. We have spoken of the clinical tests and ratings made prior to the experiment. It was hoped that it would be possible to make detailed analysis of these findings in relation to the observations in the camp situation. However, this proved too great an undertaking for this preliminary study. We are proceeding along these lines in further research. Later in this chapter, the cases of two boys who might be termed "borderline cases" in terms of their identifications are considered in some detail.

In-Group Identifications and Group Products. Along with formation of a more or less definite group structure, with which we have dealt here briefly, each group developed strong in-group feelings of *loyalty* and *solidarity* within the group and of identification of varying degrees with the group, its activities and products. This in-group identification is illustrated by the reaction of the in-groups to those members who continued to mingle or who wanted to mingle with boys in the experimental out-groups several days after the division into two groups. For example, three members of the Red Devils, Huston, Taylor, and Marshall, were branded as "traitors" and even threatened until they saw less of the boys with whom they had been friendly in Stage I and who had become Bull Dogs. By day four of Stage II, when this question was fairly well settled, they were reminded of this background and of their tendency to speak of their former friends with half-joking references to "the Bull Dogs in our midst" (meaning Huston, Taylor, and Marshall). By this time, this seemed a joke to the boys in question as well. When one of the counselors returned from a necessary trip to the out-group's cabin he was greeted with cries of "Traitor."

On the fifth day, when one of the Bull Dogs informed his group that a Red Devil wanted to get into their group, the Bull Dogs called this Red Devil a traitor for wanting to leave his own group. (This boy had, at the time, had an unpleasant encounter with Shaw, the Red Devil leader.)

A most inaccurate impression is conveyed, however, if these manifestations are taken to imply hostility between the groups at this stage. On the contrary, even though the boys of both groups expressed a desire to meet the other group in athletic events, there was not any consistent hostility or enmity between them. On day five, three of the higher-status members of the Bull Dogs paid an informal visit to the Red Devil cabin and they were hospitably received.

Becoming a group member implied identification with the group, which was unmistakably manifested by members of both groups. A striking example was Hall of the Bull Dogs asking Crane, his leader, if he had certain equipment at home. Crane asked, "Which home?" and Hall replied, "Our cabin, I mean." When packages of candy, comic books, etc., arrived in the mail, they were invariably shared with one's group.

Identification and loyalty to the group involved loyalty to the individual group members. On the eve of Stage III, with a series of competitive games in the offing, a Bull Dog said to Hall, who was fretting over his great responsibility as athletic leader for the group: "Don't worry. We won't hop on you if you blow. I mean we won't care if you lose."

Along with the group structure and the increasing identification with the group, products were standardized within the in-group which served further to crystallize and stabilize the in-groups. One example of such standardization was, of course, the names of the groups. In addition, most of the boys were quickly given nicknames. For example, because their real names were associated with brand names of these products, one boy was dubbed "Radio," and another was called "Cough Drop." Other nicknames clearly referred to individual characteristics of the boys. In the Bull Dog group, Hall, the athletic leader, was admiringly called "Horrible Hall"; others were called "Bonehead," "Screwball,"

"Bugs." Interestingly enough, the leader of this group, Crane, was the only boy respectfully called by his own first name. The leader of the Red Devils, Shaw, was tagged to typify his toughness and attractive blond appearance as "Baby Face." Lee, who had a rather long head, was called "Lemon Head"; a thin boy was named "Bones," others "Midget," "Bibi Brain" and "Madman" (the latter apparently in a flattering way, for this was Miller, one of the lieutenants).

Each group came to prefer certain songs. In some of them they inserted their own group's name in a glorifying fashion and the name of the other group in a less complimentary way.

Both group standardized methods of punishment. In the Red Devil group, sanctions were imposed by Shaw, the leader, through threats or actual "roughing up." In the Bull Dog group, a more elaborate system of sanctions was devised. They were always imposed by Crane, the leader, but it should be noted that numerous instances are recorded in which members of the group supported Crane in his decisions and felt that he was "fair." Although Crane was once observed verbally threatening a boy, Crane relied on two methods of sanctions rather consistently. The first, and least important, was added K.P. duty for the offender. The more frequent punishment was the obligation to remove a certain number of heavy stones, usually ten, from Bull Dog Pond. Later different numbers of "points" were given for different sizes of stones, the points being judged by Crane. This method started when the boys were improving their secret swimming place by damming it and removing rocks. They succeeded in raising the water level six inches.

On the second day of Stage II, Crane instituted an oath of secrecy which was sworn to by each Bull Dog and by any staff members who ventured to their secret camping place and pool, as follows: "I swear not to tell our secret swimming hole or any of the secrets of the Bull Dog Cabin."

The colors which had been assigned to the groups for identification purposes acquired symbolic value. Shaw, the Red Devil leader, was placing an order with Mr. Mussee for crepe paper and other supplies needed for craftwork and decoration. He specified that the paper should be red. Mr. Mussee said, "How about some other colors, green, blue, etc.?" Shaw replied with a sneer in his voice, "Not *blue!* Not *that* color. We just want red and white."

All of the decorations in the cabins, stenciling of T-shirts, hats (Bull Dogs), craft materials for making watch chains, lanyards, etc., were in the appropriate colors. Posters were consistently made with blue or red crayon as the case might be, although many boxes of crayons with a variety of color were provided. Harvey, a Bull Dog, insisted on leading the group to camp from a hike because his knapsack was wrapped in a blue sweater.

The two in-groups developed characteristic ways of doing things. For instance, each group made lanyards by different methods, which were not original to them but which were standardized for the respective group. The Bull Dogs had periodic cleanup by their own method, devised and enforced by Crane. The boys lined up at arm's length and walked back and forth across the grounds until they had covered the area, picking up paper, etc., as they went.

Borderline Cases in Each Group. Even the most retiring and ambivalent members were at times caught in the in-group. Of course, during the first days of Stage II as the in-groups were in the process of forming, a number of group members manifested ambivalent or conflicting loyalties (conflict between old friends and the developing in-group in which they found themselves). However, by the end of Stage II, all of the boys except two could be said to behave rather consistently as members of one or the other in-group. We will consider these cases, which have been studied intensively, in summary form for the leads they give for further work along these lines.

On the second day of camp, during Stage I, Harvey of the Bull Dog group went to the official director of the camp and complained that he was homesick. Harvey was a small boy, and one of the younger boys in camp, being almost eleven. Like several other boys in the camp (including Shaw, the Red Devil leader) he was an only child. The interviewer who had gone to his home prior to the camp had noted that he was a "lively" boy. The mother let the boy answer the questions put to him, but the interviewer jotted down that she seemed "just a shade tenser than other mothers" he had interviewed. The boy was an active member of a play clique which seemed to center many of its activities around nature study and craftwork. He was a Cub Scout. The clinical psychologist who tested him did not make special note that he was atypical, and the clinical tests revealed him to be exceptionally friendly, and not unusual in other ways except in "reactions to authority." (His responses indicated that he tended to be hostile and rebellious to authority.)

After his talk with the camp director, Harvey returned several times to ask the director to phone his parents, so that they could come and take him home. When the groups were separated for Stage II, Harvey was in the Bull Dog group. The participant observer noted that Harvey would become completely absorbed in certain group activities, such as hiking, cook-out, crafts, collecting polliwogs, frogs, and the like. During these periods, the observer noted "high elation." But when the group turned to swimming and softball, he was likely to become tearful and "beg off." He coöperated in cleanup, K.P. duties, and the like. Crane, the Bull Dog leader, was quite tactful in giving Harvey recognition, without adult suggestions of any kind. It was the opinion of the staff members associated with his group that Harvey might have become adjusted to the group, might have overcome his waves of homesickness and found some stability in the Bull Dog group; but as the handling of such a special case, which took considerable time and effort, was not the main aim of the study, it was decided not to make further efforts along these lines. Harvey claimed that he liked the camp, that it was just too far from home. He enjoyed the food, saying it was better than that at home. He had no objections to his fellow campers.

Harvey was frequently caught up in the group activities and showed signs of identification. On the second day of Stage II he made a wooden spear, saying, "This is for the Red Devils" (who were absent from camp). This spear was decorated with blue and white paper. On the fourth day of Stage II he ran it through a piece of red paper he came upon and said "That's what we'd do to the Red Devils." He was not completely isolated from the group. We have noted Crane's attentions to him. When he was stung by a bee, Biggs and Bromley were concerned and treated it for him. On day four, Crane and Bromley found an orange lizzard. Several boys yelled to Harvey to come and get it, since they did not want to harm it when they picked it up (recognizing Harvey as the "naturalist" of the group). After he did so, Crane said, "Bromley found it, I trapped it, and Harvey picked it up. It ought to go into the nature study box." The only recorded example of Bull Dogs deriding Harvey was after they had urged him to go with them on their group Treasure Hunt, so that the group would not be handicapped. When he went instead to the nurse, Biggs said, "We don't want to wait for that rotten egg." During the course of the Treasure Hunt, Harvey learned that his parents had been called. "He joined the Bull Dogs with a burst of enthusiasm, raced along with the group, offering a variety of suggestions as to where the hidden treasure notes might be."

When Harvey's parents finally came to the camp gate, some distance from the camp buildings, he was told to join them. He was in no hurry to leave. Hall was working on an airplane model and Harvey readily assisted him. He left the group with a "so long, fellows." After he had walked 100 feet or so, a cheer broke out, "Two, four, six, eight, who do we appreciate, Harvey, Harvey, Harvey." Observers reported that Harvey's meeting with his parents "was very unemotional."

Harvey's case is gone into in more detail because he was clearly not assimilated into the in-group, while the other boys were. There was, however, one boy in the Red Devil group, Huston, who was low in participation in the group and inconsistent in his identifications. This boy had made friends with boys put in the Bull Dog group and was one of those branded a "traitor" to the Red Devils during the first few days of in-group formation. Against the trend of the forming in-group, he made suggestions for getting together with the other group for a camp-wide party.

Probably because of the rough treatment meted out by Shaw, the Red Devil leader, Huston withdrew from the group on several occasions. However, on the evening of the second day, Mr. Mussee and another staff member found him wandering in the woods at dusk, looking for his group, who had gone on to campfire without him. They led him in the right direction, and as they approached, Huston said: "Gee I hope this is *my* group because we have lots of secrets that we can't give away." By the third day, the observer wrote, "Huston has definitely *joined* the Red Devil boys. At 9:30 A.M. he was seen in front of the bunkhouse carrying a red and white streamer. This fact was confirmed throughout the day during the Scavenger and Treasure Hunts. He stayed with the group throughout and helped in getting scavenger items and then helped look for the slips of paper in the Treasure Hunt." In these terms, Huston stayed a member of the group, until after Stage II, when the groups came into conflict. (We shall note the effects of conflict on the in-group structure later.)

Some Effects of the Larger Social Setting. Before summarizing the main results of Stage II, it is necessary to emphasize a finding related specifically to the general cultural background of the subjects. Along with the delineation of the "we" or in-group, the two experimental groups referred to the "they" or out-group frequently and in a clear-cut way, even though there was comparatively little functional contact between the groups.

More than this, these groups immediately and spontaneously started to make *comparisons*, not just in terms of "what *we* have or do and what *they* have or do," but in terms of "their lousy cabin," "Our pond is better," and even "those low kind." They began to express a desire to each other and to the staff to compete with the other group in games, with considerable assurance that their own group would win. We have already referred to the signs of a competitive attitude on the second day, when the Red Devils decided to set up a boundary around "their" part of the camp. This day had in large part been devoted by the groups to improving their respective bunkhouses and surroundings with their counselors' help. During this activity, comparisons between the efforts of the groups cropped up. The boundary questions led to disputes between some members of the two groups and an unauthorized visit by the Bull Dogs to the Red Devil cabin, which took on the characteristics of a "raid" because the Bull Dogs pulled down some of the Red Devils' signs and posters. As we noted, the Red Devils, led by Shaw, wanted to retaliate, but indicated when slowed down by the counselor that "We're just playing." These encounters were in a rather playful and adventurous spirit and had the effect of intensifying the developing in-group demarcations, especially of the Red Devils. After this, it will be recalled, the groups were separated physically by keeping their activities further apart as much as possible.

These instances of competitive feelings and, in some cases, of derogation, were *not* at this stage standardized in the sense that they were consistent modes of response to the out-group and its members. There was no consistent day-to-day hostility between the groups at this stage. Referring to the Bull Dog oath of secrecy given above, Evans, a member of the top-status level, indicated the possibility for future reciprocity and coöperation by saying, "We can show them [Red Devils] our pool later, if they show us theirs."

The most urgent manifestations of competition at this stage were confined chiefly to the desire to participate in the most attractive of all pastimes for American boys of this age—competition in sports. Both this desire for competition and spontaneous derogation of the other group in specific respects can be traced to the cultural background of these boys, specifically socialization in a society in which a competitive and aggressive behavior is at a premium.

Reversals in Friendship Choices in Stage II. One of the crucial tests of the study was whether or not these experimentally introduced in-group relationships would bring shifts or reversals in the friendship ties nascent in Stage I on the basis of personal likes or affinities. At the end of Stage II, friendship choices were again obtained through informal talks with each boy. It should be emphasized that the wording made it clear that the boys were free to mention those boys they liked to be with best *in the whole camp*, i.e., from the other group as well as their own.

Such reversals in friendship choices were found, and were quite clearly indicated by behavioral observations as well. (During Stage II, there were frequent instances of former friends' ignoring one another, or failing to respond to the call of a former friend.) Table 3 gives the choices of friends for the two groups at the end of Stage II.

TABLE 3.   Total Choices of Friends, End of Stage II

| Choices Made By: | Choices Received By: | |
	Red Devils	Bull Dogs
Red Devils	95.0%	5.0%
Bull Dogs	12.3%	87.7%

For comparison purposes Table 4 gives the choices of in-group and out-group members at the end of Stage I, before the experimental groups were formed, and at the end of Stage II. It is sharply evident from this comparison that friendship preferences of these boys were at first predominantly for individuals who were placed in the experimental out-groups. The in-group formation of Stage II resulted in shifts in friendship choices which were definitely in the direction of the developing in-groups.

TABLE 4.   (Composite Table) Total Choices of Friends at the End of Stage I and End of Stage II (Note the Reversals)

| Choices Made By: | Choices Received By: | |
	Eventual In-Group	Eventual Out-Group
End of Stage I Eventual Red Devils	35.1%	64.9%
Eventual Bull Dogs	35.0%	65.0%
	In-Group	Out-Group
End of Stage II Red Devils	95.0%	5.0%
Bull Dogs	87.7%	12.3%

SUMMARY OF MAIN RESULTS OF STAGE II

Briefly, in line with our predictions, it was found that when groups experimentally formed were placed in situations and engaged in activities calling for group coöperation toward common goals, unmistakable in-group structures developed, each with hierarchical positions and roles within it. These group structures were not static, but changed within limits in differing situations. The structures of the two experimental groups differed somewhat, in terms of the effectiveness of the respective leaders in maintaining and increasing in-group solidarity. As the groups formed, the members of each achieved positive in-group identifications along with the acquisition of certain statuses and roles. This identification resulted in shifts or reversals in friendship preferences of in-group members *away* from previously budding relationships of Stage I with individuals who became out-group members *toward* friendship preferences within the in-group. In short, the developing in-groups became the *reference* groups of the individual members. In the process of in-group formation, by-products of group interaction were standardized as *social norms*. Among these by-products were those relating to loyalty to the in-group, nicknames for different members, catchwords, preferred songs, ways of going about group activities, and sanctions for behavior deviant to group norms or contrary to the direction of group activity. These norms related to the in-group structure and in-group activity. Although coming from the larger society there was a tendency for making unfavorable comparison of the out-group to one's own group in this period. social norms relative to the out-group had not yet been standardized. There was also a tendency for the groups to have friendly encounters with one another, to refer to unfriendly trends as "play," and to hold the possibility of reciprocity for future exchanges of in-group "secrets." Thus, attitudes toward the out-group were by no means consistent from time to time or for various members of the in-group. This inconsistency is in striking contrast to attitudes toward the out-group after the groups were brought into functional contact in competitive and frustrating situations in Stage III. This period of intergroup relations and its consequences are presented in the next chapter.

REFERENCES

1. Guetzkow, H. S., and Bowman, P. H. *Men and Hunger.* Elgin, Ill.: Brethren Publishing House, 1946.
2. Sears, R. R., Hovland, C. I., and Miller, N. E. Minor studies of aggression: I. Measurement of aggressive behavior, *J. Psychol.*, 1940, 9, 277–281.
3. Thibaut, J. An experimental study of the cohesiveness of underprivileged groups, *Human Relations*, 1950, 3, 251–278.

꒰꒱꒰꒱꒰꒱꒰꒱꒰꒱꒰꒱꒰꒱꒰꒱꒰꒱꒰꒱

CHAPTER 10

Formation of Out-Group Attitudes and Stereotypes: Experimental Verification

In this chapter we continue the study dealing with the experimental production of reference groups conducive to internalization of appropriate in-group and out-group attitudes. Experimental in-group formation was summarized in the last chapter. Here we shall report the results of the focal period of the study to which prior stages were preliminary, the period of intergroup relations. In the last part of this chapter, a related experiment on the rise of positive and negative group stereotypes as a consequence of interaction between groups is presented.

STAGE III: INTERGROUP RELATIONS

The stage of *intergroup relations,* which lasted formally nearly five days, involved bringing the two experimental groups—each with varying in-group structures and strengthening friendships within the in-group—into functional relationships which were competitive and mildly frustrating to one another. The frustrating situations were planned in such a way that on the whole they seemed to one group to have been caused by the other.

At breakfast on the first day of Stage III a series of competitive games was announced as though giving in to the boys' requests. The plan was for each group to receive a certain number of points or credits for winning athletic events during the coming days and for excellence in performing camp duties, such as cabin cleaning, K.P., etc. This point system, which was explained and given to each group orally and on typed sheets, was simple and clear. However, it allowed for some manipulation by the staff in the points given at cabin inspection, K.P., etc. It was possible, therefore, to keep the number of points attained by each group within a surmountable range until near the end of the contest, thus keeping up the strivings of both groups to win. A daily tug-of-war counted 5 points; softball, soccer, and touch-football games counted 15 points each. Bunkhouse inspection allowed 10 points to the winner, while K.P. and sweeping each could be varied from 1 to 10 points for each team. Since such duties were performed separately, this manipulation did not arouse much suspicion. The staff agreed at the outset that the two groups were evenly matched in sports in terms of the size and skill of individual members.

The prize to the winning group was displayed and much admired—12 four-bladed camping knives, one for each member of the winning group. A poster with two thermometers was placed on the bulletin board and the rising score of each group filled in. This poster became a center of attention for the competing groups.

The effects of this period of competitive games will be clearer if the number of points collected by each group for the three days is known:

Cumulative Points

Day	Bull Dogs	Red Devils
1	26	16
2	46.5	41.5
3	89.5	49.5

The effects of competitive games were not immediate. Observers all noted considerable "good sportsmanship" on the part of the two groups at the start. For example, after the first contest, the winning Bull Dogs spontaneously gave a cheer for the losers;

Plate I. Overall View of Camp Site.

Plate II. Camp Grounds.

Plate III. Bull Dog Pond.

Plate IV. Tug-of-War.

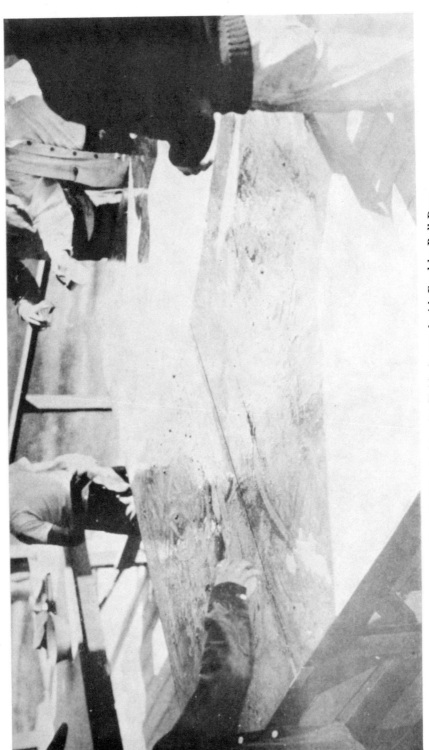

Plate V. The Red Devils' Table Smeared with Food by Bull Dogs.

Plate VI. Bull Dogs Raiding Red Devil Bunkhouse.

Plate VII. Red Devils Collecting Ammunition.

Plate VIII. Bull Dog Ammunition Pile.

Plate IX. Red Devil Ammunition Pile.

Plate X. Two of the Posters Made by Red Devils.

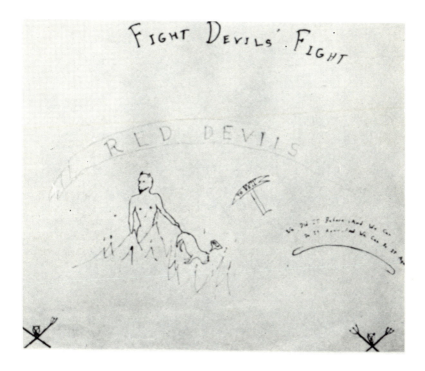

Plate XI. Two of the Posters Made by Bull Dogs.

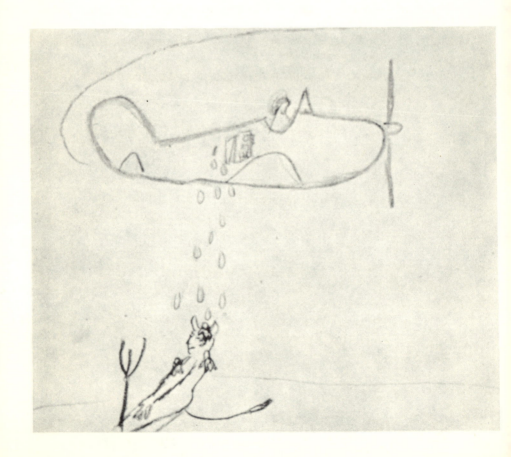

and the losing Red Devils, though still scattered around the field, responded as a group with a cheer for the winning Bull Dogs. This was repeated after the soccer game on the second day. However, as the contest progressed, the cheer changed. It started out as "2–4–6–8, who do we appreciate," followed by the name of the other team. It changed to "2–4–6–8, who do we appreci-*hate*."

The first three days of Stage III began with a tug-of-war between the two groups (see Plate IV). The group members organized themselves and exhorted each other in the intense common effort. The Red Devils lost the first contest. Their reaction to the loss represents one of many *perceptual* distortions occurring in these competitive group situations. All Red Devils were convinced that they lost because "the ground was against us." They spent most of the morning discussing this and their strategy for the next tug-of-war. On the following day, the Red Devils had pulled four Bull Dogs across the line and it looked as if they would win. But the Bull Dogs' leader began a series of shouts and encouragement to his boys. This apparently made possible a "second wind" in which the Bull Dogs regained their lost ground and finally defeated the Red Devils again. This time, the Red Devils rationalized their defeat by agreeing that the Bull Dogs "must have done something to the rope."

Especially during the first two days of this tournament of games, the contests tended to solidify further the in-group structure and loyalty. Biggs, a Bull Dog, became ill and was unable to participate in the games. When Hall, the athletic leader, went to see him, there were tears in his eyes when he learned the news; and Biggs sobbed. (Hall had not chosen Biggs as a *special* friend when the friendship choices were obtained on the previous day.) After the first game, the Bull Dogs all visited Biggs in the infirmary. They gave him glowing accounts of the game. The considerable prestige of the group's leader, Crane, is revealed here. Although Crane had not played an especially good game, Hall said, "You ought to see Crane. He stopped a line drive with his bare hands!" Biggs, the ill boy, said that if the Bull Dogs won the series he would not accept a knife because he had "let them down." The Bull Dogs shouted down the idea of such a sacrifice, gave him a cheer, and reassured him loudly that Biggs is "one of us."

The Bull Dogs spent a great deal of time rehashing their victories, dwelling on each individual's feats and lavishing praise on individuals and the group as a whole. It was typical of Crane's leadership that he credited the winning of the second tug-of-war, in which they were nearly defeated, to Bromley, a low-status member. He described in great detail how he himself was slipping and how Bromley dug in his heels and made it possible for him to anchor the rope. The Bull Dogs recognized the solidarity of their group. "You know we are winners because we have an organization." "Yeah, those guys don't pull together like we do" (referring to Red Devils). Even Lambert, who had struggled in his attempts to rise and displace Hall, felt stable and prideful identification with the group. When the Red Devils accused his group of unfair tactics, he replied, "*We* got organization!" At a crucial point in a game, he objected to a team decision as to who was to kick: "No, let Hall [his former rival] kick! He's best."

In the Red Devil group, one of the members low in status revealed increasing identification with the group during the first game. The Red Devils were trailing the Bull Dogs in softball and had two outs with no one on base. Fenwick came to bat and was tagged out with a ground ball. He sobbed for some time and went off by himself, saying to a counselor, "I lost the game for us." He was almost afraid to show his face in the Red Devil cabin; but his group never mentioned the incident and were, in fact, considerate of him. This incident typifies the manner in which group efforts and goals become intensely *personal* ones for the individual members. Another low-status member, Marshall, distinguished himself in soccer, and achieved prestige for his actions. The leader, Shaw, played around with him for quite a time after the game. (However, the next day when the Red Devils were lagging far behind, Shaw roughed up Marshall.) Marshall had been one of those Red Devils branded as a "traitor" early in Stage II. Another former "traitor," Taylor, was water boy, and carried water so enthusiastically that he had enough for both groups.

As the competitive contest went on, intergroup rivalry and hostility increased rapidly. During one game, a staff member cautioned a Red Devil not to drink too much water, because he might get sick. At this, Lambert, the Bull Dog, called in a nasty tone, "Let him drink all he can. He's a Red Devil." Such expressions of hostility became increasingly frequent.

As shown by the points won, the Bull Dog group pulled into the lead on the first day and remained there. The adult observers all agreed that the teams were fairly matched in terms of individual players, but that the Bull Dog group had much more effective team organization. We have seen that the Bull Dogs recognized this fact. Even the Red Devils were not unaware of it. Bray, a Red Devil lieutenant, said on the third day, "The trouble is we don't coöperate." But as a group, the Red Devils responded to their increasingly apparent losing position by labeling the Bull Dogs "dirty players." They were sure that they could win if the Bull Dogs were not "such cheaters." They said, "At least we play fair." During the games, epithets—"dirty players," "cheats"— were hurled at the Bull Dogs. By the contest's end, the words "dirty players" and "cheats" were almost synonymous with Bull Dogs as far as the Red Devils were concerned. Of course, the Bull Dogs vehemently denied such charges.

The cumulative effect of the competitive games caused considerable group friction and, to the Red Devils, considerable frustration. The common expressions of the winning Bull Dogs and the losing Red Devils in pictures taken immediately following the victory of the Bull Dogs in the athletic series convey this fact objectively.

The winning Bull Dogs were tremendously elated at their victory. The reward of knives was distributed by putting all the knives in a bucket which had been lined with a cloth to prevent scratching. Then each boy was blindfolded and picked a knife from the bucket. Thus, not even the high-status members had advantage in choosing preferred colors. (This was the idea of the leader, Crane.)

The losing group of Red Devils was by this time seriously weakened. In their particular case, group failure was conducive to signs of *disintegration*. Before the contest was over, Shaw, the leader, had become vindictive. After the third loss at tug-of-war he accused the front men of not "digging in." He blamed and ridiculed other members of his own group for the losses. (It was in this spirit that he "roughed up" Marshall after playing with him following his success in soccer the previous day.) At the same time, Shaw retired more and more to the company of his lieutenants. The lower-status Red Devils were overtly hostile to the Bull Dogs (Darlton of the bottom ranks was on the verge of blows with the boy he had buddied with most in Stage I—Lambert of the Bull Dogs.) But they resented Shaw's accusations. Although he made no moves to do so, Lee could have easily taken over leadership of this group at this time. Shaw tacitly recognized this fact. Whereas he had formerly referred to Lee as "my successor," Shaw now spoke of Lee as "my co-captain." Huston, the low-status member who had been lowest in participation at the beginning of Stage II but who had identified with the group toward the end of Stage II and the first days of Stage III, now began to withdraw from group activity. The other low-status members of the group were resentful as Red Devils of Shaw's behavior. For a time after the Bull Dogs' victory Shaw openly fraternized with Hall, athletic captain of the Bull Dogs. When Hall attacked Fenwick, a low-status Red Devil, taunting him about the Red Devils' loss, Shaw actually egged Hall on by saying that Fenwick "should get what is coming to him." This increased the other Red Devils' hostility toward Shaw and toward the Bull Dogs as well.

The Red Devils pretended that they had no interest in the Bull Dogs' newly won knives. The intensity with which the Red Devils actually felt the loss of the prize is revealed in Darlton's account of his dream the night after the Bull Dogs won: "You know I was thinking about those knives so much yesterday and wishing so much that we had won them that I dreamed about knives last night. I dreamed that all I could see was knives and that I began picking them up and putting them in a bag. But just when I was going to play with them I woke up." Group shame at their poor showing is indicated in this statement by a low-status member: "Gee, we better win that treasure hunt or we won't even be able to call ourselves Red Devils any more."

Primarily because of the reaction of Shaw, the Red Devil group was considerably disorganized in defeat until the day after the contest ended, when the Red Devils experienced an attack from the Bull Dogs.

Planned Frustrations of In-Groups

Following the competitive tournament between the Bull Dogs and Red Devils in Stage III, situations were arranged in which it seemed that one group interfered with or frustrated the other. As noted, the loss of the tournament involved serious frustration for the Red Devils as a group. Primarily because of the reactions of Shaw, the leader, the in-group structure was weakened for the time. Shaw's identification with his clique of lieutenants was stronger than with the Red Devils as a whole. He turned vindictively on low-status members of his own group after defeat and even attempted to fraternize with high-status members of the victorious out-group. However, in-group conflict was mingled with the increasing hostility toward the out-group experienced by most members, especially those low in status. Several situations were planned by the staff involving frustrations of the groups which would seem to be the fault of the other group. But only one was carried out because of its extreme effectiveness and the further frustrating circumstances which arose from it.

On the evening of the Bull Dogs' victory over the Red Devils in the athletic series and camp competition, both groups were asked to attend a party in the mess hall. Staff members not attached to either group openly expressed regrets that the boys were calling each other names and fighting. At this, members of the two in-groups came to the defense of their respective in-groups, placing all blame on the other group. The staff members reacted to this self-justification and blame of the out-groups by inviting both groups to a party to let "bygones be bygones." By careful timing and by indirectly interesting the Bull Dogs in something else momentarily, the participant observers were able to see to it that the Red Devils got to the mess hall for a few minutes before the Bull Dogs. None of the subjects in either group suspected that this timing was deliberate.

The refreshments of ice cream and cake were on a table. Half of them had been battered, broken, or crushed to appear as though something had happened to them in transit; the other half remained whole and delectable. When the Red Devils arrived, they were told to serve themselves and to leave the Bull Dogs their share. As we know, the Red Devils were the defeated group and had manifested considerable frustration and envy of the Bull Dogs for winning the highly valued knives.

Faced with the refreshments, half fresh and appetizing and half broken and crushed, the Red Devils, without any comment, picked up the good portion and carried it to their own table. At this point the Bull Dogs arrived. Upon seeing the sorry-looking refreshments left for them and those the Red Devils had taken, they immediately protested by sulking and by remarks of hostility against the Red Devils ("Pigs," "Bums," and more objectionable terms). The Red Devils were at first rather complacent, justifying their actions in terms of "first come, first served," which became the standardized justification for all Red Devil members.

The Bull Dogs discussed the possibility of throwing their beaten-up cake at the Red Devils, but decided against it on the grounds that, after all, it would taste good. They went to their table and proceeded to hurl insults and names at the Red Devils. Some of these names tended to be standardized at this time and later were used to apply to Red Devils. Among these was "pigs" ("low rotten pigs," "dirty pigs," etc.). This was not the first time "pigs" had been applied by the Bull Dogs to the Red Devils, although it clearly was felt applicable to this situation. They had previously accused them of being "pigs" and of "hogging" most of the camp equipment. "Dirty bums" and "jerks" were other labels standardized by the Bull Dogs for the Red Devils. (These later were recorded frequently in interchange of insults and appeared on Bull Dog signs and posters.) Other more objectionable terms were hurled at the Red Devils, including "rotten pukes" and "dirty b-----." There were frequent group cheers of "2–4–6–8, who do we appreci-*hate*, Red Devils, Red Devils, Red Devils."

Hall, the Bull Dogs' athletic captain, sauntered insolently over to the Red Devil table and flaunted his knife before them. The Red Devils ate their refreshments in righteous indignation. The leaders remained more silent and sullen than the rest of the group at the "unjustified" attack. Shaw said little. Lee, the chief lieutenant, told the group to "ignore it." But especially Darlton, Canfield, Fenwick, and Harding—all at the bottom of the Red Devil hierarchy—responded with name calling at the Bull Dogs, the most common being the already standardized "dirty players" and "cheats."

When they finished, Shaw and Lee with most of the Red Devil group dashed from the mess hall and ran down to the river. Darlton, who was leaving the mess hall, caught sight of the Bull Dogs dumping their dirty plates and ice-cream cartons on the Red Devil table. He protested and became involved in scuffling with a Bull Dog, which was stopped by the counselor when Lambert (a Bull Dog who had been especially friendly with Darlton during Stage I) pulled out his new knife, opened the blade, and had to be restrained from brandishing it.

After this party, Shaw was again seen talking in a friendly way with Hall of the Bull Dogs. He withdrew more from the group and tended to be silent with them. The observer noted that "Shaw is not acting like a leader." The low-status Red Devils, on the other hand, were incensed by the Bull Dogs' aggressiveness. When a Bull Dog hurt his leg accidentally, Fenwick of the Red Devils said: "Too bad he didn't kill himself."

This event at the party, which the Bull Dogs saw as the doings of the Red Devils, set off further frustrating situations and a series of raids and fights which soon had to be stopped by all means.

The following morning, during breakfast, the Red Devils deliberately dirtied their table by spilling cocoa, milk, crumbs, etc., to make the cleanup work hard for the Bull Dogs, who were on K.P. that day. Shaw endorsed this action, although after breakfast he and Lee were again seen chatting with Hall of the Bull Dogs. When the Bull Dogs saw the messy table, they decided to mess it up further and leave it that way. Crane, the Bull Dog leader, objected to this idea, but Hall and others prevailed. Crane then joined in helping them to smear the table with more cocoa, sugar, syrup, etc. The table was soon alive with bees and wasps. The Bull Dogs hung the walls with threatening and derogatory posters against the Red Devils, and left the mess hall (see Plate V). Most of the signs were hung near the Bull Dog table. Here are some examples of the slogans on them: "The Red Devils are Pigs," "The Red Devils are Jackasses and Bums," "Red Devils—Girls, poor girls," "We have a team."

The Bull Dogs set the tables before lunch, putting the Red Devils' table service on the sticky table humming with insects. When the Red Devils saw their table, they were furious. They tore down any signs nearby. A staff member told everyone to stand by their tables for grace. The Red Devils stood by the table, but immediately afterward moved to a table at the far side of the hall from the Bull Dogs. As the meal progressed, names and insults were hurled back and forth with increasing intensity. Finally the groups were lined up against one another throwing waste material, food, sponges at each other.

Neither side could prove who started the fight. (Adult observers reported that someone threw a sponge, but the action was so fast that there was disagreement among them as to the source of the sponge.) Both sides were, however, sure that someone in the *other* group started the fighting.

When the boys began throwing table knives and saucers and the altercation threatened to be a violent physical struggle, the staff intervened quickly and stopped the fighting with considerable effort.

At this point, it was quickly decided to stop Stage III of the experiment immediately and to concentrate on breaking down the in-groups. The decision was to stop the intense intergroup conflict by any means necessary and then to initiate a camp program in which all boys would participate on a camp-wide basis. The experiment, from the point of view of controlling the situation, was over at this point. The instructions to all staff members were to do away with the hostility as much as possible in order to send everyone home feeling good. There was no systematic attempt at integration after Stage III. However, a great deal of information and many significant leads were gained for future study of integration of hostile groups and elimination of hostility, which is the pressing problem to be tackled.

The events which followed the fight at luncheon should be viewed in this context. Participant observers and junior counselors, as well as the camp director, were making genuine efforts to prevent any further conflict and to proceed to the camp-wide activities planned. There was preaching to this effect and verbal counsel. The quarrels that did break out were stopped as soon as possible.

At about 2:30 in the afternoon the Red Devils were upstairs in the clubroom of their bunkhouse calling names at a few Bull Dogs outside, who were responding with taunts and epithets. A few green apples began to be tossed by both sides. Shortly a full-scale fight was going on, during which two windows were broken. Shaw, the Red Devil leader, first attempted to sneak around the fighting to raid the Bull Dog bunkhouse (see Plate VI). When this effort failed, he disengaged from the fighting and retired upstairs with a watermelon the group had picked from the garden. The rest of the Red Devils, led by Lee, who had previously advised the Red Devils to "ignore" the Bull Dogs, fought with the Bull Dogs around the Red Devil bunkhouse. The Bull Dogs' junior counselor rushed to the scene, blew his whistle, and told them all to stop. Slowly the Bull Dogs withdrew to their own cabin area. The staff member went inside the Red Devil cabin and saw Lee starting to clean up the mess. Lee refused the help of this Bull Dog counselor in cleaning up, on the grounds that *he* wouldn't help a *Bull Dog*. Other Red Devils wanted the staff member to leave.

They were upset at the staff's trying to make peace while they hadn't "gotten even." At this point, some of the Bull Dogs attacked the cabin again, throwing green apples. The counselor went outside and ordered them to stop. Two Bull Dogs refused, saying if he tried to stop them he would have the whole group against him. The staff member replied that if necessary he would stop each of them personally. He finally persuaded four Bull Dogs to help him clean up the Red Devil cabin. Then he went upstairs to the Red Devil clubroom where by this time the Red Devils were all eating watermelon. He said, "No more fighting." There was objection that the Red Devils hadn't had a chance to get even. Someone said, "Let Shaw decide." When Shaw agreed to a cease-fire, the Red Devils accepted his decision. When Harding complained that the Bull Dogs had entered their cabins while they weren't allowed in the Bull Dogs', this staff member sent them over for a visit to the Bull Dog cabin.

It seemed that the fighting would stop. But the lower-status members in the Red Devils still talked of revenge; and the Bull Dog group wanted to be prepared "in case." During the afternoon, both groups made unauthorized expeditions to collect green apples. The Red Devils were observed on two expeditions, and were photographed from a distance. Their secrecy and stealth indicates that they were collecting apples for a raid. This was an affair of *low-status* Red Devils (see Plate VII). When the Red Devils noticed that some Bull Dogs also were collecting green apples, they planned a raid on the Bull Dog cabin which they carried out while the Bull Dogs were away. (The Bull Dogs said they were not collecting green apples for a raid but "just in case.") When the Bull Dogs returned to their cabin, the cry went up, "Our apples are gone!" Wood, a low-status member said, "That's war." But Crane called the group together and organized a detail to raid the Red Devil cabin while the Red Devils were cooking out and instructed them to take back only the apples that had been stolen. A Red Devil, who had come back to the camp from their cook-out location, spotted the group and ran to inform the Red Devils. The Bull Dog detail returned with the apples stolen plus a few more. By this time, Red Devils were returning to the camp from various directions. The Red Devils led by Shaw went to their cabin. Their counselors had not yet arrived. An adult staff member of the Bull Dogs intervened. At his insistence that they have peace, Hall, the athletic leader who had been on somewhat friendly terms with Shaw and Lee of the Red Devils after the athletic series, was chosen to make a peace mission. He joined into the spirit, shouting to the Bull Dogs, "Keep your big mouths shut. I'm going to see if we can make peace. We want peace."

Hall went to the Red Devil cabin. The door was shut in his face. He called up that the Bull Dogs had only taken their own apples back, and that they wanted peace. His explanation was rejected, and his peaceful intentions were derided. He ran from the bunkhouse in a hail of green apples. The Red Devils were all furious. Shaw, who had been friendly with Hall, now had no use for him or any Bull Dogs. (He had not been near Hall since the fight at lunch.) They were all determined to "get even" with the Bull Dogs. But the counselors got them in bed.

In spite of the fact that the Red Devils were dead-tired from the activities of the day, they succeeded in awakening and dressing at 2 A.M. with the intention of raiding the Bull Dogs. This attempted raid was a planned "upper-crust" affair, led by Shaw and his lieutenants. The raid was stopped by the participant observer and junior counselor, who were asleep in the cabin, when one of the would-be raiders kicked over a container of green apples which were to be used as ammunition. Since it was dark, no one could be sure who did this. The boys were in general agreement that it was Billings, the boy with lowest status in the raiding party. But Billings vigorously denied the charges, saying that Shaw, the leader, made the noise. After going back to bed, the Red Devils were stopped from raiding again at 6 A.M. the same morning. Both groups were made to dump the ammunition they had hoarded the next morning (see Plates VIII and IX).

The degree of hostility between the two groups can be clearly seen in the posters which were made by the boys and hung in the mess hall (at lunch) and in each others' cabins during the raids.

(See examples in Plates X and XI.) These posters were made in every case by boys low in status in their respective groups. This fact, along with other evidence, including especially the determination of lower-status Red Devils to "get even," suggests that manifestations of intergroup hostility and rivalry of group members low in status may at times be more intense than the manifestations of members higher in status. It seems that low-status members, having greater strivings for status within the group, may go to greater lengths in trying to gain recognition by showing identification and loyalty to the in-group. In such situations as these, hostility toward the out-group is one manifestation of in-group identification and loyalty.

MAIN RESULTS OF STAGE III

In brief, the consequence of these intergroup relations in competitive situations and in frustrating situations which members of one group perceived as being caused by the other group was first to solidify the in-group belongingness and solidarity, to enhance in-group democracy, and to strengthen in-group friendships. Qualifications must be added that during the period of repeated defeats suffered by the Red Devils there were signs of *disorganization* and *internal feuds* in this group. But in the face of broadside attacks by the Bull Dogs there was closing of ranks in the Red Devil group. Second, the effect of these competitive and frustrating situations was to generate and increase out-group hostility, to produce derogatory *name calling* which came close to standardizing of negative stereotypes in relation to the out-group (*rudiments of prejudice*).

In the case of the Red Devils, solidarity was achieved once again in the clashes with the out-group. Bull Dog solidarity was at its peak. Thus we see in a concrete way that in-group democracy and coöperation does not necessarily mean democracy and coöperation with the out-group and its members, if the directions and interests of the groups are in conflict. In fact, the group which had the greater democratic in-group organization (the Bull Dogs) was the more concerted in expressions of out-group antagonism.

In dealing with intergroup relations, the vital interests and directions of the groups and especially of the power focus in their day-to-day living and plans have to be given due weight. Attempts to bring people into contact in a group situation and to change their perceptions of one another and attitudes without giving proper weight to the vital interests of group members are hardly more than playing with shadows. (Of course it is entirely possible that what group members perceive as their vital interests may in actuality be induced by the manipulation of powerful sections of the group or its leaders.) The facts of structuring and restructuring of perceptions and attitudes are not arbitrary affairs. They are organically related to the reality of motives sanctioned and regulated by actual group memberships, and of actual conditions. Actual conditions set certain compelling limits against structuring or restructuring perceptions by wish fulfillment, fantasy, and motive, no matter how strong these autistic factors may be.

Persistence of In-Group and Out-Group Delineation

As indicated earlier, after Stage III the experiment was formally over. The remaining days in camp were spent in efforts designed, by usual camping procedures, to eradicate friction left from the intergroup conflict. The post-experimental period did relieve a good deal of generated tension, in that there were no more collective fights. There is ample evidence that the boys enjoyed the camp.

During this period, tables in the dining hall, which had been put together to permit each in-group to eat together as a group, were separated so that all boys would "mix up." They were encouraged to do so by the staff members. With some persuasion by the staff members, they held joint birthday parties, campfires, and the like together. Individual competitions, such as track meets, stunt nights, etc., were held which gave the boys a chance to shine *individually* rather than as group members. While the two groups remained in separate cabins, they engaged in camp duties together.

Probably the most effective event for the breaking up of the groups was a camp-wide softball game in which a team of the best players from both in-groups elected by the boys from the entire camp competed on the camp grounds with a group coming from the neighboring town. In this game the boys participated as *campers*, not as in-group members. They all cheered for the camp (except for Thomas, who inserted "Bull Dogs" into the cheer). The camp team easily won the game, and there was considerable feeling of common pride following it. However, it should be recognized that our future efforts in studying integration between hostile in-groups should not be started by uniting the in-groups for further conflict against still another in-group. This procedure amounts to creating frictions between larger social units and conflict of larger proportions.

As noted earlier, the adult staff encouraged mixing of the boys. Under these circumstances it can be considered as surprising that there was not more mixing than there was. Seating arrangements at meals, friendship preferences, etc., *continued to follow in-group lines on the whole.* (It might be mentioned here that friendship choices were not obtained verbally after the end of Stage III because it seemed most likely that such procedure would arouse suspicion from the boys.)

This outcome is illustrated rather dramatically in Lambert's case. It will be remembered that he was the Bull Dog who had such difficulty in his status strivings, especially with Hall. Lambert did not like the idea of the groups' breaking up. He disliked the separation of the tables and wanted to sit with all of his group. When a joint birthday party was being held (for a Red Devil and a Bull Dog) each boy chipped in for the celebration except Lambert. He told the counselor that he was not going to chip in for a Red Devil, and he didn't like the idea of having the Red Devils come to the birthday party. Further, he was unhappy and would like to go home. Lambert was persuaded to attend the party, and a few days later he seemed to be adjusting to the new situation. But this behavior indicates clearly the consequence of the weakening of group lines for a member who achieved stability in his position in the group after considerable struggle.

Seating at tables was entirely up to the boys. Several boys who started to sit at a table predominantly made up of another group were called into line by their own group members. On the last day of camp, only four boys from out-groups were sitting at tables which were occupied otherwise by members of the two respective in-groups. That night four Bull Dogs requested that the campfire be separate that evening. "We want to have our own campfire"; "it's the last night of camp and we want to be by ourselves." They reluctantly agreed to a joint campfire at the staff members' persuasions.

During Stage I we noted that three boys, Crane, Hall, and Miller, who had climbed the mountain together, had dubbed themselves "The Three Musketeers" and showed all signs of becoming a little clique. Because of size and other factors, Crane and Hall were put in the Bull Dogs and Miller in the Red Devils. It might be supposed that during the period designed to break down the in-groups and to encourage mixing up among the boys, The Three Musketeers would have associated with one another again. But the previous stages had done their work. There was conflict especially between Hall and Miller. During the last days of camp, the two got into a fight. Crane, who had been especially close to Miller in Stage I, encouraged Hall and said if he had been doing the fighting, he would have done more to Miller which was his just dessert.

So in spite of the efforts of camp leaders, the in-groups tended to persist. Old names, old songs for the opposite group cropped up occasionally even though the conflict situations were past.

Concluding Remarks

This study of in-group formation and intergroup relations is a preliminary attempt to understand underlying factors producing friction and tensions between human groupings, with the aim of carrying the lessons thus learned to the study of integration between groups. It confirms the considerable literature coming from sociologists and more recently psychologists on the formation and functioning of in-groups. The results of the intergroup relations between experimentally formed in-groups in situations competitive in nature and frustrating to the groups in question substantiate the observations of sociologists and others of relations between small groups in life situations.

Underlying the conception of this study and others to follow is the guiding principle that reactions of the individual take place within reference frames, to which both internal and external factors contribute in a functionally interrelated fashion. In terms of this preliminary study, this means that the reactions of individual members must be understood in terms of the group setting in which they take place, in addition to their individual contributions to this group setting. The group setting constitutes not merely the in-group, its relationships and norms governing in-group activity, but the in-group in its relationships to out-groups and the norms which arise on the basis of these group relationships. We cannot hope to understand attitudes and behavior of individuals toward members of other groups without placing the individuals within such group settings. It is for this reason that attempts to explain group prejudice, social distance, and antagonism, or attitudes of harmony or admiration between groups in terms of the needs or motives of the individual alone are so inadequate in meeting the known facts concerning intergroup attitudes and behavior, and rather unrewarding in pointing ways to alter or even reduce intergroup tensions in a consequential way.

These findings indicate that the effects of group situations and participation as a group member will be reflected even in relatively simple discriminations (judgments), perceptions, and other reactions of the individual. The possibility which this result points to is the study of the effects of group situations, relations between in-group and out-group, changes brought about in attitudes between in-group and out-group members in precise laboratory experiments, like those currently used in judgment and perception studies. The present study offers many examples of gross trends reflected in simple perceptual responses. For example, in competitive games, the members of the opposing teams were very keen in catching even the slightest errors or fouls committed or supposedly committed by their opponents. Such errors or alleged errors instantaneously brought forth shouts of protest from the group concerned, almost to a man. Correspondingly, any success exhibited by their in-group players brought forth cries of elation. In instances of dispute where errors or fouls were not clear cut, both groups invariably lined up against each other and the referees to prove that their opponents were in the wrong, citing all kinds of "observations" to substantiate their point. Studies utilizing such lessons as these in experimental laboratory situations permitting precise measurement are under way.

FORMATION OF POSITIVE AND NEGATIVE GROUP STEREOTYPES: AN EXPERIMENTAL STUDY

As we have seen, attitudes of social distance toward out-groups are accompanied by short-cut evaluations in the form of "traits" or characteristics attributed to the out-groups and their members. These constellations of attributed traits are called group stereotypes. In Chapter 4, it was emphasized that stereotyping is not a phenomenon confined to intergroup relations. From a psychological point of view, the stereotyping tendency has roots in man's capacity to form concepts encompassing classified groups of objects, events, etc., and in a mode of mentality with long philosophical and practical antecedents which attributes causation to fundamental "essences," that is, the "substantive" mentality.

Once formed, a stereotype tends to subsume all objects or events to which it relates. Contrary cases, rather than breaking down the stereotype, are considered "exceptions" to a general rule. This is true of group stereotypes as well. Being a part of the culture through the vehicle of language and a crystallization of emotionally toned relations of man to man and group to group, group stereotypes tend to linger on even when the conditions which gave rise to them have changed.

The conditions giving rise to group stereotypes are particular kinds of functional contacts and functional relations between the groups in question, sometime in the past or in the present. In terms of the rank and file of the groups, these particular relations may be simply the picture of the aims and interests of their own group and of out-groups, induced by factions of their group with vital interests at stake in the particular intergroup relations in question. Or, these particular relations may be determined largely by actual conflict, harmony, or both between the interests, goals, and values of the groups involved as a whole.

The evidence indicates that when relations between groups are generally those of harmony and coöperation, the evaluative core of stereotypes attributed by one group to the other is generally favorable. Since few groups which have existed for a long period of time have managed to maintain completely harmonious relations at all times, some attributed traits, even in a generally favorable stereotype, will be negative or uncomplimentary. However, even such unfavorable traits are affected in some degree by the favorable evaluative core. Likewise, when relations between groups rather consistently involve conflicting aims and interests, a generally unfavorable evaluative core results; even traits which might be favorable in other contexts are affected by this negative evaluation.

In the intergroup conflict that arose between the experimental in-groups, the Bull Dogs and Red Devils, described earlier in this chapter, each group formed a generally negative image of the other, attributing derogatory characteristics to the out-group as a whole and to its members. This may be taken as an experimental verification of the hypothesis that intergroup conflict produced by incompatible group goals and directions is accompanied by the formation of unfavorable group stereotypes.

Taking her lead from facts such as those summarized here, R. Avigdor set out to investigate the formation of group stereotypes in situations in which groups coöperated with one another and situations in which groups came into conflict.[1] If, as the evidence indicates, the stereotype one group develops about another

---

[1] R. Avigdor, The development of stereotypes as a result of group interaction. Doctor's dissertation, New York University, 1952. This unpublished dissertation is reported here in summary form with the author's permission.

is a functional product of the kind of contact existing between the groups, the resulting stereotypes would be expected to be generally unfavorable in the case of conflict or tension between groups and generally favorable in the case of a friendly or coöperative relationship. Avigdor observed further that, as functional products of intergroup relations, the characteristics included in stereotypes, while not corresponding to a statistical analysis of group characteristics, would not be selected in a completely haphazard or accidental fashion. Rather, traits attributed to the out-group would tend to be those which might contribute to the group's stand in the particular kind of relationship in question.

In order to study this problem in a natural setting where the group coöperation and conflict would have real motivational significance and group goals be those arising in group interaction, Avigdor became the adult leader to groups of children in a settlement house in the lower East Side of New York City. These groups were spontaneously formed "friendship clubs" which the settlement sponsored and which met regularly once a week to engage in activities of their own choosing. The role of the adult leader was to supervise and assist in these activities. Thus, the experimenter was in a situation in which she could manipulate conditions and observe without the children's being aware that a "real life" experiment was in progress. Avigdor spent almost two months prior to the experiment gaining the confidence and friendship of the children and learning their interests and goals in order to devise experimental situations which were as natural, usual, and interesting to them as possible.

The subjects were four groups of girls, ten to twelve years of age, composed of from eight to twelve girls each. (Because of practical considerations, one group had a different leader.) The groups were similar in composition; all were from the lower or lower-middle strata. The clubs had been in existence for about three months prior to the experiment and constituted fairly definite ingroups.

In order to test the hypothesis, it was necessary to bring these groups of girls into functional contact in coöperative situations and in conflict situations. The coöperative situations were planned by the experimenter and described as follows:

Each cooperative pair, that is the Daytons and Gems on the one hand, the Melodies and the Starlights on the other, put on a show to raise money for club jackets. Getting club jackets was a goal common to all the clubs, who were paying dues for this purpose. However, they were all far from having raised enough money. This provided strong motivation to make the show a success. The money raised in each case was divided equally between the two participating groups. Left to their own choice, each group would have preferred to put on their own individual show; this however had been made impossible thanks to the coöperation of the program director of the settlement. The children were told that it was felt that a small club alone could not handle successfully a fund raising affair, and that permission for the project would be given only if at least two clubs participated in the venture. Working together with another club was thus made a necessary condition for the attainment of the common goal. Presenting this as a settlement policy had the further advantage of preventing the children from suspecting at any point that they were the subjects of an experiment.

As the adult supervisor of three of these groups, and with the coöperation of the leader of the other, it was possible for Avigdor to observe the groups as they made moves to get together to plan a show and their coöperation in putting it on, and to obtain their reactions to each other when coöperative activities reached their height. This was done by having each group rate the other for thirty-two characteristics, half favorable (e.g., careful, considerate, fair, good-natured) and half unfavorable (e.g., bossy, careless, cheaters, selfish). The pretext for this activity was that it would help the adult leader in her work. The ratings were made for each characteristic on a five-point scale, ranging from "all of them are (e.g., careful)" through "Some of them are . . ." to "None of them are . . ." In addition, "neutral" ratings were obtained at times when the groups in question were not engaged in coöperative activities.

Following the conception of the study as a "real life" experiment, the group conflict situation developed spontaneously during the experiment and was seized upon for study. Two of the experimental groups which Avigdor led were coöperating to produce a play. The other group she led was in the early stages of coöperation with the fourth experimental group led by another adult. Conflict developed between Avigdor's two coöperating groups (Daytons and Gems) and her other group (Melodies) in the following way: On the eve of the performance of the play which the Daytons and Gems were coöperating to produce, these clubs asked for a final rehearsal. This was the regular meeting day of the third group, the Melodies. The experimenter granted the request for a rehearsal and told the Melodies that they should come and watch it instead of having their regular meeting. The two groups putting on the play resented this decision because they feared that if the Melodies watched the rehearsal they would not buy tickets and attend the performance. The Melodies would have preferred to have their regular meeting. In addition, they felt that their leader had neglected them in favor of the other groups. And they somewhat resented the fact that those two groups were so near the goal of putting on a play, while they were just beginning to get together with another group to this end. The result of these mutual resentments was that the Melodies behaved rather badly, the other groups asked them to leave the rehearsal, and at last, upon their refusal, physically expelled the Melodies from the room.

Shortly after, the settlement house groups were given circus tickets. Each group was to be accompanied by an adult leader. The experimenter, being unable to accompany all three of her groups, chose to take the Melodies. This choice aroused some jealousy on the part of the other two groups and further resentment against the Melodies on their part. When the Melodies finally put on their play with a fourth group (Starlights), none of the Daytons and Gems attended. Naturally the Melodies resented this since they actually had attended the former groups' play. Finally, although the Daytons and Gems succeeded in getting the amount of money needed to purchase their jackets, the unfortunate Melodies were forced to wait until the following year to reach this goal.

In short, owing in large part to the fact that the experimenter served as leader for three groups, a conflict situation arose between two of these groups who were coöperating together and the third group. Ratings of the thirty-two characteristics were obtained at the height of this conflict situation from the two coöperating groups for the third and from the latter for the two coöperating groups.

Results were analyzed by group as well as in terms of coöperative and conflict situations to check that any trends were not a result of the reactions of a particular group, but were indeed dependent upon the experimental conditions. The latter was found to be the case.

Comparison of ratings made in coöperative, "neutral," and conflict situations showed a "general trend for Extreme Favorable judgments to decrease from Cooperation, through Neutral, to Conflict, and for Extreme Unfavorable judgments to increase in the same order." The tendency was found for all but three of the thirty-two characteristics, these all being considered as "irrelevant" to the interaction situations (e.g., "bad teeth"). In short, the characteristics attributed to the out-group in the coöperative situation tended to be favorable; those attributed to the out-group in the conflict situation tended to be unfavorable.

For unfavorable characteristics, more significant differences were found between ratings made in conflict and in coöperative situations than for favorable adjectives. Avigdor found that the reason for this variation was that, in the coöperative situations, ratings tended to be less extreme than ratings in the conflict situations. Ratings in the coöperative situations tended to pile up at a moderate point on the scale: "Some of them are . . ." That is, the stereotyping tendency was less pronounced in the coöperative situation than in the conflict situation.

Avigdor also concluded that in the particular coöperative situations used in her study, the groups tended simply to develop a generally positive image of each other, and that most favorable characteristics were attributed to the out-group in some degree. On the other hand, characteristics attributed in the conflict situation were unfavorable and tended also to be more definitely relevant to the conflict situation. This is in line with earlier observations to the effect that negative, or unfavorable, group stereotypes tend to be more definite than those for friendly or related groups.

The experiment substantiated the hypotheses formulated and serves as further verification of the conception of group stereotypes as a function of the kind of relations between groups presented in this book. At the same time it demonstrates the possibilities of experiments in "real life" settings which reduce the danger present in many group studies of elaborate measurement of artifacts.

CHAPTER 11

ЛЛЛЛЛЛЛЛЛЛЛЛЛЛЛЛЛЛЛЛЛЛЛЛЛЛЛЛ

Some Implications for Groups in Harmony and Tension

Now we have reached a vantage point from which we can view the material laid out and trace the main path leading to the formulation of a social psychology of intergroup relations which is theoretically sound, hence has realistic practical implications.

Whenever an in-group or its members, collectively or individually, react in relation to an out-group or its members, we have a case of intergroup relations. (Definitions of in-group and out-group are given in Chapter 1 and are further elaborated in Chapters 6 and 8.) This essential feature of intergroup relations imposes on the student and practitioner in this area certain crucial and distinctive considerations. In accounting for intergroup behavior, some authors have singled out deep-seated instincts inherent in human nature as the determining factors; other authors pointed out frustrations of the individual with ensuing displaced aggressions. Some have placed major emphasis on "national character" and culture. Still others sought the explanation of intergroup issues primarily through the character of the leadership.

Certainly all of these influences variously proposed as explanatory principles by different authors do enter as factors in determining intergroup behavior in various ways (see Chapters 2 and 6). But the essential feature of intergroup relations noted above requires that consideration be given these and other factors as they operate within the setting of the particular case of intergroup relations. Individual needs, motives, displaced aggressions, the undeniable role of leadership, the characteristic modes of behavior due to culture are factors interdependently related to one another and other factors operative at the time. Intergroup behavior is the outcome of internal factors (motives, attitudes, complexes, and the like) and external factors (situational, organizational, socioeconomic, and material) which jointly determine the unique properties of psychological structuring at the time. In short, intergroup behavior, like any behavior, can be understood only within its appropriate frame of reference.

The appropriate frame of reference for intergroup behavior necessitates the consideration of functional relations between two or more in-groups. The functional relationship between two or more in-groups has properties of its own. These properties are generated in the course of interaction of particular in-groups. Even though not independent of properties of the relations within in-groups, yet the characteristics of functional relations *between* in-groups cannot be deduced from the properties of in-group relations alone. Prevalent modes of behavior within the in-group in the way of coöperativeness and solidarity or competitiveness and hostility need not be the prevalent modes of behavior in intergroup relations. Intergroup hostility may, at times, be proportional to the degree of in-group solidarity. There are cases of consequential intergroup relations which effect modifications in the structure of in-group relations.

Intergroup behavior of members of any group is not *primarily* a topic of *deviate behavior*. If it were first and foremost a matter of deviate behavior, intergroup behavior would not be the issue of such vital consequence that it is today. Intergroup behavior is primarily the matter of participation of individual members within the social distance scale of the in-group in more stable times, and in the developing trends in intergroup relations of the respective in-groups which become especially prominent in periods of flux and change characteristic of our own times. This participation of individual members implies regulation of experience and behavior in relation to out-groups in terms of existing or developing anchorages provided by their reference groups (see

Chapters 7 and 8). Attitudes, hence behavior of the individual toward out-groups and their members, are regulated, on the whole,
in terms of the proximity or distance prescribed by the social-
distance scale or the developing friendship or hostility between
the individual's reference groups and various out-groups.

The motives, attitudes, complexes, frustrations, and aggressive tendencies of individual members do have a place in intergroup relations as they are modified, deflected, and even transformed within the social-distance scale and developing trends of
intergroup relations of their respective reference groups. The
organization of experience and behavior of the individual interacting as a member of an in-group has unique structural properties which cannot be extrapolated from his experience and
behavior in individual situations.

Likewise, explanations of intergroup behavior have to bring
into the picture the unique properties of the intergroup interaction in question. Only within its appropriate setting can the *relative weights* of various factors (motivational, socioeconomic,
situational, etc.) be properly singled out. In more stable and established situations and times, the social-distance scale of the
reference group in question is, on the whole, the weighty determinant. In more extraordinary times of changing group relations and group re-alignments, the dominant factor may be
situational, socioeconomic, or even military.

After noting the implications of the present-day social distance
or prejudice studies (see Chapter 4) and briefly illustrating social-
distance scales in formation in their respective historical settings
(see Chapter 5), we concentrated our emphasis on the intra- and
intergroup relations of small groups. Because of methodological
advantages they offer, we developed rather extensively the leads
derived for our problem from the study of small groups. Since
these relations yield to intensive step-by-step study in the very
process of formation and since their structural properties can be
studied in terms of reciprocal status and role relations of all constituent members including the leader, *informally organized small*

groups afford a basis for sound generalizations concerning the intra- and intergroup relations of in-groups in general.

A survey of various types of informally organized small groups suggests common minimum features (see Chapter 8). Among these are some motive or motives shared or endured by individual members, which are conducive to the interaction process and which impell members toward the attainment of common goals. As members gravitate toward one another in their strivings for common goals, the interaction process produces differential effects in the behavior of individuals. In time, the interaction process becomes stabilized in a definite pattern of *reciprocities* which are manifested in a group *structure* consisting of hierarchical statuses and roles for individual members. The established pattern of reciprocities becomes codified in terms of certain norms regulating the expectations, responsibilities, loyalties of members occupying the respective roles and statuses. Norms are also standardized concerning other matters of consequence or relevance to the existence, activities, and goals of the group.

The very fact of stabilization of a system of reciprocities implies the demarcation of in-group structure from other in-group structures. The in-group thus delineated becomes endowed with positive qualities which tend to be praiseworthy, self-justifying, and even self-glorifying. Individual members tend to develop these qualities through internalization of group norms and through example, verbal dictum, and a set of correctives standardized to deal with cases of *deviation*. Hence possession of these qualities, which reflects their particular brand of ethnocentrism, is not essentially a problem of deviate behavior, but a question of participation in in-group values and trends on the part of good members who constitute the majority of membership as long as group solidarity and morale are maintained.

Functionally related out-groups and their respective members are attributed positive or negative qualities depending on the positive or negative nature of functional relations between the groups in question (see Chapters 4, 9, 10). The positive or negative nature of these functional relationships may result from actual harmony and interdependence of the goals and values of the in-groups or from actual incompatibility and conflict of the aspirations and directions of the groups in question. Or, especially in relations of larger group units where face-to-face contacts are supplanted to a large extent by indirect *communication* including the powerful mass media, the nature of intergroup relations may reflect a picture promulgated by powerful and interested parties within the in-groups or from other functionally related groups.

In time, the adjectives attributed to out-groups take their place in the repertory of group norms as a social-distance scale of the group in question toward so many out-groups. The lasting stereotypes attributed to out-groups low on the social-distance scale are particular cases of norms toward out-groups. The rise of stereotypy is presented in our survey of prejudice studies in Chapter 4 and is verified experimentally in Chapter 10.

Because they become integral parts of the group's norm or value system, are carried through the vehicle of language, and transmitted to new group members through short-cut dictums and verbal counsel, norms or stereotypes toward out-groups tend to outlast the conditions which gave rise to them. In this light it becomes easy to understand why, in times of changed relations between former antagonistic groups, it is difficult for leadership to plunge into the line of action direly necessitated by developing conditions. "Tradition" lies between them.

The processes underlying the development of standardized conceptual symbol systems (language) in human groups are sufficiently distinctive to necessitate consideration of relations of sub-human and human groups at different levels of organization (see Chapter 3). These factors result, for good or for evil, in the "time-binding" character of human groups, in the development and transmission of culture, which is a unique feature of human groupings. Established and verbally transmitted norms may even be carried on to the point of inappropriateness to existing functional relations between groups. In such cases, the established social-distance scale conflicts with trends produced by changing functional relations between the groups in question as reflected in specific situational dilemmas, by the impact of technological changes which may affect both in-group structure and values and relations with out-groups, by changes in the structure or norms of superordinates of which the in-groups in question are parts. Then the determination of intergroup behavior is complicated by a variety of factors, one more weighty now, and another weightier in another situation or time. The established social distances tend to continue as potent factors in the frame of reference determining intergroup behavior at the time, but are overshadowed in various situations by other conflicting factors. However, depending on the nature and degree of conflict among these factors, a weakening of the established social distance scale of the in-group may be anticipated in such a setting. The outcome of such weakening could result in modifications of the established social-distance scale, in the standardization of another scale, or in its breakdown, depending both on the scope and intensity of the conflicts and the prevailing trends of main anchorages in the complex of groups.

The generalizations stated in the preceding paragraphs are derived from our survey of existing prejudice studies and intensive study of various forms of small groups in their intra- and intergroup relations. They served as useful hypotheses in the formulation and execution of the two major experiments reported in Chapters 9 and 10.

The final validity of these generalizations will lie in our ability to handle the well-known intergroup harmonies and strifes of history, and in prediction of intensified intergroup alignments and tensions now taking place. Comparison of relative weights of various factors determining intergroup relations in times of relative stability and in times of flux in historical settings will afford the testing grounds for theoretical formulations of intergroup relations. For example, detailed treatments of the American Revolution, like those of John C. Miller, reveal trends which have bearing and implications for the formulation of intergroup relations presented in this book.

The development of socioeconomic life in the American colonies in the eighteenth century brought about an ever increasing cleavage in vital interests between them and the ruling class of the mother country. A series of well-known events accentuated this cleavage. On the one hand, their being predominantly English in culture and language was coming in as a factor making it hard for them to take the fatal stand against the mother country and especially the Crown, which was perceived as the symbol of unity with their past. Yet, on the other hand, the very fact of their being English in culture, their being politically conscious of representative government (unlike other British colonies at the time), contributed to the rise of a leadership willing and committed to fight for their "inalienable rights." When the final break came in word and in action, there were still groups here and there who could not make the move in line with the revolutionary upsurge. There were groups who vacillated. It was too big a jump to make in terms of their existing mode of living and system of norms. These conservative and vacillating groups (as John Miller tells us in *The Triumph of Freedom*) changed sides back and forth as the fortunes of the long drawn-out war changed. In the case of a great many such vacillating groups, the compelling hand of events unfolding at the time came as the decisive factors to determine for them the nature of their lasting attitudes on the issue. Here we see an illustration of intergroup relations into which various factors came with their relative weights, resulting in a new pattern of intergroup relations.

Experimental Approach in Validating Hypotheses for Intergroup Behavior. The area of intergroup relations affords a golden opportunity for experimental social psychologists in validating the applicability of

1. hypotheses derived from the surveys of empirical literature on prejudice and on small groups, and
2. psychological concepts concerning the place of shared attitudes, motives, frustrations, deprivations, situational factors, and various personality "traits" in determining social behavior.

Only through the rigor and precision inherent in the experimental approach can we hope definitively to verify or reject hypotheses and concepts advanced to account for intergroup behavior—this most complicated of topics.

But if the experimental approach is to be the real testing ground that it should be, it cannot start with problems advanced in a haphazard hit-or-miss way. Problems formulated in a haphazard way because they happen to be in the psychologist's lingo at the time cannot help being pseudo-problems. Hypotheses to be tested should not be advanced on *a priori* hunches having little contact with the reality of events in question. Hypotheses advanced on *a priori* hunches can give us only an intellectual gymnastics, no matter how refined they may appear to be at first glance.

As emphasized at the very start, problems which have organic relatedness to intergroup relations can be formulated only after a great deal of familiarity with actual events in this area (see Chapter 1). This means going beyond the psychologist's tendency for exclusive preoccupation with his traditional formulations and concerns. Fruitful hypotheses can be derived only through careful sifting of recurrences in intergroup behavior in the actual events of history and in sociological observations in this area. After such a realistic formulation of our problem and statement of hunches based on factual content, we can use experimental testing of our psychological concepts, generalizations, and techniques in a way that has serious implications; otherwise we shall be dealing forever with artifacts. As Murphy, Murphy, and Newcomb stated cogently in their *Experimental Social Psychology,* experimental design and testing do not come at the start of the game in the study of human relations. But experimentation comes as the crowning touch of rigor and precision in the study of the problem attained after laborious exploration of our bearings which affords familiarity with the layout of the area. In the long run, careful and laborious exploration of the length and breadth of the layout is more effective and time-saving than haphazard testing of this or that hypothesis linked with theories which have not led us far in the study of group relations.

These theoretical and methodological considerations briefly restated in the above paragraphs were basic in the formulation and design of the experimental study of intergroup relations presented in Chapters 9 and 10. They were basic also in determining the choice of experimental conditions to be introduced and observation techniques to be followed.

To approximate, as much as possible, the natural process of spontaneous group formation and the in-group and out-group delineation with its consequences on intergroup relations so abundantly reported in literature on small groups, the subjects were kept unaware of the fact that the whole thing was an experiment on group relations. The announced purpose of the study was that it was a study on camping procedures. Contrary to the opinion of some workers in this area, it is psychologically naïve and unrealistic to have the subjects aware that the process of group formation and their strivings to achieve a status in their group, their hostility expressed in words and deeds, and the like are under study and still to assume that this self-awareness would not come as an important factor in determining their behavior.

It follows that data concerning in-group formation and intergroup functioning should be obtained through participant observers who are perceived as part and parcel of the situation by the subjects in the sense mentioned earlier (see Chapter 9). Moreover, the participant observers should not be detected by subjects while recording observations contrary to the natural functions of their announced roles. The argument that subjects cease to be mindful that their words and other behavior are being taken down is contrary to what we have learned concerning structuring of perception. The presence of a personage ever observing, ever recording our words and deeds in a situation in which our status and role concerns are at stake cannot help coming in as an important anchorage in the frame of reference of behavior in question. Therefore, in this infancy of the scientific study of group relations, substantially more will be contributed to its development in the long run if we establish the main tendencies first, rather than obtaining detailed items of everything that goes on at the cost of distorting the process itself.

Such an approximation of experimental set-up and techniques for studying the interaction process in a natural setting does not preclude the possibility of checking the validity of observed trends by precise laboratory techniques at "choice points." If there is any validity in the recent generalizations concerning perceptual and judgmental variations (distortions) as a function of attitude or motive, relevant perceptual or judgmental tasks of the type studied in the laboratory can very well be introduced at a few choice points. Such experimental tapping should be done by individuals who have not been in the situation and are not a functioning part of the interaction process. They might be introduced as "psychologists" who came to the situation to study topics of discrimination, judgment, or perception. The stimulus material used in these experimental gropings should be of an indirect and unstructured type which seemingly does not constitute direct questioning of the developing group attitudes.

Nor does this serious concern for approximating the interaction process within and between groups to that which develops in natural settings imply giving up the ideal of experimental introduction of conditions constituting so many well-defined variables. Starting with the physical layout itself, which will preclude intrusion of outside influences for the time, the main conditions which have bearing on the problem and hypotheses can be introduced and deliberately specified. This deliberate introduction of main conditions was achieved considerably in our experiment (see Chapters 9 and 10). Yet these experimental conditions and related group goals were not additional topics dragged in for discussion or solution. They were organic parts of the preoccupations and concerns of the subjects *in the situation*. In short, the experimental conditions were chosen on the basis of studying crucial ongoing interests of subjects in the interaction process. For example, individuals experimentally assigned to groups were given undivided, unprepared ingredients of a sumptuous meal when they were hungry, thus creating a situation of interdependence and coöperation for the attainment of a commonly shared goal. Suggestions of how to proceed, discarding proposals perceived to be inadequate, adoption of what was seen as the effective way to go about it, the rise of a coördinator, division and coördination of various tasks to be performed, a developing pattern of *reciprocities* were consequences of such conditions.

The formulation of problem and hypotheses and the choice of experimental variables and techniques accordingly in the interaction process of a group setting makes it feasible to pull together in one design experimental and observational approaches. Such a study, which takes the group setting as the primary point of departure, does not negate the possibility of bringing into the picture assessment of the contribution of unique personality characteristics of individual members. Having the natural flow of group interaction as our realistic concern, this personality assessment aspect also should be divorced from the ongoing activities in the eyes of the subjects. This can be achieved by the collection of life-history data and sociometric standing of the subjects in school and neighborhood, and by direct and indirect personality tests given a considerable length of time prior to the experiment by experts who are not linked to the experimental period as far as the subjects are concerned.

In our first attempt at studying in-group and out-group interaction processes, we aimed at experimental verification of in-group formation on the part of subjects who were not co-members of an already existing in-group, who were not attached to one another personally, but who, at the same time, did not have antagonisms toward one another based on socioeconomic, ethnic, or religious background differences.

In this attempt we undertook to produce the negative, that is, standardized intergroup hostility. This was done deliberately. The major area of concern in intergroup relations today is the reduction of intergroup tensions in a contemporary world of mounting friction between groups. However, by singling out factors in intergroup relations which are conducive to friction and tension, we shall be learning what to avoid in intergroup relations.

Of course, this is not enough. We have to proceed to singling out factors in intergroup relations conducive to harmony and integration. It should be emphasized again that coöperation and solidarity *within* in-groups need not *necessarily* imply solidarity and coöperation *between* groups. Harmony and tension between groups is determined at the same time by the nature of functional relations between groups. As with solidarity and morale within in-groups, it is necessary in intergroup relations to have an *actual* and perceived condition of interdependence for the attainment of common goals which are inherent and real in the process of living and interacting. But to be effective, the introduction of conditions of interdependence and common goals among groups and the trends implied by them should not be pulled and pushed asunder by practices and norms in conflicting directions within the respective in-groups. This will go a long way to insure us an ever enlarging experience of "we-ness" that is real, that is not conflicting—a "we-ness" in which the individual's particular in-group, as well as the self are perceived as autonomous and free.

Our program of research is extending along these lines.

NAME INDEX

309

SUBJECT INDEX